# GAMBATTE

# GAMBATTE

GENERATIONS OF PERSEVERANCE AND POLITICS,
A MEMOIR

DAVID TSUBOUCHI

ECW Press

Published by ECW Press
2120 Queen Street East, Suite 200, Toronto, Ontario, Canada M4E 1E2
416-694-3348 / info@ecwpress.com

LIBRARY AND ARCHIVES CANADA CATALOGUING IN PUBLICATION

Tsubouchi, David
    Gambatte : generations of perseverance and politics / David Tsubouchi.

ISBN 978-1-77041-131-9
Also issued as: 978-1-77090-372-2 (PDF); 978-1-77090-373-9 (EPUB)

    1. Tsubouchi, David. 2. Politician—Ontario—Biography. 3. Japanese
Canadians—Biography. 4. Progressive Conservative Party of Ontario—
Biography. 5. Ontario—Politics and government—1995–2003. I. Title.


FC3077.1.T78 2013     971.3'04092     C2012-907510-8

Cover and text design: Tania Craan
Cover and interior images from the author's collection.
Author photo: Seneca College
Typesetting and production: Carolyn McNeillie
Printing: Friesens   1   2   3   4   5

The publication of Gambatte has been generously supported by the Canada Council for the Arts
which last year invested $20.1 million in writing and publishing throughout Canada, and by the
Ontario Arts Council, an agency of the Government of Ontario. We also acknowledge the financial
support of the Government of Canada through the Canada Book Fund for our publishing activities, and the contribution of the Government of Ontario through the Ontario Book Publishing
Tax Credit. The marketing of this book was made possible with the support of the Ontario Media
Development Corporation.

Canada Council Conseil des Arts
for the Arts du Canada

Canadä

Ontario
Ontario Media Development
Corporation

ONTARIO ARTS COUNCIL
CONSEIL DES ARTS DE L'ONTARIO
50 YEARS OF ONTARIO GOVERNMENT SUPPORT OF THE ARTS
50 ANS DE SOUTIEN DU GOUVERNEMENT DE L'ONTARIO AUX ARTS

FSC
MIX
Paper from
responsible sources
FSC® C016245

PRINTED AND BOUND IN CANADA

To my parents, Kiyoshi Thomas Tsubouchi
and Fumiko Frances Tsubouchi, who faced adversity
throughout their lives with dignity and perseverance
and to all Japanese Canadians who shared this experience.

LEGACY

Rice paper thin
   a shroud cloaks and
   separates us from them.
A common tongue,
   fading heritage
seldom spoken memories
   all serve to heat the crucible.
We,
the children of the children
search for foreign characters
to define ourselves
and although the words are correct
and formal
they are not right.
Still we try . . . It will be the legacy of our children
And theirs.

David Tsubouchi

February 24, 1942, marked the day that shattered the lives of the Tsubouchi and the Takahashi families, as well as the day that destroyed the lives of every man, woman and child of Japanese descent living in Canada. The shock waves from that day continued on through my generation and will not stop until the Japanese Canadians cease to exist as an ethnic group as they intermarry and become assimilated into Canadian society. On that infamous date, the Mackenzie King Liberal federal cabinet passed an order in council under the Defence of Canada Regulations of the War Measures Act. That order gave the federal government the right to intern all "persons of Japanese racial origin."

In plain language, that meant that every person of Japanese descent — most of whom had been born in Canada — were put into prison camps. The conditions were deplorable. Women and children were forced to live in uninsulated shacks. Several families were crowded together with a single pot-belly stove to heat the entire shack. Most of these people were city people unused to such rough conditions. The "lucky" ones were allowed to do forced labour on beet farms in Alberta. Some men were put onto forced labour crews building roads. The real "troublemakers," the community leaders, were sent to a POW camp just outside Marathon in northwest Ontario.

When they were forced from their homes, no one would tell them where they were going, how long would they be away or even if they would ever return. Most of them assumed incorrectly that one day they would be allowed to return to their homes and the government would act as trustees for their homes, businesses, cars and possessions.

In 1943, the Custodian of Enemy Alien Property sold everything that was left behind by the Japanese Canadians. The money that was realized from the sale of all their worldly goods was kept by the Canadian government and used to pay for the imprisonment of the Japanese Canadians.

Besides the general wrongdoing caused to the entire Japanese Canadian community, these events caused some very real tragedies in my family. My maternal grandfather, Chozo Takahashi, became the first Japanese Canadian to die as a direct result of the transportation. I believe that the illness that my mother contracted in the Lemon Creek internment camp led to her loss of a lung and her untimely and early death.

No Japanese Canadian was ever found guilty of any crime against Canada during the Second World War.

The full-scale incarceration caused several generations of Japanese Canadians to feel a real sense of alienation from their homeland of Canada and also from their identity and heritage. We didn't fit in. Canadians did not view us as Canadians and we did not view ourselves as Japanese. We were told to fit in and assimilate. We spoke no Japanese at home and denied our own roots. We tried to be good Canadians, but we were standing on the outside with our noses pressed against the window.

My parents had never been to Japan. My parents were born in British Columbia, my father in Duncan and my mother in Vancouver. We never spoke Japanese at home because they didn't want any of their children to have accents. We were to become Canadians. We needed to speak like Canadians, act like Canadians and, they hoped, be accepted as Canadians.

We were living contradictions. There were few visible minorities in Canada in the 1950s and 1960s, so as much as we were encouraged to assimilate, we were different.

As much as we had the veneer of being Canadians, inside our house there were many things that were not typically Canadian. We had bacon and eggs, and my mother would occasionally make spaghetti, but many of our meals would be considered exotic to our neighbours. We would eat chow mein for days. Mom would serve rice with the bacon and eggs. My mother's attempts to cook her version of a Canadian meal were meals that I would have preferred to miss. We never ate hot dogs or Kraft Dinner. Our house even smelled different.

We went to the United Church, yet once a year we attended the Buddhist temple to show our respect for our grandfather.

Other than relatives, we had no Japanese Canadian friends.

Even growing up, I knew there was a connection to my past, but there was no way for me to express what it was. None of us can escape our past. We should celebrate and embrace it. The past is what makes us what we become, even if we are not aware of it.

Because of the attitude of my parents I adopted an attitude of optimism. I have always remembered my father saying that throughout his life and its challenges, he woke up every morning with one goal — to make life a little better for his family and himself. My mother, no matter how bad and desperate things got, always had an encouraging word and a hug.

There is a word in Japanese, *gambatte*, that literally means "do your best." Culturally, it conveys a sense of love, like when a mother says it to her child before sending him off to school. Or it expresses a sharing of good fortune, as when someone is embarking on a new venture or trip. When the double disasters of the earthquake and tsunami devastated the Tohoku area of Japan in March 2011, people would say "Gambatte." It symbolized hope and encouragement. It meant that the sun would rise again over Japan.

I was fortunate in that the feeling of *gambatte* was stronger in my life and my heart than my struggles with identity, but the struggles of my family have never been far from my mind and have inevitably shaped the course of my life.

# CHAPTER ONE

# THE TSUBOUCHI CLAN

My grandfather Hyakuzo Tsubouchi immigrated to Canada shortly after the turn of the last century. I remember my grandfather as large for a Japanese man of that time. He was about five feet, nine inches tall. He lived in Duncan, B.C., on Vancouver Island and worked in the bush as a lumberjack. My grandmother Ume Hisatsugu came to Canada just after the First World War. She added to the family income by cleaning the homes of wealthy white people. My grandparents Tsubouchi raised six children — my aunts Chizu, Nobu and Setsuko and my uncles Kenji and Eiji, and my dad, Kiyoshi. In the Tsubouchi household, my grandmother obviously had no difficulty producing children. She once jokingly said to me that she would jump onto the table, have the baby, jump off and get back to work.

My father's middle name was Thomas. It was an acknowledgement by my grandparents that he was a Canadian. He was born on November 20, 1921. As in most large families, everyone had responsibilities. It was a humble household and everybody was expected to pull his or her weight.

My dad was the oldest male child and with that position carried more responsibility. Even as a boy, my dad reigned over his sisters. His brothers were much younger than the older sisters. In Japanese families the eldest son is held in great esteem; he will be the heir. This is significant even to a poor family. In Japan when a family had no male child, the family would arrange for a male from another family to be adopted so that the family name would continue. My aunts told me that when they were older, they all jumped when my father came home from work, and that he was an authority figure they obeyed. My Aunt Pat (Chizu) used to say, "Kiyoshi will be home soon — is the rice on?" That used to be the watchword. My father, on the other hand, said it was his three sisters who used to tell him what to do. As with most families, the truth is somewhere in between.

My father always took his responsibilities as the oldest son seriously and at an early age, during the Depression, tried to earn money to help out the family. My dad did any chore that he could get paid for. At the age of 11, he decided that the way to make money was to become a caddy at the local golf club.

Every morning he would put on his painter's hat (he did not own a real golf cap), walk down to the golf club and line up with the other boys hoping to be chosen as a caddy. Every night he would return home disappointed.

Unfortunately my dad had two strikes against him. He was the smallest boy and he didn't look as if he could even carry a golf bag. The second strike was that he was Japanese, and in British Columbia at that time, there was considerable prejudice against both the Japanese and Chinese, who were seen as cheap labourers taking jobs away from "real" Canadians.

If there was one trait that my father had, it was persistence. I think this hard-headedness is a trait that all of his children inherited. He had a determination to succeed no matter how long it took or how many times he was rejected. The next morning he would return again.

My father told me that this had gone on for almost the entire golf season.

It was difficult for my father because he had to endure rejection and bullying and name-calling from the older boys, but the hope that he might get a job and be paid five cents to caddy, an enormous amount of money to my father, kept him coming back.

Some of his enthusiasm had been eroded by the older boys calling him a "dirty Jap" and telling him to go back to Japan, but he was used to this by now. He had earned his place to wait for work as a caddy. He was so small that he usually got roughed up, but the older boys knew that he wouldn't back down and finally gave up. The older boys also knew that my father would never get hired anyway.

One day my father thought he might get a chance to caddy because there was a tournament at the club, even though he had never been picked to caddy in any tournament before. It was special as well because my grandmother had been home that morning and had encouraged him.

All morning the golfers came over to the caddies to make their selection, and one by one, the other boys were selected. My father said that he tried to stand straight and puff up his chest to look as big as he could, but he was hopelessly small. His disappointment mounting, for the first time in his life he was considering giving up and going home. He then heard someone say, "You over there with the painter's hat. Do you want to caddy for me?"

He couldn't believe his ears. He was the only one who wore a painter's hat. When he looked up he saw a big man who had a very distinguished air about him. Everyone seemed to be making a fuss over him.

The man said, "Yes, you, the little Japanese fellow. Do you think you can handle my bag?"

All my father could say was, "Yes, sir!"

He was quite surprised that the man had asked him to caddy. This was the greatest thing in the world to my father. It was his first job as a caddy. The only experience that my father had in golf was watching people play from afar. No Japanese family could afford to buy a set of golf clubs or to play, nor would they even be allowed to play at the golf and country clubs, which were almost all white-only. When my father told me this story, I was quite surprised to learn that he was even allowed to be on the golf course as a caddy.

My father knew nothing of how to play golf, and any golfer would know that. He had only his determination to carry the large bag. My father realized that the man had done himself no favour, but my father was a quick learner, and with the patience exercised by the man, my father figured out which club was used in each situation. When they finished the front nine, the golfers stopped to have lunch. The man gave my father 50 cents and told him to buy some lunch. This was the equivalent of a day's wages for a man. It was more money than he had ever held in his hands.

My father ran home and gave the money to my grandmother, who made some rice balls for him to eat for lunch. My father then ran back and was waiting for the man when he finished his lunch.

The back nine went smoother as my father began to understand what he needed to do. When they had finished the round, the man gave my father a dollar and in front of everyone proclaimed loudly, "The next time I come back to play, I want Tommy to be my caddy."

My father had no trouble after that getting a job as a caddy. It was only years later that my father discovered that the distinguished man was the Honourable John Hart, who was the member of the provincial legislature for Victoria and who later became the premier of British Columbia.

I learned two lessons from this story my father told me. There are a lot of doors that will be slammed in your face, but if you keep on knocking, one will eventually open. The second lesson was that no matter how important you are, remember your roots and who you are. My father was telling me to be true to myself.

A great passion was born that day for my father: golf. Until the day he died my father loved golfing. My father bought golf magazines, golf videos and, like most guys, golf gadgets. My father always had time for a game of golf and had a great short game. When he was 83, some days he could almost golf his age.

My father always said that he was shy, but wherever we went he somehow ended up talking to everybody. He was never in need of golfing partners. He used to golf at a public course in Markham, and I was always being surprised by complete strangers who would walk up to me in town just to tell me that they had been golfing with Tommy last week or last month or last year. There were a few times near the end of his life when my father joined us for a tournament. He couldn't drive the ball very far anymore, but from 100 yards in, he was deadly accurate.

As a teenager, my father went to work in the bush as a lumberjack. My father used to say that he was five-foot-six, but if he was, then I am six feet tall. Working in the bush in those days was very dangerous. Maiming and death were not uncommon. There was no such thing as workplace safety laws. My father used to say that working in the bush toughened him up.

My father was wiry and strong and nothing seemed to frighten him. He was also very intelligent. He once said that he learned how to survive, play poker and smoke cigarettes when he worked in the bush. The smoking was a habit he carried on until I was about 12, when he quit cold turkey. I don't recall ever seeing my father smoke in front of any of us but we knew that he did. If anyone went to our one bathroom in the morning after my father, we did so through a cloud of smoke.

My father told me he was introduced to smoking when he was eight years old. He and his friend managed to snitch a cigarette and matches from his friend's father. They went to a farmer's field and sat down, lit the cigarette with the match and started to smoke it. Unfortunately, their experiment ended fairly quickly when the match that the two boys used to light the cigarette set the farmer's field on fire. Soon the fire department appeared on the scene.

My father and his friend had since got rid of the matches and the cigarette and were watching the firemen putting out the fire that they had started by accident. When the fire captain approached them to ask if they had seen anybody who might have caused the fire, the two boys blamed the school bully.

My father was a good athlete and played baseball and hockey. He passed on his love of sports to my brother and sister and me. When he was a young man, he was considered to be quite handsome by many of the girls in his community.

Like many working people, my father didn't pay attention to politics unless politics imposed itself on his life. Those circumstances included when some level of government raised his taxes or told him that there was yet another thing that he couldn't do. He would rather play golf or watch his precious Maple Leafs or Blue Jays or Argonauts on television.

It was only after I entered provincial politics that he started to pay attention and realized that many of the values in his own life were being espoused by Mike Harris. My father believed that he should take responsibility for his own life and that if he worked hard he should be rewarded and, most important, that the government should not waste his money.

My father, like almost every Japanese Canadian, lived a life that was affected by prejudice and unending challenges, and yet he lived with determination, optimism and courage.

He would talk occasionally of the courage and determination of his parents but not about his own. My father's view — and mine — was that our own lack of money and status in our early lives was not so great an obstacle because we were both blessed by wonderful parents who did what they could to make life better for us and who did their best to not allow us to believe that we had very little. We had nothing, but we were not disadvantaged.

Although it was far from idyllic, my grandparents lived with the same beliefs as most Canadians, that hard, honest work would eventually reward a person. This philosophy carried them through establishing themselves in a new country, the Depression, the Japanese Canadian internment and starting all over again with nothing.

I don't remember much about my father's father, as he died in 1964, when I was 13 years old. My grandparents lived in Fort William, which eventually joined three other regions to form

Thunder Bay, and we lived in Toronto. I saw my grandfather only when we went on one of my father's maniacal non-stop road trips to Fort William. My mother did not drive in those days, and my father refused to stop, in part because he didn't want to spend money for a motel room while en route, but mostly because he just wanted to get there faster.

My mother would pack food and we would eat while my father drove. I remember once when Lynne was two, Dan was six and I was 10, and Dan needed to urinate. When my mother urged my father to stop so Dan could go off somewhere in the woods, my father pointed out that he had brought a small plastic pot and let us know what its purpose was. The little pee pot served its purpose several times. My father, not wanting to stop, slowed down and emptied the contents of the pot out his window. It was only when we had other reasons for stopping that my father took mercy on us and reluctantly pulled over. Not surprisingly, we made good time.

When we reached Fort William we all could finally relax. Most times we stayed in Fort William with my Uncle Paul Oda and Aunt Sets and my cousins Mike, Noreen and Jay. Since Mike, or Mickey as I called him, was about my age and Dan was about the same age as Jay and Lynne was about the same age as Noreen, it was ideal.

The first place we would go after setting up with the Odas was to visit my Bachan (Grandmother) and Gichan (Grandfather) Tsubouchi. My grandfather was always a bit of a mystery to me. Even when we visited Fort William I didn't see much of him. I remember him as a big friendly man who seemed to be ailing. I would visit him while he was lying in his bed, and he would give me these tiny Japanese puff pastries. Unfortunately he didn't speak much English and I didn't speak Japanese.

The only time I saw him on his feet was the time he visited us in Toronto when I was five years old and we visited Niagara Falls for the first time. He was quiet and kind and had large hands.

My grandmother Ume Tsubouchi was a whole different kettle of fish. They were a true example of opposites attracting. While my grandfather was quiet, if there was a stage to stand on, my grandmother would be on it. She had an opinion on everything.

Once when I was a little boy, walking on the street with her in Fort William, she muttered something in Japanese about a woman who walked by. I asked my mother what she had said, and my mother told me that my grandmother said that the woman had a face like a can of worms.

When the mini-series *Shogun* starring Richard Chamberlain was appearing on television, the local photographer had taken an ad that featured a photo of my grandmother. That was a great source of pride to her. It wasn't long before the extended family knew of her "fame."

My grandmother Ume Tsubouchi was a typical grandmother. She liked nothing better than to spoil her grandchildren. She never had any money to buy things but spoiled us instead through her cooking. Bachan was a great cook.

Despite the geographical distance between us, I had a chance to become very close to Bachan when I was 12. My mother had been hospitalized in the Weston Sanitarium for tuberculosis for a period of time for treatment, and Bachan came to take care of us. My brother Dan was eight and my sister Lynne was four.

As soon as Bachan walked in the door, everybody knew who the boss was. Even my father used to jump when Bachan told him to do anything. This came as a complete surprise to the three of us children. My father thought he was the undisputed boss of our family. I never understood how my grandmother, who was not even five feet tall, could tell my father what to do. As I got older I really understood the power of women in the Tsubouchi households past and present. I understood later that my mother was the real power behind the throne and had persuasive power over my father, just as my grandmother had over her family.

My father used to visit my mother every day after working from 5:30 in the morning to 6:30 at night at the dry cleaners. He would sit with her at the sanatorium. Often he would eat something with my mother, but when he came home and Bachan had prepared his dinner, he would have to eat it, hungry or not.

Bachan believed in feeding us great quantities of food and told us that it would make us grow and become stronger. One Saturday morning, when I got up I passed my brother as he was coming out of the kitchen.

"You're in big trouble," he said to me as he smirked.

"What are you talking about?" I asked him.

My brother, who was eight years old at the time, said, "Bachan just made me breakfast and she made me four eggs and tons of toast. I had to eat it. But she's making you pancakes."

Pancakes have always been my nemesis. While I enjoy pancakes, the ultimate number of pancakes that I am capable of eating is two. I was afraid that my grandmother, who had occasionally watched cartoons with my sister, had seen *The Flintstones*. I was hoping that she did not get any ideas about making a huge stack of pancakes from the show.

My greatest fears were realized as soon as I saw the stack of 10 pancakes sitting on my plate. I knew that this was going to be an undoable task, but my Bachan never understood that anyone might not be able to eat everything that she made. So I sat down and tried my best. Her pancakes were perfect — fluffy and round and made from scratch — but perfection does not necessarily offset the gag reaction after you have eaten five pancakes. Finally I just could not eat another pancake and told Bachan.

My Bachan never got mad at me but looked at me and asked me why I didn't like her cooking. I sat down guiltily and ate one more before giving up completely.

In those days, we lived in Agincourt. My parents had scraped together every penny they could to pursue the Canadian dream and bought a very modest bungalow in a working-class neighbourhood at Finch and Kennedy in an area called Lynnwood Heights. When we first moved to Agincourt, Kennedy Road was an unfinished road in the middle of nowhere. Finch Avenue was a dirt road and ran through a marshy area that we called the Swamp. Bachan used to wander off in the early spring and pick fiddleheads and cook them as part of a meal. She also had a green thumb and made a small garden in the backyard to supplement the food budget.

Bachan was the ultimate recycler. She recycled not because she was a huge proponent of ecology but because she had survived the Depression and imprisonment in an internment camp. She understood what having absolutely nothing meant. Nothing went to waste. If Bachan made potatoes and there were leftovers, they were used for the next meal and if there were still leftovers they were used again until nothing was left. Every container and every elastic band had a use. When Bachan stayed with us on garbage collection days, there was only a small paper bag at the foot of our driveway, the size you might use to carry home a chocolate bar.

Bachan was also the ultimate judge and jury of all disputes. All of the Tsubouchi clan is very competitive at everything from contact sports to Scrabble. A few years later, Bachan was visiting when Dan and I were both in our teens. My brother was big as a teen. When he was 15 he towered over me at just over six feet tall. We were playing a game of Monopoly when typically we came to a dispute about some rule or another. It didn't take long to escalate because at the time we both had short fuses. Soon we were grappling with each other and just as I was about to throw the first punch, Bachan walked into the room and looked at us. Instantly we both stopped dead in our tracks. Our Bachan never had to say anything. All she had to do was look at us and we knew what she meant. If the UN had drafted Bachan, we would have achieved world peace by now.

Elaine and I visited my Bachan together for the first time as a couple shortly after we were married. Bachan was very independent. She was in her late eighties but was as spry and alert as ever. She lived in her own apartment with its own entrance at my Aunt Nobu's house in Thunder Bay. My aunt had told me that Bachan knew we were coming over for lunch and she had been up since 5:30 a.m. cooking.

When we arrived, her kitchen was full of Japanese food that she had been preparing for days. She had made many of my favourite dishes, including the "bags" that were officially known as inari sushi and manju, the Japanese pastry that was filled with sweet red bean paste. The aromas of the food filled her house and my mouth was watering the instant that we walked in the front door.

My Bachan did not speak much English and Elaine did not speak any Japanese, but Bachan took an instant liking to Elaine and somehow they seemed to be able to communicate with each other. Bachan led Elaine into her bedroom, where she had arranged photographs of her grandchildren. I had not seen the photographic display before. Bachan had devoted an entire wall to my photos. As the eldest male of the Tsubouchi line, I was clearly Bachan's favourite.

In January 1992, the entire Tsubouchi family was going to converge on Thunder Bay to celebrate Bachan's 100th birthday. Elaine and I had booked our plane tickets when we got the news that Bachan had passed away peacefully in her sleep, a few days short of her birthday, the ultimate milestone. Bachan had been independent, healthy and as bright as always up to her death. It was a crushing time in my life. Instead of gathering together to celebrate her life with her, we celebrated her life at her funeral. I was privileged to be asked to speak at her funeral. It was hard to believe that Bachan was gone.

# CHAPTER TWO

# THE TAKAHASHI SIDE

My maternal grandfather, Chozo Takahashi, was born in Japan on January 12, 1889. He immigrated to Canada in 1907. My grandmother was born in Japan as Suga Kishibe on January 19, 1899. In 1916, my grandfather went back to Japan to marry my grandmother and bring her back to Canada. They lived in Vancouver, British Columbia.

My mother, Fumiko Frances Takahashi, grew up in a large family. There were seven siblings in the Takahashi family: my aunts Kazuko, Kiyoko and Haruko, my mother, and my uncles Hideo, Akira and Toshio. Altogether they produced 19 children.

Fumiko was a quiet girl and was very close to her younger sister, Haruko. Auntie Haru was like my second mother and played a very important role in my life. Auntie Haru told me that when she was a teenager and later as a young woman, my mother was very beautiful and most of the boys had crushes on her. She said that my mother was slender and had a beautiful face. The boys ignored my aunt (according to her), but my mother always included my aunt in everything that they did. Auntie Haru adored my mother because she truly wanted to include her younger sister.

When I was a little boy, I would look at photos of my mother when she was young and I always thought of her as glamorous in the June Cleaver/Barbara Billingsley way. My Auntie Haru once said that my mother got both of the best assets of my grandmother: good looks and intelligence.

My mother never spoke much of her life as a child. She was much younger than my father and was born on April 16, 1928. She enjoyed school and played the piano at Sunday school. When I asked her about it, she would just say that she was a good girl. Auntie Haru would tell me that my grandmother was very strict and never allowed the girls to do anything. They had to come directly home from school and do their homework and chores, which included shining the family's shoes after Sunday school. My mother was self-taught on the piano. She used to say to me not to watch how she played because it was all wrong, but it sounded fine to me.

My mother spent her teenage years behind barbed wire, living in crowded barracks with no privacy. She became very close to Miss Hurd, the missionary who taught at the prison school. My mother maintained a friendship with Miss Hurd until the day that Miss Hurd passed away. I met her when I was a child and always thought of Miss Hurd as a very nice lady.

People who question the relevancy of Christianity, the church and missionaries do not know of the small joys and kindness that they brought into the lives of many families. If they did know, they would give them the proper respect they deserve for their dedication and commitment to their mission. Years later, I was having lunch with Toronto Councillor Kyle Rae and was talking about my family's experience in the internment camps when he told me that his uncle had been a United Church missionary who had served in them.

My mother and her family had a life of drudgery and endless deprivation at the hands of the Mackenzie King Liberal government, living in despicable conditions. The lack of animosity that they had towards the people who did this to them never ceases to surprise me. This is representative of the view held by almost all Japanese Canadians.

Even after the Takahashis had settled in Toronto after the war and my mother and Auntie Haru enrolled at Central Commerce Collegiate, my grandmother continued her strict ways and did not allow them to go to their prom.

After being released from POW Camp 101, my uncles Hideo and Akira went to Toronto before the rest of the family arrived in order to prepare the way. Hideo worked at a mushroom farm in Port Credit, and Akira worked at some kind of packaging plant.

The first place that my uncles secured for the family to live in was 148 Manning. They were proud of their ingenuity, but it was a source of great embarrassment to my mother and Auntie Haru. It wasn't a house; it was an old store. It had one light bulb hanging from the ceiling. There was no basement. There was only the kitchen stove in the entire house to keep them warm. My aunt said that they were always cold. The worst part for the girls was that it had been a store, so it had a big display window in the front, which presented a problem for their modesty.

While I remember my Tsubouchi bachan as a rough and ready woman who wore her emotions on her sleeve, my Takahashi bachan was a dignified and educated woman who was very proper. She was a very shrewd woman who fought to make life better for her family. She was as tough as nails.

After my grandfather died en route to a POW camp, she had to raise her family of seven children as a single woman in a new city and province with no resources other than her own wiles.

Everyone in the Takahashi family had to work. It was a story typical of most immigrant families who start with nothing, except that it was the second start from nothing thanks to the theft of all their worldly possessions by the government of Mackenzie King. Everybody's money was pooled together, with my bachan watching the pennies and controlling the money and the spending.

From the time I was a little boy, all my cousins referred to Uncle Hideo as Uncle Nisan, which meant the second boy, but as far as we knew he was our oldest uncle. We didn't know that my grandmother's first baby died in childbirth. Our parents all called him Nisan, so he became Uncle Nisan to us. Only when we were teenagers did we discover that his real name was Hideo, but we still call him Uncle Nisan to this day.

After his job at the mushroom farm, Uncle Nisan then got a job at a factory and eventually got a job as a clerk at the unemployment insurance office, where he worked for 37 years. He was always pleasant and had the same corny humour that all my Takahashi uncles had. He was, by consensus, the intellectual of the Takahashi clan.

Uncle Nisan had a strange hobby, at least for most people. He subscribed to the printed records of the proceedings of Parliament. He was the only family member who seemed interested in politics. Looking back on the times he had lived through, it may have been a survival instinct to want to know what the enemy might be thinking. At least the next time he might get some advance warning. When I had an opportunity in the legislature, I mentioned his name during a debate and had a copy of the Hansard records sent to him. He was very pleased.

Uncle Akira went to work for an electroplate company and made a success of it. He married my Aunt Kathy, who became a principal in the Toronto separate school system. Uncle Toshio got work eventually at Zenith Electric as a television repairman and married my Aunt May. Auntie Kay worked at Simpsons and married my Uncle Mitz Yamada.

When my parents got married, they lived in the Takahashi house. When I was born, I spent a lot of time with my bachan. I couldn't say "bachan" when I was a baby so I said "baba." Bachan was very happy to be called Baba.

We lived with the Takahashi extended family. Later my mother would tell me that I was very spoiled with affection. After all, I had nothing but uncles and aunts and my grandmother surrounding me.

I discovered years later that my bachan used to write haiku that she sent back to Japan, where they were published. When I told my mother that Bachan must be the reason I had always been interested in writing poetry, she told me that my grandfather Tsubouchi also wrote haiku and that both sides of the family wrote poetry.

My Bachan Takahashi was also not above favouritism. Although I was neither the eldest grandchild of the Takahashi family nor did I carry the Takahashi name, my bachan always treated me with a great deal of preferential treatment.

My bachan was the glue that held her family together through very difficult times. She was very proud of my achievements, but she passed away in 1987, the year before I was first elected to Markham Council. Her funeral, held at the Toronto Buddhist Church, was packed to overflowing. It was a very special day and I was honoured to deliver the eulogy.

In the Buddhist religion, the lives of our relatives who have passed on are celebrated in a service on the first Sunday in the month in which they died. We all gathered for this annual event to celebrate the life of my grandfather.

All Japanese Canadian families are a mix of intermarriage and religions. Today Japanese Canadians are, at a rate of around 95 percent, the most intermarried ethnic group in Canada. Religion is similarly mixed. Most Japanese Canadians adopted the religion of the missionaries who taught school at the various internment camps where they were imprisoned. My mother was brought up in the United Church; hence, I was brought up in the United Church. My Aunt Kathy Takahashi was brought up as a Catholic and became a Catholic school principal after the war. Others were Buddhists. There was one thing that we shared in common: we respected each other's religions and we all went to the Buddhist church for our grandfather's service.

The services were held in Japanese. Since none of the grandchildren spoke Japanese, it was a great source of amusement to us. The service became a contest to see who was going to make the other laugh first. It always had the same conclusion: someone was going to get heck.

The highlight of the day for all of the grandchildren was gathering back at Bachan's house for dinner. This dinner at Bachan's was special because my aunts and my mother had all worked together to make a potluck dinner. This would be the only day that we could eat our fill of all the homemade Japanese food that we could eat. Most of the food would be what is known as "camp" food. This was the kind of cheaper quasi Japanese food that the Japanese Canadians had learned to scrabble together in the internment camps. The food was cheap and plentiful and it was delicious.

Recently I attended a Nostalgia Night at the Japanese Canadian Cultural Centre in Toronto. As a feature, they served food that had been eaten in the internment camps. "Delicacies" included spam sushi, which is rice made into a ball with a piece of fried spam on top, fiddleheads that they had picked in the camps, pickled radish, tinned fish and other cheap or found food. They also had a table of sushi and other Japanese food from Edo, one of the finest high-end Japanese restaurants in Toronto. Not a scrap of the camp food was left.

There is a certain sweet taste of survival.

For us grandchildren, the gathering at Bachan's was a feast. It was also a great opportunity for us to get into trouble, and we always did. This is when we learned the few words of Japanese that we did know: *yancha* (bratty), *yakamushi* (noisy) and *urusai* (pain in the neck).

We earned those words.

# CHAPTER THREE

# THE LOSS OF DEMOCRACY

One of the darkest periods in Canadian history, both for Japanese Canadians and for Canada, was the imprisonment of every man, woman and child of Japanese descent, regardless of whether they were Canadian-born or naturalized. The suspension of all democratic rights was enacted by Mackenzie King's Liberal government by an Act of Parliament through the War Measures Act.

All Japanese Canadians were denied the few rights they had. The excuse was that Canada was at war with Japan, yet similar measures were not taken against the German Canadians or Italian Canadians as ethnic groups. This was clearly a measured and premeditated opportunity to exercise legalized bigotry and economic exploitation. There was no opportunity for the Japanese Canadians to fight back. They did not have the franchise to vote until after the Second World War. They had no power.

The measures taken against the Japanese Canadians were not based on a spur-of-the-moment decision. This was an opportunistic decision, one that was based on years of anti-Japanese sentiment. While continually trying to prove their loyalty to their new country, Canada, the Japanese Canadians had not been pushing for equal rights, but rather the right to be left alone, to make a living and a life for their families. During the First World War, more than 200 Japanese Canadians tried to volunteer to serve their country overseas. Those who tried to enlist in British Columbia were turned away, but determined, they travelled to Alberta and there joined battalions of the Canadian Expeditionary Force and went on to serve in Europe. Fifty-four Japanese Canadians were killed in action and 92 wounded.

In 1919, when Japanese Canadian fishermen held more than half the fishing licences in the country, the Department of Fisheries reduced the number of licences issued to Japanese Canadians and stripped more than two-thirds of the licences owned by them. In Victoria in 1930, Shige Yoshida formed the first Japanese Canadian Boy Scout troop in the British Empire when he was barred by a local Scout troop. In 1936, the Japanese Canadian Citizens League was unsuccessful in obtaining the right to vote for Japanese Canadians as a group. In 1937, all Japanese Canadians over the age of 16 years were required to register with the RCMP. Later a special committee of the Cabinet War Committee recommended that Japanese Canadians not be allowed to volunteer for the armed services.

Japanese Canadians were non-persons. They had no vote. They were not welcome at professional schools in British Columbia. They were excluded from working for the civil service and from teaching. British Columbia was moving towards a segregated public school system — one for whites and one for Asians.

Today, we as Canadians pride ourselves on our fairness and non-discriminatory views, but the history of our country paints a very different picture. A most disturbing social development was the formation of the Asiatic Exclusion League.

The Asiatic Exclusion League was originated in the United States by white labour leaders. The goal was to spread anti-Asian propaganda and to stop Asian immigration. There was no doubt that this was a hate organization that targeted Japanese, Chinese and Korean people. The Canadian labour unions followed the

American lead and formed the Canadian arm of the Asiatic Exclusion League in 1907 in British Columbia. Their goal was simple: keep Asians out of B.C.

In September of that year, this group organized a mob riot of more than 10,000 people who marched into Chinatown and assaulted people and caused great property damage. The mob then turned towards Little Tokyo, where the Japanese Canadians fought back and repelled the mob.

Later, at its height, boasting a membership of more than 40,000, the Asiatic Exclusion League pushed for the creation of the Chinese head tax and the internment of the Japanese Canadians.

After the attack on Pearl Harbor by Japan, government measures against the Japanese Canadians accelerated.

On December 8, Canada declared war on Japan. The same day, all fishing boats — more than 1,200 of them — owned by Japanese Canadians were seized. All insurance policies owned by Japanese Canadians were cancelled. Later that year, the light on the Japanese Canadian War Memorial recognizing the contribution of Japanese Canadians in the First World War was extinguished.

The government created a 100-mile protected area on the west coast to exclude male enemy aliens. A month later, all Japanese Canadians between the ages of 18 and 45 were excluded from the protected area, despite being Canadian citizens and not aliens. Additional measures that were taken against the Japanese Canadians included the confiscation of all property and belongings of the Japanese Canadians by the Custodian of Enemy Alien Property, as a "protective measure." As a result, 572 farms owned by Japanese Canadians were confiscated and, by Order in Council 469, all Japanese Canadian property was ordered to be sold.

The British Columbia Security Commission then commenced its program of forced labour and imprisonment. By the end of 1942, more than 12,000 Japanese Canadians were imprisoned in internment camps, almost 1,000 men were in forced labour camps and 699 men were imprisoned in POW camps in Ontario.

Despite the despicable treatment of their families, when the British government asked for Japanese Canadian volunteers to serve in the Far East, 150 Japanese Canadian men volunteered for service.

In Canada, all Japanese Canadians and persons of Japanese descent were imprisoned. This included the Issei, who were the immigrants to Canada, and the Nissei, who had all been born in Canada as Canadians. All property — personal possessions, money, businesses and real estate — was confiscated by the Canadian government and sold to pay the costs of the imprisonment of the Japanese Canadians. In Vancouver, the families were herded to the Pacific Exhibition Grounds and housed at the Livestock Building. Families were separated. The women and children were to be transported to the internment camps separately from the men. The men who objected to being separated from their families, out of concern for their wives and children, were branded security risks and imprisoned in a POW camp at Angler near Marathon, Ontario.

This was quite different from the treatment of Japanese Americans in the United States. Under the Enemy Alien Act, all Japanese Americans were relocated from exclusion areas that were designated by U.S. government officials. They had very little time to relocate, but they were not required by law to be imprisoned. Japanese nationals were required to be interned. The personal property of Japanese Americans was indexed, warehoused and receipted and was returned at the end of the war. Farms owned by the Japanese Americans were tended and the proceeds of the sale of their crops were deposited and held for them. Their homes were not confiscated and sold. The Americans did not suspend all the rights of the Japanese Americans. They took a clear alternative that the Canadian government did not choose to exercise.

The sweep to evict the Japanese Canadians out of their homes was done in quick fashion with no information. Some families were given just 24 hours to leave their homes. They were allowed to take only what they could carry. No cameras or radios were allowed. Most of what people took were the clothes that they would need to survive in the winter. They did not know where they were going or how long they would be gone.

One of my aunts had just been married and had left all of the wedding presents at home. Most of the items were stolen by their neighbours, and those that weren't stolen were taken by the government and sold.

Years later, through a colleague and fellow sansei (third-generation Canadian), Gabrielle Nishiguchi, who worked at the National Archives in Ottawa, I was able to obtain the records of the Public Custodian on the disposition of the property of both the Tsubouchi and Takahashi families. The question was really a moot one, as no matter what the valuation of the property was, it had been stolen and sold by the government.

This is the reason why no Japanese Canadian family has any heirlooms that were in their family's possession in Japan. The Nissei and Issei were dispossessed and stripped of everything that they had owned and worked for. But the government could not take away their dignity.

The documents set out the details of the sale of all the property of both sides of my family. The Takahashi family had owned a house in Vancouver. The file contained an official appraisal that set the value of the house at $1,800. There was a sale of the house for $2,000. The government had realized $200 over the appraised value. The file contained another unofficial appraisal of the house at $2,800. It seemed evident that someone had managed to get a bargain, somehow profiting on the misfortune of my family.

It was sad to read about all of their worldly possessions being sold at auction. The most disturbing sale was the sale of my mother's and Auntie Haru's dolls for 10 cents. Somehow that was shameful.

Someone once said to me that my family was lucky in that they had lost only material things, but we lost so much more. My grandfather died as a direct result of the imprisonment. Some of the "things" that have been lost forever were the only connections that my family had with their past. We have very few photographs of my family in their early days in Canada and had none from their lives in Japan until relatives in Japan were able to provide a few. There are no photos of my father or mother as children. There are no records of great joy or sadness. There is nothing of friendships of youth or personal triumphs.

Most Japanese Canadians have no heirlooms or precious items from their past. It is as if existence started only after the Second World War. I am lucky to have my grandfather Takahashi's sake cup. That is everything that I possess from a man I never met.

My father was one of the many Japanese Canadian men who protested the separation of the men from the women and children. In the United States, families were allowed to stay together during the relocation. It was a simple policy that cost nothing and would have allayed the fears of ordinary people as they were uprooted. His penalty for protesting this measure was to be incarcerated as POW Number 606 at POW Camp 101 at Angler. POW Camp 101 was an actual military prisoner-of-war camp under military discipline and law. German POWs were also held there.

My father never considered himself to be a man of principle, but he was, in his own quiet way, through his actions. He knew what the consequences were for his actions and beliefs and went ahead with them.

Grandfather Takahashi, who was in poor health, was arrested when he was out for a walk and was, after little less than a month in custody, sent to Angler. My uncle Akira, not wanting my grandfather to be alone, voluntarily entered custody and was also shipped to Angler.

My father and my uncle Akira — my mother's brother — became best friends in the POW camp. Because the camp was a POW camp, the security was far greater than at the internment camps. My uncle Hideo was also an inmate in the POW camp. The camp had two groups: the older men who talked and gambled, and the younger men who practised martial arts. I always thought that it was ironic that my father was a POW and was practising his martial arts skills while armed guards surrounded the POW camp, providing security against prisoners — most of whom were experts in unarmed combat. Both my father and Akira were kendo students. My father became a black belt in both kendo and judo. My father was also one of the few young men in the POW camp to finish high school through a correspondence course. He spent some of the best years of his young life behind bars for committing no crime.

As Hideo was one of the more educated men in the camp, he became one of the camp recorders.

When I would ask my father about the POW camp, he never seemed interested in sharing the stories. This was typical of most of the Japanese Canadian community. Most did not want to talk about the internment, as if they were ashamed of the experience. Yet there is no shame in being a victim of bigotry. The shame is on the bigots.

Robert Okazaki later wrote a book about the experience, *POW Camp 101*, but my uncle Akira was the source of most of my knowledge. There are two stories my uncles told me that point out why the Japanese Canadian POWs had respect for the First Nations community.

Angler was located in northwest Ontario just outside of Marathon, where in the winter there is lot of snow and it is very cold. My uncle Akira and a few of the POWs in his barracks were crossing the distance between barracks in a snowstorm. They had their coat collars up and hats down and were trying to avoid getting a face full of snow, as there was a blizzard. Apparently none of them had realized that they had passed an officer and they failed to take off their hats and bow. Because of their oversight, they were all charged with insubordination.

My uncle and his friends realized that they had no chance of justice, as it was their word against that of an officer with no excuses accepted. The matter came before an officer by the name of Captain Kay, who happened to be a First Nations man. Captain Kay, to the surprise of my uncle, dismissed the charges. Years later my uncle saw Captain Kay at a subway station in Toronto and thanked him. Captain Kay had forgotten the incident that had meant so much to my uncle.

My uncle Hideo told me the other story. The POWs wanted to form a camp band. There weren't many instruments and they had no music. One of the guards was a Private Stonefish, who heard of the problem and brought some sheet music to my uncle. His explanation for his generosity was that his daughter was finished with the music. No one is ever finished with sheet music. I still have music that I haven't played for years but still might. If he had been caught smuggling in music to the POWs, he would have been in trouble. Private Stonefish did what he did because he had empathy for people who had nothing and had been abused by the Canadian government. The only people who had shown any empathy for my father and uncles were First Nations people. They truly understood what it was like to be separated from the general population and treated differently.

My mother was incarcerated at Lemon Creek internment camp in the interior of British Columbia. Life was not as difficult for her as it was for my father, but being housed in rickety, uninsulated barracks with no privacy is not easy. Being deprived of many of the basic rights and things that we take for granted and living behind barbed wire would not be anyone's definition of an idyllic life.

My grandmother tried to make the most of the situation, and my mother attended a school run by the missionaries from the United Church and played piano for the school. There is a photograph of my mother in the internment camp in the book *Years of Sorrow, Years of Shame*, by Barry Broadfoot. While my father was making friends with her brother, my grandfather Tsubouchi had seen my mother and had made plans that she should one day marry my father. My Auntie Haru tells me that my grandfather always had sweets for her and my mother, and kept boasting about how good-looking my father was. While my father was being described to my mother in Lemon Creek, my uncle Akira was no doubt mentioning his sister Fumiko to my father in Angler.

Sometimes out of the most difficult of circumstances a love match finds its way.

My grandmother Takahashi, who had very high standards in what she expected of her children, had similar ideas as to the suitability of potential spouses for her children. Fortunately for my parents' future and my own, my grandmother knew that my grandfather Tsubouchi was educated, because both of them wrote haiku and both of them had had their poetry published in Japan, but my father would have to overcome other obstacles to get her approval. Bachan Takahashi maintained strong opinions about everything and everyone.

Auntie Haru told me that after the postwar release from the internment camps and the eastward exodus of the Japanese Canadians, when their train stopped in Fort William, my grandfather Tsubouchi had tried to persuade my grandmother Takahashi to settle the family in Fort William with the ultimate goal of setting up my father with my mother. Unfortunately, Grandmother Takahashi had sent Uncles Hideo and Akira ahead to Toronto to establish a place for the family. My parents' love story took a small detour.

As POWs, my father and uncles were the last Japanese Canadians to be released from incarceration on April 30, 1946. My father first joined his family in Fort William to ensure their financial stability and then, at the urging of both my grandfather and his best friend, Akira, my father travelled to Toronto.

# CHAPTER FOUR

# BACHAN'S STORY

My Bachan Takahashi wrote an account of my grandfather's arrest in Vancouver for the crime of taking a walk. My grandfather was ill and Uncle Akira had joined him to look after him. En route to POW Camp 101, he was taken off the train to the military hospital. Akira was not allowed to detrain with him. On May 23, 1942, my grandfather died all alone. He had the inauspicious notoriety of being the first Japanese Canadian to die as a result of the internment. Here is the story in my grandmother's eloquent words:

> My 52-year-old husband, Chozo, had been ill since October of 1941, and in January 1942, he took a turn for the worse. At that time, we had all but given up all hope that he would ever recover. However, during the latter part of February, his condition improved somewhat, for which we were very grateful.
>
> On April 13, 1942, while out for a stroll, he was stopped on the street by a Mountie and hustled off to the Immigration Building.

On April 21, word leaked out of the Immigration Building that my husband was very ill. I immediately hastened to the B.C. Security Commission to obtain a special permit to visit my husband in the Immigration Building. My request was flatly denied. I then went to the RCMP Headquarters, but also with no success. I then decided to go to the Immigration Building with or without a permit and was able to speak to Sergeant P… I asked the Sergeant for permission to speak to my sick husband.

He replied, "I have no authority to allow you to do that."

In the meantime, I learned that my husband's condition became worse day by day and finally the authorities had decided to transfer him to a hospital.

I went to the Immigration Building and asked, "Which hospital will he be taken to?"

"He will be sent to the Essondale Mental Institution."

"But he is not insane. The doctor knows that. Why do you have to send him there?"

"There is no room in the Vancouver General Hospital."

"That is not possible."

After much haggling, it was agreed that he would be taken to the Vancouver General Hospital. With that problem settled, my daughter and I requested and obtained permission to see my husband.

What we saw was beyond belief. In a dimly lit cell, my husband was lying forlornly on a cot on top of a single army blanket and nothing else. Why, even a cat or a dog would receive better treatment! Gazing at that pitiful sight I couldn't stop the tears from running. I wondered how anyone could expect to get well in such a dismal surrounding. Is this their idea of humane treatment?

On April 24, he was taken to Vancouver General Hospital. During the six days he was in that hospital, I was able to visit him, but the door to his room was always kept bolted.

On April 26, I met with Dr. Dobson of the Hospital and said, "Since I am able to provide good nursing care for my husband, I would like to take him home and care for him myself."

The doctor said, "If you take him home now and later on find that you wish to have him hospitalized again, he will not be allowed to come into this hospital. Is this agreeable with you?"

I replied, "Once I have him home, I will not bring him back here."

However, my attempt to bring him home failed, although I was able to exact a promise from the doctor, "He will not be moved out of this hospital without your approval."

In the early afternoon of April 27, I received word that the Security Commission had given its approval to have my husband taken home and I should go to the hospital at either 3 p.m. or 7 p.m. When I arrived at the hospital at 3 p.m., I was informed that the Security Commission had refused my request and consequently my husband could not be discharged.

The following day (April 28), I went to see Dr. Hodgins at the Hasting Park Manning Pool and explained the conflicting stories I had been given. His reply was that the timing was not good but that I could probably take him home in two or three days' time. In any case, he added, he will not be taken from that hospital without my approval.

On April 30, when I went to visit my husband, I was told by a nurse that he was transferred to the Essondale Mental Institution. How could they do this to me? Why should he be sent to an insane asylum? He isn't crazy. What about the promise that he would not be taken out of that hospital without my consent! I went to see Dr. Hodgins and demanded an explanation. All he would say was, "That is as good a place as any to recuperate."

On May 2, my son Akira and daughter Kazuko visited him in the mental hospital. Although no evidence of inadequate treatment was noted, my husband was deemed to be a "dangerous element" and therefore was not even permitted to see the movies as did other patients. As a form of exercise, he was compelled to wash the floors, which he found to be extremely tedious.

In the eyes of the doctor, my husband was considered to have recovered and he was returned to the Immigration Building on May 13.

Concerned about his father's well-being, my second son, Akira, requested of the Mounties that he be allowed to be with him. The request was granted and Akira therefore marched into the Immigration Building.

On May 16, my husband was placed on a train with other inmates to be sent to the prisoners of war camp in Petawawa, Ontario. Akira was also placed on the train to watch over his father, and I am sure he found some measure of comfort in this fact alone.

Furthermore, my eldest son, Hideo (then 22 years old), had been previously arrested and sent to the POW camp at Petawawa on April 10, 1942. I was confident that Hideo would look after his father as soon as he arrived there. I was awaiting the opportunity to correspond with him.

At 4 p.m. on May 23, two Mounties knocked on my door and said they were bringing bad news to me. They said, "Takahashi became ill on the 18th and was taken off the train in Winnipeg and hospitalized in the Military Hospital but died at 1 a.m. on May 23."

I was really stunned to hear this news. If he was so sick, why could they not have notified me?

I asked, "What was the cause of death?"

"Natural causes. If you want his body to be sent here, you will have to pay the cost."

"I don't have a penny to my name but I want his body sent home to me.".

"If he had died at any of the road camps then the Government would accept responsibility and send him back to you. But since he was an internee, we can't help you at all."

"Will you put that down in writing, that you cannot help me at all?"

"We can't do that."

"We will bury him in Winnipeg."

I told him to wait and immediately contacted a friend and arranged to borrow some money. Arrangements were then made to have my husband's body sent home.

Receiving information that my husband's body would arrive at the CNR station on May 27th at 8 a.m., my friend offered to go there and bring him back. A short while later he returned empty handed, saying that he didn't see any casket being unloaded.

Did my husband actually die? There followed some moments of anxiety and uncertainty.

It wasn't until much later when I learned that an undertaker had taken the body directly to the funeral parlor. A funeral service attended by just a few friends was conducted the next day and cremation followed.

It wasn't until the end of the war when I learned that at the time my husband was taken off the train at Winnipeg, my son, Akira, had pleaded to accompany him but this was denied. With sadness in his heart, Akira was given no alternative but be taken away to the POW camp at Petawawa, Ontario, for the duration of the war.

Thus ends my grandmother's account.

My grandfather had committed no crime. My grandfather had never been charged. He had been arrested as he was walking by his house. He became a victim simply by being Japanese Canadian.

I never met my grandfather Takahashi, but my grandmother had an iron will and a determination to protect her family.

The senseless death of my grandfather, which I lay at the feet of the Mackenzie King government, caused countless difficulties for my grandmother and my mother. Their survival is a testament to the family's courage and strength.

# CHAPTER FIVE

# AFTERMATH AND A NEW LIFE

After they were freed from the internment camps, the Japanese Canadians were told to show their loyalty to Canada by getting on a train and moving east. There wasn't any choice. It was either that or be deported to Japan. They were put onto trains with no money and possessions and told to keep going.

My father's reaction was typical. He asked, "Why should I go to Japan? I was born in Canada. I've never been to Japan and don't even speak Japanese that well."

Since my father was being processed out of the POW camp in northwest Ontario, the Tsubouchi family settled in Fort William, the largest city in northwest Ontario. The family settled on Simpson Street, which was at the time a working-class area. As in all other Japanese Canadian families, everybody worked and contributed to the family coffers.

This experience of settlement is one that is shared by almost all Japanese Canadian families. I once asked my friend Bruce Kuwabara, the world-renowned architect, why his family settled in Hamilton. He said it was quite simple. As the train that his father was on stopped in Hamilton, he saw a sign that said "jobs." He said to himself that he needed a job and got off the train.

After the family was settled, my grandfather encouraged my father to go to Toronto, where the Takahashi family had gone, to meet my mother. At the same time my uncle Akira had written to my father and invited him to come to Toronto to visit. Being encouraged by both his father and best friend, my father headed to Toronto.

According to my Auntie Haru, when my father and mother met, it was love at first sight.

Both of my parents agreed with Auntie Haru's assessment. Years later, my mother told me that when she met my father she thought he was very handsome. My father similarly fell for my mother like a ton of bricks.

My father started courting my mother. My mother had just finished high school at Central Commerce and had begun working at the MacMillan Book Company with Auntie Haru as stenographers. Both of the sisters took pride in their typing and shorthand skills. Until they were married they were under the very strict rule of my grandmother, so going to work was a welcome relief.

My Bachan Takahashi had very strong opinions about who her children should marry. When I asked my Auntie Haru what Bachan originally thought of my father, she said that at first she didn't approve because even though my grandfather Tsubouchi was educated, she thought he was a flirt. She had never met my father but she had seen his photograph. She thought that he was very handsome and, like father, like son.

As it turned out she couldn't have been more wrong, as my parents were dedicated to each other throughout their life together. My parents began to see each other in secret, and during this secret romance my Auntie Haru stood steadfastly by my mother despite the fear of the consequences for herself from my grandmother. Despite her original opposition, even my grandmother came to realize that love conquers all.

My father started to look for work and discovered that no one wanted to give a job to a Japanese Canadian.

This was a common experience facing all Japanese Canadians across Canada. There were jobs, but not for them. If it wasn't for the empathy of the Jewish community in Toronto — and specifically the Jewish clothing industry on Spadina Avenue — very few Japanese Canadians would have been employed.

My father got a job as a dry cleaning presser and learned quickly. He preferred to be paid by the piece because the faster you worked the more you made. Once he had gained some experience he went to work for a Jewish man who owned Apex Cleaners at Bathurst and Fairlawn. All the customers were Jewish and everyone treated my father decently.

My parents were married in 1950 and a year later I was born.

When I was very young, I rarely saw my father, as he was working two jobs. I do remember the security of being with my mother. She made all of us feel loved and happy even in the worst circumstances, and she made us all better people. One of my fondest early memories of being with my mother is when she made a slide out of snow for me to ride down when I was three.

When I was four, my parents moved to 129 Kingsmount Park Road in Toronto. My brother, Dan, was born the next year. When I turned five I went to kindergarten at Bowmore Road Public School. Since the time he could smile, Dan could charm anyone with his bubbly personality. While I was the serious older brother, Dan had the personality. Anyone who calls him Danny knew him when he was a kid.

One of my duties as the older brother was to look after Dan. He would quite often tag along. If I played hockey, Dan played hockey. If I played baseball, Dan played baseball. Because he was always hanging around with us, he became very competitive. As he grew a little older, I always wanted Dan on my team because he was better than most of the kids my age.

Things change an awful lot as we get older. I seem to remember as a five-year-old walking several blocks to school with other kids.

These days, small children would never be allowed to walk on their own.

I remember when I attended kindergarten that I was not cooperative at times. When told it was time for a nap and I wasn't tired, I didn't lie down and sleep. I didn't like to skip either. I do remember enjoying juice time. I had never tasted apple juice before and found it delightful.

I also have a strange memory that for the class picture, I was standing next to a boy who had smelly feet.

Years later I found out from my mother that because of my "contrary nature" (that is, my unwillingness to sleep at nap time and to skip when ordered), the school thought I might be too uncooperative to go on to grade one. From my perspective I had never accepted doing something just because someone told me to do it or just because everyone else was doing it. I wanted to know why. This attitude would plague my less understanding and less patient teachers throughout my school life.

I didn't realize until a lot later that we didn't have much of anything, especially money, in those days. My mother would explain to me that when she was a girl she would make sugar sandwiches by sprinkling sugar on bread toasted on the wood stove, telling me that it was one her favourite treats. If it was one of my mother's favourite treats, it became mine. So I had sugar toast. It was only years later that I found out what jam was. We couldn't afford jam at the time, so my mother made sugar toast sound good.

In the winter when my mother got milk, and the cream rose to the top of the bottle, I received my mother's version of ice cream: cream, snow and sugar. The first time I had real ice cream at another child's birthday party I couldn't believe the wonderful taste. I don't eat sugar sandwiches anymore but I do enjoy ice cream.

My clothes were clean and in good repair but were rarely new. I knew other kids wore new clothes but it never occurred to me to ask for them. When I was a young child it didn't make any difference to me but later, when I was a teen, it became an issue.

We celebrated Easter and Christmas like any other family. We never felt deprived or envious, because my mother and father wouldn't let us. One of the advantages that we had was great parents. Both of my parents had positive attitudes despite the difficulties they both had to endure. And we all had each other.

When I was five and Dan was one, my mother had us dress up in our best clothes for a photograph that was to be taken by my friend Robert Foyer's older brother. He was an aspiring photographer and didn't charge us a fee.

The Christmas when I was five years old was one of my favourite Christmases. Both of my grandmothers had sent underwear and socks. My uncle Stan (Toshio) worked for a company called Zenith Electric as a television repairman. The company had a special on television sets and was promoting the space age with a silver cardboard punch-out space helmet. We didn't get a television set but I got the free promotional cardboard space helmet. My parents bought a toy radar set for me that cost a dime from Kresge's. That was my big haul at Christmas. There was a budget of ten cents, but at the time, I thought that it was a wonderful Christmas.

I started grade one at Bowmore Road Public School, but my father moved the family out to what was then the country, to Agincourt. He was proud that he had saved enough to put a down payment, albeit with a big mortgage, on a small bungalow at 10 Deblyn Drive. Just before we were to move, my old school had changed its attitude and said that I should be advanced to grade two, but I finished grade one at Lynnwood Heights Public School when we moved to Agincourt.

In 1959, my sister Lynne was born. After two rambunctious boys, my parents were ecstatic to have a baby girl. It also made changes for Dan and me. We now had a bunk bed and shared a small room, but it was no big deal. Even though Dan was four years younger than me, he was not a pesky younger brother. He was always good company.

My parents continued to struggle. My father had a lot of debt but was a very proud man who insisted on meeting his obligations.

As children, Dan, Lynne and I had no idea of their struggles. My mother took in sewing jobs and my father worked crazy long hours.

Growing up in the country was terrific. The neighbours were blue-collar workers and we couldn't have better people around us. Mr. Chaney drove a streetcar for the TTC. Mr. Robinson was an elevator repairman for Otis. I never knew what Mr. Kearns did. Mr. Ferry produced a lot of artistic shows for the CBC.

If anyone's car wouldn't start, Mr. Chaney would be there in a second with jumper cables. When my mother was in a car accident, it wasn't long before the neighbours were at the door with food. They were hard-working, good, decent people who struggled to make a better life for their children. There were a lot of life lessons to be learned by being around them.

Because we were in the same grade at school, I would stop at Jimmy Chaney's house on the way to school every morning and we would walk together. This was particularly great because Mrs. Chaney would give me an apple every morning. A bunch of us lived on Deblyn Drive and hung around together: Jimmy Chaney, Yopi Sevenhuissen (who changed his name to John), Larry Pickering and some of the younger kids as well, my brother Danny, Dewey Robinson and Peter Sevenhuissen.

Nobody had any money, so we just had a lot of fun.

The neighbourhood we lived in was ideal for kids. Deblyn Drive was a dead-end street that ended at the park and playing fields for Lynnwood Heights Public School. We had two alternatives for ball hockey. If there were a lot of kids, we would play up on the asphalt at the school. If it was just the neighbourhood kids, we would just set up on the road. We also played a lot of softball. Dan and I would take our bat, ball and mitts to the diamond and within a few minutes, kids were showing up and a game was started.

Living in the country also gave us great places to explore. At the end of Bellbrook when the houses we lived in were being built, the builders had created a huge mound of earth. The water drained down to this area through the ditches into a natural pond. The earth had been there for some time and was firmly packed and had all kinds of flowers and plants growing in it. We called this place the mountains. There was one really big hill and one that was smaller separated by a stream.

The pond had all the usual wildlife. We watched tadpoles turn into frogs. Wild pheasants frequented the area. We caught dragonflies and grasshoppers.

Some days we would keep going past the mountains and walk along the railway tracks to Finch Avenue. The area around Finch Avenue in those days was a swampy area that we naturally called the Swamp. It became an area where people would throw away their junk. Further along Finch Avenue there were forested areas. Some days when we were feeling adventuresome we would ride our bikes along the Swamp.

South of the public school there was a huge field of clover that had been lying fallow for as long as I remember. On the other side of the field was Linwood Avenue, where a couple more of my friends lived. Billy Bullock, who is now a doctor in Vancouver, soon became my best friend. Next to Billy lived Harold Green, who had a pet rabbit that he kept in his house, which necessitated keeping an eye out for the little rabbit pellets. Across the road lived Kenny Holden.

I remember sleeping out in Billy's backyard in a tent when we were seven years old. The next morning Mrs. Bullock had made breakfast for us — bacon and home fries. It was a wonderful meal. Normally I did not have breakfast, so the home fries and bacon together were an unbelievable meal to me.

Just off Linwood Avenue was another source of great fun for us, Lawson's Orchard. Lawson's Orchard was an abandoned apple orchard that also had one pear tree. As kids we were always hungry and in season we ate as many apples and pears as we wanted. The first thing we did, of course, was build a treehouse out of every piece of wood that we could get our hands on. This is where John Sevenhuissen came in handy. He was one of those kids who could build anything with his hands. If you gave him string and wood he could probably build a space shuttle. John was in charge of building the tree house and he did a great job.

Since the orchard was abandoned, weeds were allowed to grow up to the height between my waist and my chest. The weeds allowed us to have great games of hide-and-go-seek. One day we decided to go further than we had ever gone before and followed a path through Lawson's Orchard towards Havendale Avenue. We pushed our way through the weeds and met a couple of kids who went to public school in the village, John Barnett and Donnie Edwards. We all became friends in high school.

There wasn't much in organized recreational activity in those days. The first real activity that I participated in was Cubs and later Scouts. I joined Cubs when all the other kids did. I had to persuade my mother to buy me the uniform. My mother understood, because the first and only organization that she had belonged to was Canadian Girls in Training, a youth organization of the United Church.

Cubs and Scouts opened up a whole new world for me. In those days being a Cub was cool. I learned skills that I still remember today. I can still tie a reef knot or clove hitch. I can start a fire in the rain. Most important, Cubs and Scouts taught me about respect. The Cub and Scout leaders were wonderful fathers who volunteered their time.

Mr. Douglas was a stern man who ran our Scout troop like a military organization. We all had a lot of respect for him and we learned a lot of bush craft from him. Norm Humphries, our other Scoutmaster, was a very modest and quiet man. We listened to him because we liked him. Norm Humphries was viewed a little differently in the community because he lived in a house that had only a basement and nothing above the surface. I think it was because he never got around to building the house above. One day he ran into a burning house and rescued a family. Norm Humphries was a brave man and a hero.

Through Scouts we were able to go outside of our own community. My patrol leader in Scouts for the Antelope patrol was James Stanbury, whose uncle Robert had been a cabinet minister in the Trudeau cabinet. Occasionally we would have to meet over at James's house. To all of us, his family lived in a mansion on Kennedy Road just north of Finch Avenue. Years later, I realized that the house wasn't a mansion, but it certainly seemed like one compared with the modest houses where the rest of us lived.

My most memorable camping trip was to Markham. We carried our camping equipment off a country road and along a railway track. We found a place next to one of the tributaries of the Rouge River. We took the usual supplies: beans. In those days we were able to catch fish from the Rouge with our fishing lines. We knew a lot about edible plants from Mr. Humphries, so we had plenty to eat. The great discovery was a large patch of wild raspberries. At that camp, I stuffed myself with them. To this day I love raspberries.

One of the other great discoveries of my childhood occurred when I was 11 and the school PTA held a strawberry social. My parents always tried to fit in and insisted that we participate. I had never eaten a strawberry before. They were almost as good as the raspberries.

If there is one thing the Tsubouchis were, it was competitive. It didn't matter what it was, no one liked to lose. We were sore losers. We were gracious in victory but obnoxious in defeat. It didn't matter if it was a team game or a board game played at home, it was always a life-and-death struggle.

Some of the toughest competitions took place at home over a Scrabble board. The primary argument was who would have the board facing him or her. This is when I learned to read upside down. At the end of the "negotiations," the board usually faced my mother. She was the undisputed decision-maker and was beyond challenge, even by my father. This continued until one day I finally bought a Lazy Susan to put the game on. The game with its challenges usually resulted in someone with the Tsubouchi temper blowing his stack. Thirty seconds later the dispute was forgotten and the game continued until the next blow-up.

My father eventually bought Apex Cleaners from his boss, Mr. Smith. My father had a reputation for doing good work and being skilled at removing difficult stains from delicate clothing. His customers included Larry Grossman, who became the leader of the PC Party of Ontario, and Stompin' Tom Connors. Because of the quality of his work his dry cleaning business was very busy.

My mother started working for Apex Cleaners, doing the mending work, before my father bought the store. My mother was a very good seamstress. After my father bought the business, my mother used to work the counter. She was a natural. My mother had a great memory for detail. When a customer came in, she recognized him or her on sight and she greeted every customer by name. She knew their addresses and the names of their spouses and children. Quite often she would know about birthdays and anniversaries. My mother was always pleasant and accommodating, even when a customer had a complaint. She lived the motto that the customer was right.

Unfortunately there were times when even my very diplomatic mother was stymied. On those rare occasions she would have to call my father from the back, where he was processing cleaning. This was not an option that was exercised lightly because it was the equivalent of pushing the button to start a thermo-nuclear war. If the customer still persisted in unreasonable behaviour, she would yell "Tom" and my father would come to the front of the store, his face dark with thunderclouds.

When I saw the Seinfeld portrayal of the "Soup Nazi," I thought immediately of those occasions when the unfortunate and unsuspecting customer caused the "Call Tom" option to be exercised.

My father always assumed that when someone had caused my mother to call him, that customer was being mean or abusive towards her. This was something that he did not tolerate, ever. It always started with my father giving heck to the customer, even before he knew what the complaint or cause was. My father gave only two options. The first was to apologize to my mother and he would give the customer a second chance. The other option was to get out and never come back again.

Surprisingly the second option very rarely had to be exercised.

My father was the strong, no-nonsense backbone of our family.

My mother was the heart of the family.

No matter what had happened, my mother was there for all of us. It wouldn't matter how bad things were or how down you were, she was there with comforting words or a hug. My mother was very petite. She was about five-foot-one and weighed maybe 95 pounds. She was very shy, but if you did anything bad to her family, she turned into a wolverine.

My mother and my Auntie Haru were both shy. Auntie Haru told me that many of their girlfriends when they were young were jealous of my mother's good looks and would call her stuck-up but she was just very shy.

I remember once when I was five years old, coming home upset because some older kids had called me names and pushed me around. My mother sat me down and asked me what was bothering me. When I told her, she looked at me and asked me if I was injured. I answered that I wasn't. Then she asked me if I was ashamed of her and my father. I said that I wasn't. Then she asked me if I was ashamed of myself. I said no. My mother then said if I let someone hurt me by something he said, that I let him win, and that he doesn't win unless I let him. Then she gave me a hug and everything was fine.

When my father came home, he told me to punch the bully in the nose. The next day I took his advice. It led to my first trip to the office. I also found out that bullies don't like to be punched in the nose.

My mother was soft spoken and I don't remember her ever getting angry at us or raising her voice at us. We simply didn't want to disappoint her.

My father was a reminder that opposites attract. We were in awe of my father. He was not big in stature, but to us he had the presence of Zeus. The greatest threat that we could ever hear was, "Your father will not be happy to hear this."

My father was never home because he was working such long hours. He would leave before the sun rose and get home after dark. My father never complained once about how hard he had to work.

I do remember that he did attend all the really important dates with my mother — like the father and son dinner for Cubs or my grade eight graduation.

Since my father was always working, everything else defaulted to my mother. She never missed anything. She would be at the Christmas pageant at the school even if Dan's part was just banging on a pot with a wooden spoon. When I was sick, she would deliver my newspapers.

On Saturdays when the CBC and Channel 11 from Hamilton used to televise professional wrestling, my mother I would watch wrestlers like Sweet Daddy Siki, Billy Red Lyons, the Tolos Brothers, Lord Athol Layton and Whipper Billy Watson. It might seem like a strange mother and son activity, but I remember it fondly. My mother used to root for the good guys. Years later when I was the Minister of Consumer and Commercial Relations, I would work with Chris Layton, who was the son of Lord Athol Layton. Chris was the director of communications for the LCBO. He also inherited his father's size. Chris is a big man and a really nice man.

I have picked up some different likes and dislikes when it comes to food because of my mother. My mother used to drink tea with sugar and Carnation Evaporated Milk. Today I still occasionally put Carnation Evaporated Milk in my tea despite the cloyingly sweet taste because it reminds me of my mother.

My brother Dan was a mischievous kid who would always test boundaries. Occasionally he might stretch the truth. One day when he was 10, Dan decided to climb onto the roof of the public school so he could retrieve all the tennis balls that we had shot up there playing ball hockey. When he was climbing down the flagpole he slipped and scraped his face. When he walked in the door at home, my mother asked him what had happened to his face. Dan explained that he had tripped at the school and scraped his face on the pavement.

Unfortunately my mother knew what had happened; before he'd returned home, she'd already received four calls from other mothers asking if Danny was okay after falling off the flagpole.

Caught red-handed!

Typical of my brother's philosophy as a kid was his response to my mother's warning to both of us not to cross the railway tracks. I never would. Dan walked up to the tracks and looked them over. He then balanced on one rail and walked along the rail but he still had not technically crossed the tracks. Then he would balance on the far rail. Then he was on the other side. Nothing bad happened, so to Dan, there was no problem.

The most despised meal that my mother made for us when I was a kid was liver and spinach. Both liver and spinach are theoretically good for you. This was in the early days of my mother's ability to cook. When I was a young boy, my mother was not the greatest cook. My Bachan Takahashi hated to cook and never really taught my mother how. By the time I was a teenager, however, my mother had become a very good cook. But back then, my mother would cook the liver until it was the consistency of leather. I used to kid my mother later in life by telling her that her liver used to be like a train, "chew, chew, chew." Adding the boiled spinach to the liver was adding torture to torture for us. This was when I was 11 and Dan was seven. But like a dutiful son I would eat the meal.

Dan had a very different view. Our kitchen table was an old '60s-style kitchen table with an Arborite top and steel legs. It was a little larger than a card table and had a drawer for cutlery but my mother used the drawer to hold pencils. One day my mother needed a pencil and discovered where Dan had been hiding two months' worth of liver and spinach.

My brother followed his own way in life. For a kid who didn't eat his spinach, and who worked the front counter of the family dry cleaning business for free, my brother has been very successful.

Nothing we did cost money and we had great childhoods that were full of mysteries and discoveries.

# CHAPTER SIX

# GROWING UP

After we moved to Agincourt, into a relatively small community, our lives seemed to settle into a comfortable routine. Lynnwood Heights Public School had just been built in 1955. The kids who went to the school included our neighbourhood, Highland Heights from across Kennedy Road, and the kids from up Kennedy Road in the more rural areas, who were the bus kids.

You remember certain teachers from when you were young who were wonderful role models. I was lucky to have two teachers who had a big impact on my life.

Mrs. Margaret Britain was my teacher in grade three. There were times when it was challenging for me at school because I looked different and I was as a result self-conscious. I was the only visible minority in the school until my brother went to kindergarten. Most of the kids were pretty good to me but there are always a few older kids who want to make fun of anyone who is different. That of course meant me. I can't recall exactly what Mrs. Britain said to me but I felt better as a result. She was a no-nonsense teacher who had a big heart. Years later when I met her at the Markham Fair

Dance she told me that she still had the little perfume bottle that I had given her at Christmas 40 years before.

Mrs. Britain was my teacher when it was decided to have three of the grade three students also complete grade four in the same year. My best friend, Billy Bullock, Susan Hibbert and I ended up doing double duty that year, but I don't really remember it as extra work. Mrs. Britain was our mentor and teacher. It was fun and easy.

Grade five found the three of us taking time out from every day to study away from the class, and we had special classes in the small school library. We learned French and studied Prester John. It was one of the first gifted programs of its sort.

The most special place for me in the school was the library. I loved it because it was filled with books. By the time I was in grade three, I had read all the biographies. Other kids were reading books like *The Space Ship under the Apple Tree* and *Curious George* while I was fascinated by the life of George Washington Carver and Thomas Edison.

One day Billy told me that he had to go to the Agincourt Public Library to return a book and asked me if I wanted to go with him. We rode our bikes over a number of farmers' fields and through a forest and up to Midland Avenue to the library, which was located in a small house. Walking into the public library was almost like Christmas morning for me. I eagerly got a library card and signed out three books. From that day on I rode my bike two miles to the library every week.

When you come from a family who can't afford many things, you live within a world of limitations and lack of experience. I couldn't afford to go to see a movie and I had no money to buy books. My family did not go on vacations to interesting places. We certainly did not go to see performing arts. There were so many things that I didn't realize that I did not know.

What the library did for me was open the world of possibilities. It taught me what I might be able to do with my life. The library gave me the opportunity to aspire. The library showed me that there were worlds to explore, places that I never thought I would ever see.

Suddenly I knew that I could do something other than what my parents did. At least I could dream that I could. I loved and respected my parents and, although I was a very hard worker, I could never envision myself pressing clothes, even at the age of seven. I now had something to work towards. What exactly it was, I was not sure.

The concern about skipping grades is that the children who move ahead will not fit in socially because they are then younger than the rest of the class. As far as I could tell, we all seemed eventually to be able to make the transition. Bill became a doctor and I got my law degree.

The other great teacher I had was in grade eight. Ed Vine brought an energy to teaching that I have not seen since. Mr. Vine truly cared about each and every student, no exceptions. Going to school was fun. Mr. Vine expected that we would all live up to our potential. We tried to not disappoint him.

Ultimately, schoolwork and getting good marks was not that difficult. I never had homework in public school. Later, in high school, parents were expected to indicate on the report card how many hours of homework the student did. To be diplomatic, my mother used to write in a half hour, even though I never did homework.

The three of us caught up socially in high school, but in grade school, for Billy and me, the one-year difference in our ages seemed a lot, especially at the grade eight dance. Now I had four big social obstacles. I was younger, a brain, the only visible minority and I had no money.

I was also very self-conscious of my appearance. Not only was I a year younger, but I was small and wiry. I had a very uncool haircut. My father bought hair clippers and cut my hair because that way the haircut would be free. And the easiest haircut that someone who had no training could do was a brush cut. This only made me feel more self-conscious. I thought that my ears stuck out as well. In any picture I was the smallest kid. When I had a haircut that looked like it was copied from a picture of Curly of the Three

Stooges at a time when long hair was in style, I definitely felt like an outsider.

No one ever invited me to any parties. Other than with my friends like Billy, I was a persona non grata.

Even though I spent grade school feeling excluded and alone at times, my mother would never let me feel sorry for myself. My mother had a wonderful sense of optimism. She and my father had only one goal: to give us the opportunities they had never had.

Another asset I had was my own determination that I would do better than anyone else. My social outcast status gave me a drive to succeed. I didn't want just to fit in: I wanted to be better. I was a shrimp but I wasn't afraid of anything. I also had to consciously think about what I needed to do to make my own life better, even when I was young.

One of the things that I was most self-conscious about was my clothes. My clothes were clean and neat but, much like my haircut, they were out of style with what the other kids wore. I begged my mother to let me get a paper route for the *Toronto Star*; a boy I knew wanted to give his up because it was too much work. My mother agreed on the condition that I would live up to my responsibilities. I was allowed to spend the money in any way that I wanted.

In the early '60s, the *Toronto Star* cost 10 cents. For every paper I delivered I got two and a half cents. The paper route had 40 customers. The *Star* was delivered six days a week. I made $3.60 a week delivering papers. I collected for the papers once a month. If I was short when I had to hand over the money to the *Toronto Star* rep, it came out of my pocket. If even one customer didn't pay me, it was worth almost one week's labour. I had to be relentless in collecting. With some customers, I had to go back to collect five or six times. There was no such thing as a tip except at Christmas. I would get an occasional tip at Christmas of 25 or 50 cents. Most people did not tip.

I never missed delivering my papers. As soon as the papers were dropped off at Kennedy Road and Bellbrook, I would be waiting, and my customers got their papers as soon as I received them every day. I was never late on my own account. I had one grouchy old man who complained that the paper was always late. I had no choice but to listen to his unfair ranting every day.

I also looked for any opportunities to make even more money. I mowed as many lawns and shovelled as many driveways as I could.

Every penny I made delivering papers and doing other jobs when I was in grade school, I spent on clothes. These were not cool clothes but ordinary clothes that normal kids would wear to school. Wearing funny clothes was one social stigma I could do something about, so I did.

Whenever I wanted to buy candies like other kids I would ride my uncool bike with the paper carrier rack to Austin's Pharmacy miles away and look for empty pop bottles that I could turn in for two cents each. I didn't want to waste my hard-earned money on extras. This was a funny discipline.

I had another liability. I didn't like to take crap from anybody. I disliked the older kids who called me names. The taunts usually came when they were in a large group. It's funny how gutless people seem to get braver in large numbers.

The only time I ever got the strap in grade school was in grade seven. I remember this because my grade seven teacher, Mr. Gough, was the one who administered the punishment. At recess I was being harassed by two kids who were in grade eight. One of the boys was holding me while the other boy was going to hit me. I kicked the one who was going to hit me in the balls. The one who was holding me ran off to tell on me. The two older boys never got into trouble but I got the strap. I don't remember the strap hurting me but I remember feeling a deep sense of unfairness.

The school called my mother and I thought that I was in a lot of trouble when I got home. My father was a tough disciplinarian. I was fearful that I was going to get it worse at home. The worst part was the anticipation while I was waiting for my father to come home. When he did, he asked me to tell him what happened. I truthfully told him everything. When I finished, all he said was, "Don't ever take crap from anyone. You need to stand up for yourself." That was it.

This outsider status continued into grade nine. When I was in grade nine I was barely five feet tall and 95 pounds. I was small but I never forgot what my father told me. I only found out later the "crap" he had taken from the Canadian government.

The first day of grade nine, I was lucky because Billy was in the same homeroom as me. One the bigger kids in the grade who had been held back a year decided that it would be funny to stuff a little kid into a locker. He made a big deal about it and grabbed me. He was almost six feet tall and was laughing at me. I hoofed him hard and he collapsed on the ground. He never tried it again. Later, after I grew in size, I made him suffer every time he had the misfortune to play any sport opposite me. I went out of my way to get him.

Grade eight at Lynnwood Heights Public School — because of Mr. Vine and despite being a social outsider — was as good as it could have been. My siblings and I found academics easy and we breezed through our studies. My father was a really good athlete and we also seemed to inherit his abilities.

I realized even in grade school that if you were a good athlete, it went a long way to making you acceptable and less of a pariah. Every sport that I tried, I found that I was good at — except swimming, where I sank like a stone. I played soccer and softball for the school. I was one of the fastest runners in track. The one sport that my brother and I became obsessed with was hockey. I first started skating when I turned ten. Dan laced up the skates at age six.

I played hockey on the grade eight team with boys who were at least a year older than me. I was always a good hockey player. I could score my share of goals. My biggest asset was that on the ice I was fearless. I didn't care how big anyone was. If someone went into the corner with me, I went in with bad intent. I didn't care about the puck, I went in simply to take out the other guy. Maybe this was a product of being smaller, but in the days before it was illegal to crash someone into the boards from behind, I would. I found that many bigger boys started to fear going into the corners or behind the net when I was coming.

I also learned when I was playing bantam hockey that I was good at fighting. I never stayed down and wasn't afraid of being hit. Eventually I found that I enjoyed fighting even more than scoring a goal. In the intramural league in law school, if you got into a fight you were suspended for the next game. In three years of playing hockey at Osgoode Hall, I played only every second game. I only ever picked on someone who was bigger than me or who had done something bad to one of my teammates.

My rough-and-tumble style came about because I had a bad temper and it didn't take a lot to get me started. I never took offense at a clean check. If someone decked me because I had my head down, that was my mistake. If somebody threw an elbow, I would drop my gloves and start throwing punches. When I realized that everyone on the ice was afraid of me, I could do what I wanted. That's when I started playing with a lot more unpredictability and bad intent. I also realized that most guys playing hockey have some fear of getting into a fight, so if you are willing, you win most of the fights. I also realized that if I took down the biggest and toughest guy on the other team, I owned them.

I played all contact sports the same way. One hundred percent forward. No backing up. If I could hurt you, I would. My father used to say I played contact sports like Mr. Hyde. Off the ice or playing field, I was Dr. Jekyll.

Most of my teammates appreciated that I would protect them in a scrap. One of my law school teammates was afraid that someone might retaliate against him and asked me to dial it down.

In grade nine I was too small to join the football team but I was determined to do something. I decided to run cross country. Nothing in my background could have possibly led me to the conclusion that I would be a good cross-country competitor.

My friend Freddy Campbell, who was originally from the United States, was a hurdler, and he asked me if I was interested in running track for a club team. I had always done well in school meets and had been caught up in all the hype in Canadian track and field with the success of Harry Jerome. I went with Fred one day to the Scarborough Lions Track and Field Club, which was being coached by John Hudson. I tried out for the club and Mr. Hudson decided that I had some potential as a sprinter, so I became part of the team. Training for track gave me a new discipline that I had not experienced before. The warm-ups and constant reps were new to me. There were tests that seemed irrelevant to me, like vertical jump measurement. I ran both the 100-yard dash and the 220. I was pretty fast, but honestly, I was never good enough to win. If I had a good competition I could finish third. When you consider the regional meets that we competed in, that wasn't bad, but it was enough to know that I wasn't going to the Olympics.

We competed in regional meets all over Ontario. Freddy was good enough to win or at least be in the top three almost all of the time, but I loved the competition. My track career ended when I was 16 and I tore the cartilage in my left knee while returning a kickoff playing football. I remember that day like it was yesterday. It was a home game. I received the ball on the 15-yard line and headed towards the sidelines to let the blocking form up. Just as I was rounding the corner somebody planted my left foot and someone else hit my left knee. There was a terrible snap and my leg collapsed. At first I thought that I had broken my leg. I would have been better off if it had been broken. I was knocked clear out of bounds and was lying there in agony. I looked up and saw that the cheerleading squad was standing over me. I remember specifically hearing Mary Lou Little cheer "Go, Tsubouchi, go!" All I could think of was, please go away. I was helped off the field and sat down on a bench in the dressing room. When I tried to stand up, I couldn't. My leg seemed locked. My coach called my mother, who came and picked me up in her little car.

The next day we made an appointment to see the family doctor. He told us that I had two choices. They could either do radical surgery on my knee or we could see if it could be treated by physiotherapy. We opted for physiotherapy, which was a long and painful process. My knee has never been the same. My knee injury affected every sport I competed in. I had to wear a brace that slowed me down, and in track, parts of seconds count. My days as a sprinter were over.

I don't believe that Mr. Hudson thought I had a career beyond the level I was competing at, because I was short and my father was short. I remember Freddy being upset one day when John Hudson suggested that Freddy might not have a future as a hurdler, as at the time he was as short as I was and ideal hurdlers were tall and had long strides. If John Hudson had looked at Freddy's father he would have thought differently, because Mr. Campbell was a big and tall man. Fred eventually took up competitive cycling and was good enough to compete internationally. He grew up to be over six feet tall.

I went to Sunday school at Knox United Church in Agincourt. One of the kids in my Sunday school class told me that he was training in the pole vault. He had built a pole-vault pit in his backyard. Freddy and I had done the same thing because, as fans of Rafer Johnson, we had visions of competing in the decathlon. He told us that one day he was going to compete at the Olympics. Years later, I was thrilled when Bruce Simpson came in fifth at the Munich Olympics and also won the gold medal at the Pan Am Games and the Commonwealth Games.

Sadly I had my first experience of discrimination from an adult in authority when I was 13 and waiting for Mr. Campbell to pick us up after track practice. Freddy and I had just finished our workout at Birchmount Stadium. We were wearing our Scarborough Lions shorts and shirts and had our track shoes hanging around our necks. A police cruiser drove up to us and the policeman rolled down his window and pointed to me and not Freddy. He told me that if I was still there loitering when he came back, he was going to take me down to the station.

I was terrified. I had never been in trouble with anyone, let alone the police. There was no place for me to go, as we needed to be there to be picked up. Freddy was as concerned as I was. We decided to leave and started walking up Birchmount Road, looking out for Freddy's father's car. It was the first time that I had been overtly picked out and treated that way because of the colour of my skin by someone in authority. I had received my share of crap from kids and occasionally adults, but never from a policeman. It left me feeling scared and ashamed and later angry. Discrimination is a terrible thing to experience.

Cross-country running is a totally different world than training for sprints. I found that I enjoyed the training. This was in 1965, long before people jogged for leisure. I would occasionally wear Adidas sneakers. No one wore Adidas. I would train every night by starting at the high school. I would run down Denison to Brimley Road, then along Brimley almost to Finch Avenue and cut across a farmer's field for a concession to McCowan, then back on McCowan to Sheppard and back to the school. Running all by myself was peaceful.

I found out that running cross country was the lowest of the low in high school. The cross-country team would compete at half time of the football games. We would travel in the bus with the football team to other schools. I remember the rule, "Cross Country Stand." I thought to myself then that I was not going to stand the next year.

That year I also competed on the wrestling and track teams. All of the sports that I competed in in grade nine were the unpopular sports. I enjoyed the competition nonetheless. I also continued to play minor hockey, where I competed against kids my own age and excelled.

That summer the miracle of growth happened. I grew to my present height of five-foot-seven and put on a lot of weight. Because I was always training, both for cardiovascular and weight, I was 165 pounds of muscle and meanness ready to be unleashed. (I added another 20 pounds of muscle the following year.) I tried out for the football team and became the starting running back. I liked the position because I could run over people and around them. I loved the glory. The *Toronto Telegram* covered the high school sports and would report on the results of the games and named the stars of the games. I loved to see my name in the paper when I scored a touchdown.

When you are on the football team and are scoring touchdowns, all of a sudden you have status and popularity. I also found that I was a decent gymnast and competed successfully on the pommel horse. I did a little wrestling and ran track. I continued to play hockey.

By the end of high school I had included playing on the volleyball team. Even though I was not tall, I had a pretty good vertical leap. Bill Clarke and I formed one of the top badminton doubles teams in Scarborough.

Just after my growth spurt before grade 10, I was finally able to convince my father to let me have a cool haircut. My father's hairstyling was not so bad when we were younger, but with the advent of the popularity of the Beatles, long hair was the ticket to looking cool. This was a fantastic breakthrough for me. Of course, I had to pay for my hair to be cut myself, and I did, along with any new clothes I got. Both helped me to fit in better.

My brother Dan was a far better athlete than I was. I had good talent in almost anything I did and could elevate my game through pure determination and drive. Dan was a naturally gifted athlete. As soon as he picked up a hockey stick as a tyke, you knew he had talent. He could skate, even as a five-year-old. When he was playing MTHL, he was scoring four or five goals a game.

He played for the Wexford teams. His tier-two Junior A team went to the finals against Chatham. His team was filled with players who were later drafted by the NHL — Mike McEwen, Mark Napier, Mike Marson, Billy Hazard and my brother.

Dan was smarter than most of the other guys playing Junior A with him. First, he has an IQ of 140; second, he was more interested in economics than stats. When he was 16, I was nosing under his bed looking for *Playboy* magazines but all I found were economics books. He didn't want anyone — especially his teammates — to know that he was a closet economics and finance junkie.

My brother was wined and dined by every university and college of significance in the United States, offering him scholarships to play for them. Every weekend he was flying off to an Ivy League university or top hockey school. He finally decided on St. Louis University, where he eventually became the captain of the team and was a late-round draft selection of the Pittsburgh Penguins and the Calgary Cowboys of the WHA. He never played professionally in North America. He played a year for Davos in Switzerland because he wanted to see Europe and then returned to Canada, where he got his MBA at the University of Toronto and played for Tom Watt on the U of T hockey team.

Dan, true to his nature, went out west to work in the oil industry and became very successful. No one can outwork my brother, and he is one of the smartest people I know. He is currently the vice chair of GMP, one of the largest investment banks in Canada, and is one of the top experts in oil and gas in Canada.

My brother, despite his very competitive nature, is a really decent person. One day when Dan was 16, we were tossing the ball around at the basketball court at Lynnwood Heights Public School. There were a couple of young boys watching us. Finally one of them approached Dan and asked him for his autograph. At the time he was playing for the Wexford Raiders Junior A team. Dan patiently signed the pieces of paper and talked to them for a while. My brother had class even at that age.

Sports allowed me and my brother to overcome much of the social stigma of being different.

Agincourt Collegiate was almost all white. Now that I had started to become somewhat accepted in high school society, there were a few other hurdles. My clothes were still a problem. I heard from a couple of new friends from school, Frank Gardner and Bill Hazlewood, that they got summer jobs at the Tam O'Shanter Golf and Country Club as waiters in the hockey school that was run by former Toronto Maple Leafs great Harry Watson. They told me that they would be making one dollar an hour. They also told me that you had to be 16 years old to be employed.

A dollar an hour was a lot of money at the time. We would be paid for eight hours a day for six days a week. For eight weeks of work, I would be paid just under $400 for the summer. That was more than enough to pay for my clothes and other things that I could never have afforded before.

I walked down to the "Tam" and applied for the job. I lied about my age and, though I still looked young, I looked willing and they must have been desperate for help. I was hired.

After I started working there, I realized that it was the best summer job ever imaginable for a Canadian kid. Harry was a true gentleman. All of the kids who worked for Harry respected him. Years later, when I was the member of provincial parliament (MPP), he introduced me at one old-timers' event by saying he gave me my first job.

In addition to being paid a dollar an hour, we were given free meals. After all the kids had been served their meals, we were allowed to eat the leftovers that had not been served. That meant eating food I had never had before. We could also drink as much Coke, Orange Crush and 7-Up from the soda fountain as we wanted because we served the kids pop as well. These kids, many of them from the States, paid a lot to go to the hockey school.

We also got to meet the hockey players who were instructing at Harry Watson's Hockey School. These stars included Frank and Peter Mahovlich, Kent Douglas and the notorious Howie Young. John D'Amico, who had been a long-time linesman, was the strongest. One day he was horseplaying with Peter Mahovlich, who at the time was probably the biggest player in the NHL. John D'Amico was tossing Peter around like he was a boy. The player who was nicest to the kids was Kent Douglas, who had been rookie of the year with the Leafs.

The best perk of the job was that after 7 p.m. every night the staff for the hockey school were allowed to play shinny for free. Most hockey-crazy Canadian kids in the '60s would have worked for free in return for ice time in the summer. Eventually some of the older kids from the hockey school who were from New York or "Baastan" and who thought that they were pretty good at hockey found out that we were playing shinny after hours. They thought they might put us in our places because we were just waiters who couldn't afford to pay to come to the school. We were challenged to a game.

It was true that we were kids who worked during the summer because we needed the money and we lived in a rural area, but we lived and breathed hockey 365 days a year. As soon as the ice froze outside we were playing on outdoor rinks and ponds. All it took was one kid with a puck, and a game broke out in a matter of minutes. The basic skill that you need to play hockey is skating. Because there was plenty of ice and we skated every day, all of us could skate. We didn't skate at a scheduled time once or twice a week. We skated until we couldn't see in the dark or, more often than not, one of our mothers came to holler at us to come home.

The game was no contest — country boys who lived on skates versus rich American kids. We poured it on until finally they quit. We never heard disparaging remarks again from the hockey school kids, because we owned them that night.

I can also thank the Tam for the opportunity to learn how to golf. Golf to me was a sport for the rich people. The Tam allowed us to play for free after 7 p.m. as well. My dad scraped up the money to buy me what looked like a discarded golf range set of clubs and I found all the balls and tees that I needed to play. I had no lessons and just learned how to play by the hack-and-whack school of golf.

I started to grow and gain confidence — especially after I learned that I could grow sideburns — and I announced to my father that I was going to let my hair grow long. By the time I returned to school in grade 10, I was armed with my athleticism and decent size, new cool clothes and a new haircut. During the summer I also discovered how to talk to girls. One of the girls who worked at the snack bar had a crush on me and gave me free hot dogs and chocolate bars whenever I saw her.

My friend Billy Bullock drifted to a different group of friends deep into music and a kind of hippy culture. I had a couple of other good friends — Rick Ferry, who lived across the road from me, and Billy Fifield, who lived just down the street. Billy was a real cool athlete who had played for the Markham Waxers Junior team and eventually got a hockey scholarship at Michigan State. But Billy was more than a jock. I found out in high school that I really didn't like hanging around with stupid people. Although Billy was the ultimate jock, when we hung around we played chess while we listened to Santana and CCR. We did things most high school kids in the '60s didn't do. Billy once got the bright idea to take a couple of dates down to see the National Ballet in grade 12. Billy and I also hung around with John Barnett and Donnie Edwards at Donnie's house.

Donnie's parents, Hector and Mary Edwards, were very permissive parents and allowed Donnie and his sister Anne to have parties at their house all the time. We had some wild parties for that time at the Edwards' place. Mr. Edwards worked at Burroughs and was one of the early researchers into computer technology. I used to disappear from the parties from time to time to go upstairs to talk to Mr. Edwards about science. He was a brilliant and very nice man.

Billy and I hung around with the jock and cheerleader crowd and at the same time viewed this crowd with disdain because of their shallowness and lack of interest in the world at large.

Rick Ferry was an interesting friend. Rick was fairly tall and very good looking. I was still involved in some uncool activities at school. I played clarinet in the band. Eventually I played first clarinet and was the president of the band. Rick played trumpet. The main goal that Rick and I shared was to meet girls. Since we both played music, we taught ourselves how to play guitar at the same time. We also realized that playing folk music drew a whole new crowd of girls. So we played folk music.

Music gave me a new confidence and cockiness. Grades had never been a problem for me in school at any level. There were two subjects that had given me trouble, however. The first was writing. Not creative writing, but penmanship. I was always in a hurry. When I learned penmanship in grade school, we were taught with ink wells and straight pens and blotters. My attempts were a mess. To this day, my wife, Elaine, tells me that no one but she can decipher my chicken scrawl. This is a skill I have never been able to improve.

My other Achilles heel was oral composition. If I had to speak in front of more than one person, I froze from fear. In grade seven I had to do an impromptu speech of two minutes from a topic chosen from a slip of paper pulled from a fish bowl. I chose "baseball." Since it was a topic that I knew a lot about, I thought that I might have a chance. I gave the entire speech in monotone staring at my shoes. I was terrified.

My teachers showed me a lot of sympathy, since the rest of my marks were very good. I got 51 out of 100 in writing one year and just a little bit better in oral composition.

Rick persuaded me in grade 10 that we should perform "Richard Cory," a Simon and Garfunkel song, at the high school variety night. There would be a whole different bunch of kids performing. He thought that we would now have access to these girls as well as any girls who liked folk music. Despite my misgivings, my bravado trumped my stage fright. Once on the stage I realized that it wasn't so scary, and we did a pretty good rendition of the song as we played our guitars. I realized that once you have performed on the stage, speaking in front of people was easy.

Despite our obsession with meeting girls, Rick was not one-dimensional. His father directed a lot of CBC productions that were based in the arts. I learned about classical music as I played it and enjoyed it. Mr. Ferry owned a huge library of sci-fi pocketbooks and had all the giants: Robert Heinlein, Isaac Asimov and Arthur C. Clarke. Both Rick and I became big readers of sci-fi.

When the high school was doing a production of *Finian's Rainbow*, our band leader asked me if I could pick up how to play a tenor sax because they needed a tenor sax for the pit band. I thought it would be fun, so I learned tenor and alto sax. Rick played his trumpet in the pit band and, surprisingly, Billy Fifield played the sheriff in the musical. The production was directed by Alex Barris, whose two kids, Katie and Ted, went to school with me. Ted was a year ahead of me in school and Katie a year behind. Mr. Barris was a celebrity in our community. He wrote an entertainment column for the *Toronto Telegram* newspaper and was a panelist on the CBC show *Front Page Challenge*.

The next year Mr. Barris, along with the music teacher, John Rutherford, decided to put on *The King and I*. I thought I would play in the pit band again. When the auditions were taking place I was watching them with a few of my football teammates. We were making smart-aleck remarks about everyone who was auditioning. Finally, frustrated at the catcalling, Mr. Barris looked daggers at us and singled out who he thought was the ringleader. I remember him pointing at me and saying, "Dave Tsubouchi! If you think you can do any better, get up on this stage. Otherwise, there's the door!"

Both choices were not appealing. Either I left with my tail between my legs or I got on the stage. Again, bravado and ego won out, so I stepped on the stage. I was given some sheet music for "I Have Dreamed" and the pianist played the first verse. After I finished singing the song there was silence. Mr. Barris looked at me and told me that I was no longer in the pit band . . . I had the part as Lun Tha, the young lover.

Many of my friends became part of the cast. John Barnett played the Captain. Dave Forfar was the prime minister. Ann Edwards was Anna. I sang two songs, "I Have Dreamed" and "We Kiss in the Shadows." My parents came to see the production. My mother told me later that she didn't know that I could sing like that. My mother had heard me singing when I had played my guitar at home, but she meant that she had never heard me sing songs that she knew as stage songs. I could only respond that I didn't know that I could sing like that either.

When my mother started to work the counter for my father at the dry cleaners, I had the job of looking after both Dan and Lynne until my parents came home. My sister Lynne was born eight years after I was. Lynne and Dan are much closer than she and I, as they are much closer in age. As the only girl child in the family, she was treated with kid gloves. Lynne had plenty of personality and friends and was very pretty. My parents were ecstatic to have a little girl.

Dan had a lot of the responsibility of looking after Lynne at school, and then I took over when they got home. That included making dinner for everybody. This wasn't a very difficult job until I turned 15 and started to work at my part-time job and had to leave for work when my parents came home. I was in pretty good shape then and would run a couple of miles to work.

We got into a routine after school. *Star Trek* had just come to television and was my favourite show. Dan liked the show too, but in order to get Lynne on side we had to agree to let her watch *Family Affair*.

Years later I was fortunate to be meet and become friends with George Takei, who played Lieutenant Sulu in the original *Star Trek*. I told him why I loved to watch *Star Trek*. Before that series, every Hollywood portrayal of an Asian was either a grotesque caricature like Mickey Rooney in *Breakfast at Tiffany's* or was an evil character or a war enemy. My parents had always told us to be proud of who we were, but their actions said the opposite. We were made to assimilate into the Western culture and hide who we were. Then George Takei came along as Sulu. He was an action hero. All of a sudden it was okay to be Japanese. I never thought of myself as Captain Kirk, I thought of myself as Sulu.

When I told George this, he then went on to tell me about the *Starship Enterprise* as a universal symbol of coexistence. At a time when black rights were the social issue of the day, here was a black communications officer, Uhuru. At the time of the cold war, there was Lieutenant Chekov.

If you knew George Takei, you would admire him as a strong advocate on behalf of the Japanese American fight for justice. He is also an activist on behalf of gay and lesbian rights in the United States. He still continues to live his life as a hero.

Throughout high school I was known more for being a jock than anything else. When I reached grade 13, I dropped a lot of sports when I realized that, although I enjoyed the competition, I was never going to achieve the level of skill that was needed in the sports that I played to go anywhere beyond being a better-than-average athlete. Determination and fearlessness could take me only so far. I had seen how effortlessly my brother Dan had played hockey and golfed. He had an innate sense of athletic direction that I did not possess. I had to think about what I needed to do. I thought quickly but that was not the same as instinct. I still participated in a number of sports but at a more casual and less intense level. I still wanted to train and keep in shape. I dropped all the team sports and still competed in gymnastics and badminton. I worked out with the wrestling team.

My interests had obviously evolved. The major change in the direction of my studies occurred because I got angry at one of my teachers. Getting good marks in grade school, with the exception of penmanship and oral composition, was easy. I had an exceptional memory and the ability to absorb information. I also wanted to understand the foundation of any lesson being taught. I never accepted a bald statement: I wanted to know why. This was obviously irritating to all but my bright teachers. I am happy to say that with only a very few exceptions I was blessed with understanding, patient and smart teachers. I never studied throughout high school and usually ranked in the top-three students in my grade.

Other than penmanship and oral composition in grade school, I received only one bad mark in school. In an interim report in grade 13 English I received a D. The interim report was not an official report and was supposed to be only an indication to your parents. I blew my top. All the written assignments that I had turned in to the teacher, Mr. Proctor, had been marked with my typical A. I assumed that it had been a mistake.

I immediately went to see Mr. Proctor and asked for an explanation. He advised me that the mark did not reflect my written works and assignments but rather my lack of effort, and that I was not living up to my potential. I asked him whether my assigned work was better than everyone else's in my class, to which he responded that it was but that I could do better. My response was that I should be marked on my assigned work and not on my potential.

When I gave my interim report to my parents, they were shocked. Nobody in our family had ever received such a mark for an academic subject. My father agreed with me and did not question the written work that I had been marked on. My father went down to meet with Mr. Proctor, and I assume that the meeting went the way it did when my mother called him to the front of the store for a troublesome customer.

All through school my best marks had been in mathematics because I appreciated its logic. Once in an examination in high school I achieved 105 percent because I had answered all the questions correctly along with the bonus mark. Science was a close second in marks. That is not to say that these subjects held the most interest for me. I enjoyed history and I really enjoyed creative writing. I was shocked at the mark for English. I was also disturbed that I was marked on the basis of potential and not merit.

I had read that there was a national creative writing contest for high school students, so I thought that I would enter a story to see how I would do and, if I did well, to rub it in to Mr. Proctor. The Canadian Students' Prose and Poetry Contest had more than 1,200 entries and the top 16 were to be published in an anthology of prose and poetry called *Solitudes* by Scholastic Books. My short story, "The Love Song," was selected and published. The news was well received by my high school when it was announced.

Two things were accomplished. My final mark was an A in English, and for the rest of the year I read extensive essays on the books that we studied, including *Macbeth*. I was fully prepared to challenge any statements made by the high school curriculum or Mr. Proctor and to be a real pain in the ass. I also learned that I loved to write, and that had a huge impact on my university studies. I will grudgingly give Mr. Proctor some credit for pushing me to do more.

No one in my family had gone to university. I had absolutely no idea what that entailed nor did I have an inkling of what the experience would be. I did know that in order to have a better life I would need to go to university. I also had no idea of what to study.

Getting into university would not be difficult from a marks perspective, but I would need to earn the tuition and the cost of books and transportation. I also didn't know what skills I might need to qualify in case I needed to compete with others for acceptance. There was an awful lot I didn't know. I couldn't turn to my parents or aunts and uncles. All of my friends were from blue-collar families. Intuitively I knew that I would need experiences other than as a better-than-average athlete or a decent-but-not-gifted musician.

I got involved in almost every extra-curricular activity and committee — United Appeal Committee, Christmas Cheer Committee, debating team and current affairs club. I was the president of the band, editor of the yearbook and the Simpson's rep. The Robert Simpson Company was a large department store that selected one student from each high school in Toronto to be their rep. This involved going to a meeting once a month to Simpson's, where they treated you to a meal and gave you opportunities for fun activities like ski trips or to be models in fashion shows where you could keep the clothes you modelled. You received a blazer and a pair of slacks and a lapel pin.

When I was in grade 12 I also had my first foray into politics. Through the encouragement of several friends I was persuaded to run for the president of the student council. I had not been a member of the student council, but I had been involved in a lot of school activities. I thought to myself, how difficult could it be? The campaign involved basically putting up a few posters and giving a speech at the assembly before the entire student body. I had never given a speech in front of the student body but I had performed.

My competition was Stephanie Prince, who was one of the cool kids who lived in the village and not on the outskirts as I did. She had been involved in a lot of the committees just I had been involved with the sports teams and the band. The kids seemed to be aligned into pretty even camps, and it became evident that the big speech would actually make a difference. I learned a very valuable lesson about political speeches from my high school speech. It's not what you say but how you say it. Ideally you have to have both substance and sizzle, but people listen less and form an impression more.

I took the speech seriously and gave a speech with promises that I knew I could keep. I was straightforward and plain-spoken. Stephanie Prince was amusing and funny. She also won.

I had assumed incorrectly that the students were paying attention to what I had to say. My failing was that I did not get their attention. I didn't give another political speech until 1988 but I remembered the lesson. Adult voters were no different from high school students. If you didn't get their attention, no one listened to the message.

I had a small connection with the Conservative Party when I was in grade 13. I explained this connection to Premier Bill Davis at a function shortly after our government was elected in 1995. I was chatting to Premier Davis when I asked him if he remembered the first time that we had met. He replied that he hadn't. I explained that it was in 1969 when he was the Minister of Education and he was on one side of the barrier and I was on the other side yelling at him. I explained that I had helped organize a protest against the government's intention to increase the high school year by a week. I also explained that my motivation was apolitical. In those days I couldn't have cared less if someone was Liberal, Conservative or NDP; my motivation had been purely pragmatic. I needed that one week to earn my tuition. The government was going to take away my ability to work for one more week during the summer and that might prevent me starting my post-secondary education.

Premier Davis turned to me and said, "David, sometime the biggest rebels become the biggest Conservatives."

I also learned that the more activities that you were involved in, the less the teachers would question where you were. As the editor of the yearbook I received my own key for the school so that we could work on the yearbook on the weekends. In theory, the staff adviser should have been with us but he trusted us. I took the opportunity to exercise a lot of my own sense of humour in the yearbook.

In grade 13 I got involved in a lot more intellectual activities. I was a member of the debating team and enjoyed the challenge of taking up sometimes unpopular positions and succeeding. Our high school entered *Reach for the Top*, the Canadian high school quiz show that was hosted by Alex Trebek before his fame on *Jeopardy*. The school made their selections based mainly on marks but tried to be strategic as well.

Our team consisted of Bill Hazlewood, Wendy Hammond, grade 12 student Vince Letke and me. Bill had studied classical music, so music questions would be his expertise. Vince apparently had a background in art. I am not sure what area of knowledge Wendy had studied and I was apparently a jack of all trades and master of none. I am certain that the school staff did not know of my unquenchable thirst for knowledge and what my parents thought was useless trivia. Even as a boy and young man, I had eclectic tastes in my reading. One day I would be reading a sci-fi, the next, e.e. cummings or a book on the theory of infinity.

*Reach for the Top* got my interest quickly. The school had been provided with sample questions from the TV show. My colleagues studied the questions, but I pointed out that the questions were context and meant only to give us some familiarity with the style of questions. The sample questions were not likely to be used on the show and were representative of the questions of past shows.

I knew a fair amount about classical literature and poetry because of my interests and about classical music because I played it. I realized that although Vince was our expert on art, I did not know much about artists. Art was not in my parents' sphere of interest. I did not like relying 100 percent on anyone else so I embarked on my own crash course in how to recognize the different genres, ages and styles of art. My simplistic method was to train myself to connect the piece of art with the artist and to recognize the artist quickly.

I found that I was able to familiarize myself easily, as I did not think that the show would use examples other than well-known pieces from famous artists; after all, this was a high school show.

Simple things jumped out at me. Modigliani painted long noses. Dali was self explanatory. Miro was also easy. I loved Impressionism, so it was not a task but a joy. I found that I was viewing the artists with an interest beyond my original intention.

Having general or specific knowledge is quite different from accessing that knowledge under the pressure of being on a TV show with time limitations and a live audience. Before the show started I found myself trading quips with Alex Trebek and the audience. It seemed that everyone else, both on my team and the other team, Danforth Tech, was very nervous.

As the show started I realized that it was more important to get the opportunity to answer the question and therefore buzz early even before the question had been fully asked. The only penalty was that if you anticipated the question incorrectly, it was read out to the other team and they could answer. This was not really a downside. I started buzzing early when I felt I knew what the question would be. My teammates seemed to be a little shell-shocked by the whole TV experience. I found that I buzzed in on about 90 percent of the questions. The final score had us winning by over 200 points. The strategy was successful.

We did not, however, advance as far as we could have, and I attribute that to my reluctance on a subsequent show to buzz in as early as I had been doing because, for some reason, I got cautious. That was not a winning strategy. Fortune favours the bold.

High school gave me my breakout years. I gained self-confidence but I also found that I needed to rely on myself for almost everything. I also learned how to network and the advantages of being able to access all the different subcultures of high school. It was in high school that I gained an interest in music, art and literature. Other than the books that I had brought into my home when I was growing up, we had a set of encyclopedia volumes that my mother got for free, one per week from the grocery store. School introduced me to an entirely new world.

# CHAPTER SEVEN

# UNIVERSITY AND THE SCHOOL OF LIFE

It strikes me that many of the current generation who are attending university or college seem to have a lot of choice of where to attend. There are surveys done ranking all the institutions on their programs, services and quality of life for their students. The surveys are published, usually in special edition magazines and newspapers. Students read the surveys and so do boards of governors, who then try to address any of the shortcomings in the surveys.

When I was choosing which university to attend, my decision was based strictly on which was the most affordable. Budget trumped everything. I had an old Austin 1100 car that was on its last legs. Sometimes it started, sometimes it didn't. In the winter I would put an old rug over the engine and used a block heater to keep it warm. I needed the car so that I could get from school to work as quickly as possible. I took into consideration the distance to school and the cost of parking. I also determined if there was a discount gas station on the way to either school or work.

The closest school to where I lived was the Scarborough College campus of the University of Toronto. My decision was made. A few of my high school friends had chosen to attend Scarborough College as well, and they decided to carpool with me. The gas money that they contributed paid for the trip to and from school. Having a couple of extra passengers also came in handy if my car wouldn't start. We could push my car to the top of the hill and hop in and I would pop the clutch and we would be on our way.

I soon made some new friends at Scarborough College. I also found a few other students who liked to play cards for money. I was able to supplement my income from my job by winning at euchre and hearts, and that paid for my books and other expenses for the year.

Like most first-year students who use their freshman year to find their way by taking a variety of courses, I registered for a number of different disciplines including economics, psychology, sociology, English and political science. After my first political science class I came to the conclusion that it was a waste of time and dropped it for anthropology.

I discovered that despite the fact that the reading requirements were quite different from high school, namely several books a week rather than several weeks for one book, I enjoyed my English literature course. I also realized that I wanted to continue writing poetry and prose. I enjoyed the creativity. If I was to pursue my writing, staying at Scarborough College was not an option. I would either have to transfer to the downtown campus of U of T or transfer to York University. Since I was still working part time at Lansing Building Supplies during the school year, trying to save money for my tuition and expenses, I made the decision on purely budgetary reasons. The parking at York University was cheaper.

The transition from the intimate atmosphere of Scarborough College to the campus at York University was fascinating and full of new challenges. Since I was new to York and the program, I had to take one science course and one humanities course to comply with the requirements for first year. I took a sociology course and a physics course. My other courses were English and creative writing with my favourite professor, Frank Davey.

The fact that I didn't have any friends at York wasn't really a problem, since any spare time I used to go to my part-time job at Lansing Building Supplies as a shipper and fork truck driver. Throughout my university and law school education I was able to concentrate all my courses on Tuesday, Wednesday and Thursday so that I could work at my part-time job for the rest of the week. For me, going to school was not a period of leaving home and spreading my wings for the first time; it was an endless cycle of going to class and going to my job. It was also not a time of making new friends, because other than being in class I had no time to socialize. I was not involved in activities. This was totally different from high school because I had to pay for my own education. It wasn't free.

University was uneventful. It became extremely important to complete any assignment as soon as it was given because otherwise I had no time to do it. The weekends were filled with my job. This was how I learned not to procrastinate. What I enjoyed about the university experience in the English department at York was the willingness of the faculty to promote free thinking. I was to learn later that this was totally different from law school.

For those who believe that there is no value in a liberal arts education, I can only disagree vehemently based on my experience at York University.

Frank Davey was a wonderful teacher. I remember meeting with him in his office and discussing writing in general and my writing specifically. He was talented and creative but he was also kind and understanding. It was my best experience in university.

Although my strength was in free verse, it was at this time that I was encouraged to experiment with other styles. At some point I tried concrete poetry and submitted some of my work to bpNichol, who had a publication called *grOnk*. When Canada's and possibly the world's most renowned concrete poet published some of my writing, I was ecstatic. He would occasionally send me some of his work, which he inscribed for me. In those days many of the Canadian poets would have their work "published" on mimeographed paper in very limited quantities.

This was when I started my lifelong hobby of collecting first edition books signed by the author. I had not been able to buy books up to then because I didn't have enough money.

I then tried my hand at doing book reviews for some magazines but soon found that I didn't like negative criticism of someone else's work. Years later when I started the Markham Group of Poets, we concentrated on sharing our work and motivation and positive criticism.

York was a very sparse campus in those days. There were few buildings and few students. We were in the boondocks compared with the sophisticated University of Toronto. In the winter, the wind howled across the bare fields with little to dissipate the cold. But I still liked York. The campus was the antithesis of elitism. The students who went to York were equal to one another. It didn't matter if your father or mother was a judge or doctor or if he pressed clothes or cleaned houses. There was equality among the students and the faculty. There were no fraternities or sororities.

I can't comment on the clubs or the political activities on campus because I did not participate. I was just too busy trying to survive and earn my tuition and expenses. When you had to count pennies for your gas, there was no time for fun.

But York provided me with an opportunity. I was the first Tsubouchi to go to university. I had to work like heck to earn it so I appreciated it. I respected York because it was a university of first opportunity for so many of us. Instead of building more doors that closed in our faces, the doors opened to the future.

I didn't make lifelong friends at York but I was able to create a positive image of my own self worth. I also learned that anything is possible if you work for it.

Years later my father said to me that I must be proud of how I put myself through university and law school. I told my father that at the time, I thought that it was the greatest injustice in the world. While I was working, unloading boxcars in the middle of winter sometimes by hand, most of the other students were having fun, partying and boozing. I also told my father that I appreciated it more because of my experience of how he had sacrificed everything for all of us. We both understood what I meant.

Working my way through university and law school had some real life benefits. I had been working at Lansing Building Supplies (now RONA) at Kennedy Road and 401. Before I got a car, I would walk there from Finch and Kennedy, a trip of about three miles. My mother would pack me a lunch in a lunch box. It was nothing to walk there and back because it was in the country. We walked everywhere.

Working at Lansing meant that I was working with real men. Because of the nature of the job, you didn't work there if you were a weakling. You were constantly loading concrete, lumber, drywall or plywood sheets, basically all heavy building material. I started working as a shipper. I would load the trucks along with the truck drivers. Sometimes I would put together a load and put steel straps around the load and use the fork truck to load it on the truck, but most times it required putting several retail deliveries together and planning the route the truck would take and loading it accordingly. These retail loads were mostly done by covered truck, so loading was labour intensive but easy.

Sometimes the plywood or lumber needed to be cut to certain specified sizes and this is how I learned to use industrial power tools and equipment. It was mostly simple to do but there were some tasks that I preferred not to do. One of the jobs that I disliked most was bundling loose bats of fiberglass insulation in the heat of the summer, as the loose fibres got on your sweaty skin and I probably breathed in a lot as well. The other was ripping two-by-four lumber into two-by-two. You had to really pay attention when you were feeding the lumber in if you didn't want to lose a finger or two, because there was not a lot of leeway for error.

Occasionally, I got a break from the humdrum of loading lumber or unloading boxcars full of lumber when a driver needed someone to help them deliver a load that he couldn't do himself. Even though the task usually involved delivering drywall up five flights of stairs it was a nice relief.

As long as I worked hard and didn't take any crap, I found that I really enjoyed working with the guys. I had a really great boss, Jon Berlinghoff, who was in charge of the shipping department. Jon was a bright and surprisingly optimistic and cheerful person. He also gave me a lot of opportunities to work overtime. As I went from high school to university, he gave me more and more responsibility, which I enjoyed. More often than not he would put me in charge for the evening even though I was a part-time worker and a student.

The guys who worked at Lansing were good, decent people. Just like me, they came from working-class families. There were no pretentions. What you saw was who they were. Any real disputes could be settled with fists behind the lumber pile. I know because I ended up there a couple of times. There were a couple of old curmudgeons who worked in the yard with me. Stan White was the foreman in charge of receiving. He was a strict, no-nonsense man. There was only one way of doing something: his way. If it wasn't done properly, it was redone until it was.

One of the guys who had shown me the ropes was Malcolm Thistle. Mal seemed be the target of all and any scorn that Stan White had for "college boys" because Mal was working on his university degree. As long as I stayed out of the way, Mal took the flack, partly because Stan acknowledged, grudgingly, that I was a hard worker. More important, I never tried to show that I was smarter than everyone else. Mal Thistle didn't try to show he was smart but he was a bit of a wise guy, and that meant he got the worst jobs from Stan.

On Friday nights, there was only a skeleton crew on in the warehouse and the yard and our responsibilities were to load the trucks for the Saturday deliveries, which were mainly retail and to service any retail customers for the evening. It took us only about an hour to load the trucks and there weren't a lot of customers. One of the other young guys, Jimmy Atkinson, who ran the wholesale office of Lansing, which was located in the back, always had a football to throw around. The usual suspects were Mal Thistle, Larry Shaw, Jimmy Atkinson and me.

One day, Jimmy Atkinson, who fancied himself somewhat of an athlete, saw a note in the lumber industry magazine that there was to be a lumber industry fastball league created. Jimmy immediately volunteered Lansing Building Supplies to enter as a team. We had enough young guys to play and the question was, did we have the talent? As it turned out, one of the older fellows, Willie Featherstone, had pitched in the Beaches years ago and, although his fastball had lost a little, he still had an unhittable drop ball and changeup.

With great enthusiasm we played the season and, to some amazement, we won the championships. I played shortstop and hit around .800 and had a great time. To celebrate, Bill Kitchen, the distinguished and wealthy owner of Lansing, invited the team to his house for a barbecue. I had never seen such a big house in my life. Although I didn't have much call to see or speak to him, he always seemed like a classy person to me.

After that success, Jimmy decided to organize the very first company golf tournament at the Tam O'Shanter Golf Club. Despite the fact that most of the employees had never picked up a golf club, a great time was had by all.

I had my first real connection with politics while I worked at Lansing. One summer I was asked to show the ropes to a young fellow who was just a few years younger than me. Apparently he had gotten the job because his father was a friend of Bill Kitchen. In those days, I couldn't have cared less about politics. I was just trying to earn as much as I could.

He was a bright person and very personable and we got along very well. One day in August he asked me if I had any interest in the new cabinet of the federal government. I didn't and said so. I realized later that Doug really knew because his father was Senator Keith Davey, otherwise known as the "Rainmaker."

The lesson I have learned continuously in my life is that with good people the journey is much more enjoyable. I can say with gratitude that the guys at Lansing made that part of my life enjoyable despite the hard work. They were good people the same way as my neighbours in Agincourt were good people.

During my time at university I still tried to make time to play hockey. I played in a couple of industrial leagues and one year, at the encouragement of my father, I played in the Japanese Canadian Men's Hockey League. That turned out to be a bit of a mistake.

Even if I tried to, when I laced on the skates, I couldn't control my competitiveness and my desire to run anyone I played against through the boards. My behaviour playing minor hockey and industrial hockey followed me around like a bad scent. On my first shift at George Bell Arena, I got caught up the ice and these two brothers did a really nice give and go and scored. They celebrated as they skated by me, high-fiving each other up the ice. I punched one of them in the face and when the other brother stood up for him, I knocked him down too. The funny thing was that all three of us got two minutes each for roughing. My team scored on the power play. There is no justice in hockey except frontier justice.

All of this bad stuff that I did was never premeditated. I just played the game with a mean streak. On the plus side, other teams were afraid to come into the corner with me. They didn't know what I would do. I used to drop the gloves at the slightest provocation. The only hockey fight that I ever lost was because the linesman was holding me alone while my opponent kept pummelling me. But I have never been hurt in a hockey fight. I don't count lost teeth or stitches as being hurt.

The only time that I was ever really out to get someone was over an insult to my brother. At the time in 1975 after Dan was drafted by both the Pittsburgh Penguins and the Calgary Cowboys of the old WHA, he was being pursued by the Japanese corporation Seibu to play hockey for their corporate team and then for the Japanese national team. Dan had huge attraction for the Japanese national team. The average size of the Japanese hockey players was more like me except lighter. Dan was a six-footer and played at well over 200 pounds.

Seibu had agreed to fly Dan to Japan and then wined and dined him for two weeks. At the same time there were other possible recruits but none had the hockey pedigree of my brother. For two weeks the executives tried to persuade my brother to move to Japan. They offered him financial terms that were more than competitive with professional hockey. They offered him a place to live and a job with the corporation in the off season. They offered him travel. In the end there was one big problem.

Although Dan was of Japanese descent and looked Japanese, he was 100 percent Canadian. His normal diet when he was young was hamburgers and French fries. He was a big meat and potatoes guy. The only thing close to being Japanese in his diet was when he would fry up a big pan full of fried rice. The only vegetable to Dan was a potato.

When Dan got back, I asked him what he had thought of Japan. He looked at me and said that he didn't like the food, he didn't speak Japanese and everybody stared at him because he was so big. He had declined the very generous offer to play in Japan. The consequence of Dan's decision was that the other possible recruits for the team were not needed or wanted because the company had not signed their main target.

When one of the other possible recruits came back he started bad-mouthing my brother. This eventually got back to me. Coincidentally, this guy's first game upon his return was against my team. I remember that day distinctly. My mother had decided to come to the game with my father to watch me play. As soon as I stepped on the ice, the entire arena exploded into a chorus of boos. My mother was so embarrassed that she never came to watch me play again. My father thought it was funny. I got even more revved up.

I was on the ice at the drop of the puck. I played right wing and so did the alleged bad-mouther, so we were on opposite sides of the rink. That was a mere detail to me. It would not be the first time that I charged at someone from across the rink. The puck was dropped and I took a full-speed charge at him and put him in the boards. As he tried to get up I cross-checked him to the ground then I skated away. I was kicked out of the game and never played another game in the league. But no one got away with screwing with us.

As a Japanese Canadian family, we lived in a kind of voluntary isolation. No community in Canada in the '50s and '60s had more than one Japanese Canadian family. Other than my cousins, I didn't see any Japanese Canadians on a regular basis. We didn't attend the Japanese Buddhist temple nor did we go to the Japanese church. We didn't socialize with other Japanese Canadian families other than mainly Auntie Haru and Uncle Tosh and my cousins Bruce and Gary. We had started our process of assimilation.

As I got older I started to appreciate how important cultural centres were, especially to the Japanese Canadians. My family from my generation going back is 100 percent Japanese ancestry. My extended family from my generation forward is more than 95 percent mixed marriages. As the Japanese Canadians intermarry, we will no longer look Japanese and we will likely lose a lot of the cultural connections of language and customs. It is through these cultural centres that we can explain and show our grandchildren where part of their ancestry comes from.

The Japanese Canadian Cultural Centre in Toronto is the perfect model for such an institution. More than half the membership and board of directors are not of Japanese descent. The JCCC is used by many outside organizations and welcomes visitors. The Japanese cultural courses, whether they are for martial arts or flower arranging, are enjoyed by the community at large. What I like most about the JCCC is that it builds bridges and understanding.

# CHAPTER EIGHT

# OSGOODE HALL

Becoming a lawyer was never a conscious aspiration for me. Just achieving a university degree was an accomplishment. Other than seeing episodes of *Perry Mason*, I had no idea what a lawyer really did. No one in my extended family had anything to do with the law nor did any of our family acquaintances. If anything, to most of the Japanese Canadians, the law was the means used to strip our community of everything we had. The law was to be suspected, not trusted.

The other notion I had was that in order to be a lawyer, you needed to come from a privileged family. Your father had to be a lawyer or judge and so had your grandfather and so on. The law profession at the time was by and large a very exclusive club. The entry fee was pedigree and wealth. It was just another case of pressing my face against the window at Simpsons and looking at the Christmas toys that others would receive.

I thought that after graduating with my degree in English I could teach English. I loved the creative thinking and analysis of Frank Davey and John Lennox, the professors who taught at York University. They were positive and intelligent teachers.

There were not many teaching jobs at the time, unfortunately. I was contemplating this and what I had to do to get employment when I happened to chat with my high school friend Peter Dudding, who told me that he was going to try writing the LSATs and that I should as well. After finding out what the LSATs were, I decided to sign up.

I was always good at standardized tests. I still love logic puzzles and cryptic crosswords. There would be no pressure because I had no real expectations. Today, students take courses on how to write the LSATs or buy instruction books. Back then, I just showed up on the day of testing.

I didn't find the test very difficult. In fact, I was finished early in every section.

When I received the results I applied to Osgoode Hall Law School mainly because it was at York University and fit my gas and parking budget. I must have had a good result, as I was accepted.

Fortunately in the early '70s the tuition for law school was not a lot more than regular tuition. Unfortunately I had to continue to work a part-time job during the school term, but I was used to it. The scariest part of going to law school was that I had no idea what that would mean. I had never even seen the inside of a law school. I had no idea of the amount of work that was expected. I had no friends who were going to law school.

I remember the usual speech on the first day of law school about how dedicated and hard working you must be to graduate and be a privileged alumnus of Osgoode Hall. "Look to your right and then look to your left, one of you will not be here by the end of the year." Sure enough, our first-year class started with 300 students. By the end of year we were down to almost 200 through attrition. We had been warned.

The other thing that the students told us was, "The first year, they scare you to death. The second year, they work you to death. The third year, they bore you to death." This too was true.

When I got my course materials I knew that I didn't have any time to waste because of my job requirements, so I read the entire semester's reading in the first week. I wasn't sure what to expect in class, as I was used to the acceptance of creative theorizing in the arts. I soon learned that I was in creative hell. Like legal precedents, we were bound to follow conventional wisdom.

I soon learned to dislike the Socratic method of teaching and the snide comments of some of the wimpiest students. They were in their element where the weapon was sarcasm and not a punch in the nose. They could hide behind the phony decorum and not be accountable. We were being programmed like little robots.

In fairness, I had some pretty good professors who made their classes interesting. I was privileged to have Peter Hogg for administrative law, Louise Arbour for criminal law and Ron Atkey for constitutional law, all of whom went on to greater achievements.

I discovered that there was an intramural hockey league and that each of the five sections of the first-year class was going to field a team. It was 1972, the year of the Canada–Russia series, and the first time there was a Team Canada. One of the guys had the bright idea of naming our team after Team Canada . . . sort of. We decided to call ourselves Team Cannabis and, instead of featuring a maple leaf on our jerseys, we would have a big marijuana leaf. The other sections named their teams similarly.

I didn't really have the time for hockey, but it really never leaves the blood of a Canadian kid. I loved hockey because it allowed me to mete out justice to anyone I chose. I loved throwing a hard bodycheck more than scoring. The second year I played I was having a brutal year scoring. I was playing right wing. I finally scored in a game that I was playing with a sprained wrist. When I shot the puck it floated like a knuckle ball — much slower than the goalie expected — and somehow ended up in the net.

There was another Japanese Canadian kid in first year, Glen Wakabayashi, and even though we were in different sections, we hung around a little. In the cafeteria there were some pinball machines Glen and I would play. We also discovered that in the business school they had better machines. In my third year they held a pinball competition. I was the champion of Surf Side.

One day, Glen told me of an incident that occurred during his hockey game. The goon from the other team had called him a "slope head." I had never heard the slur before but I didn't like it. Unlike me, Glen was a really nice guy who was more of a fancy stickhandler than a fighter. I filed the incident for future reference.

The next week when I was playing against the goon's team I kept an eye on him. He was a lot bigger than me. He had me by about half a foot and about 30 pounds, but that didn't really matter to me.

Our games were refereed by only one official. When the play had been whistled dead, the goon skated by me. As he passed I said, "Try calling me a slope head!" and speared him in the back. He then tossed a punch at me. The ref turned and separated us and gave him a penalty for roughing. As the goon skated away from me, I speared him again in the back. He then skated at me again and got another penalty for roughing. Finally he skated away again and for the third time I speared him in the back. This time I engaged him, and it was a pretty even fight. I love justice.

One game when Glen was playing against me, an awkward thing happened. He was carrying the puck over our blue line. I was backing up and waved my stick at him. Unfortunately his knee caught my stick and deflected it into his groin. Glen dropped like a stuck pig. I clearly did not intend to do that. I was soon surrounded by his teammates and I knew that there was going to be an accounting, especially considering my reputation.

From the ground where he lay, Glen croaked out, "It was an accident."

The incident was over.

Things seemed to be going well and then all of a sudden I had no energy and was tired all the time. I lost my appetite and I started to lose weight at an alarming rate. I went to see my doctor, who told me that I had mononucleosis. He told me that I would be likely experiencing the symptoms for weeks.

I contacted the law school authorities who advised me that because of my medical condition I could restart my year the following autumn with no penalty or I could continue but I would be subject to the same conditions as everyone else. For better or worse, I decided to continue on. I couldn't afford a year off.

Law school is very competitive. Everyone wants to make sure that he or she is not going to be the one person out of three who does not make it through the first year. It only takes one or two real idiots to make conditions bad. Someone had been razoring reference books in the library. In other words, someone had cut out pages or partial pages from reference books to prevent others from getting the same source for an assignment.

Later in the year, the day before the property law exam, I had left my property law notes in the library when I went to get a coffee with some friends. When I returned, I discovered that they had been stolen. My notes would have helped no one, as I used short forms that were a combination of Latin or made-up symbols that only I could understand. My notes almost looked like an alchemist's. In some classes when I was bored I wrote the notes backward so you would have to use a mirror to read them.

Fortunately, I always felt that studying the day before an exam was a waste of time if you didn't know it by then.

The point is that law school is not just competitive, it is über competitive.

It was in this context that I discovered who my friends really were. I couldn't attend class and needed notes other than the textbooks. My new friend Nancy Toran would take a bus from York University once a week and bring a copy of her notes to my parents' home in Agincourt. It is still a very long trip even today by bus. Nancy, her husband, Victor, and my wife, Elaine (whom I met after law school), and I are still friends today. It was largely because of Nancy that I managed to get through my first year and not be one of the one-third who didn't.

Nancy herself was a bit of an anomaly. Nancy was the youngest student in our class at Osgoode. I was 20 years old when I entered law school. Nancy was two years younger than me. Nancy was an odd fit for law school. She was a free spirit who would sometimes fight the system in clandestine ways. It was great to be Nancy's friend, but it would be a very bad to be on her list of enemies.

I had another good friend in law school, Dave Hunt. Dave was very slight and unathletic. I had long hair in law school that used to hang out the back of my hockey helmet, but it was the early '70s. Dave's hair made him look like a stoner. Dave was never into drugs but he looked like Spicoli in *Fast Times at Ridgemont High*. Dave was also a walking encyclopedia of rock music and could recite artists and songs, dates and B-side songs. He used to come and watch our hockey games.

Dave was raised by his mother, Mary, and like me, lived in Scarborough. I didn't have much when I grew up and Dave came from a similar background. I always admired Dave because he made his own way through university and law school too. I also admired his willingness and guts. Dave couldn't have weighed more than 140 pounds soaking wet yet was always competing with us when we threw the football around. He would get knocked down and dust himself off. He would never complain.

When we attended the Bar Admission Course, I used to pick up Dave on my way downtown. Dave lived in a tiny one-room apartment on MacPherson Avenue. I used to say to Dave that his apartment was so small, you had to stand in the hall to take a leak. Every day he would have a bologna sandwich for lunch. That was his budget.

In the Bar Admission Course you have an exam once a week for half a year. It is a pretty intense time since you have already invested, in most cases, six years of post-secondary education plus a year of articling. No one wanted to screw up now. People would use most of their time studying.

Dave Hunt and I along with another friend, Don Fiske, used to go play pickup hockey after the morning classes at an outdoor rink. As much as Dave Hunt was a non-athlete, Don Fiske was a very talented one. Dave had more determination than his body was capable of producing. He was not a good skater. If there were three, four or five other people playing hockey, Don would challenge them to play against the three of us. We had a simple strategy. We told Dave to stand by the net and Don and I would get the puck to him. More often than not when we did, Dave would land on his behind but he would get back up.

You could never keep Dave Hunt down. He is now a Justice of the Peace and doing a good job, according to his peers.

Law school was again a time of work and study. There was very little time for fun and good times because that required having leisure time. As a result, when others might have been creating networks and sharing their mutual interests and backgrounds, through circumstance, I was again on the outside.

# CHAPTER NINE

# TO BE OR NOT TO BE

I never had a burning desire to be on the stage or in front of the movie cameras. Other than my brief foray as Lun Tha in *The King and I* in high school and before the camera on *Reach for the Top*, I had no experience.

In the early '80s I served on the board of the Japanese Canadian Cultural Centre. One evening during a meeting the phone rang and I answered. It was Doug Barnes from the CBC, and he asked me if I could post a notice that they were looking for extras to appear in an episode of *Home Fires* that dealt with the Japanese Canadian internment during the Second World War. I told him that I would. He then asked me if I was Japanese Canadian. I said yes and he asked me if I would consider being in the show. I told him that I wasn't an actor but I would think about it.

My curiosity got the best of me, so I called Doug Barnes and went down to the CBC to meet with him. And so I became an extra. The day of the shooting I was fascinated by the behind-the-scenes preparations. The crew and cast members were all very nice. In addition to the entertaining day, I got paid. I thought it could be a very interesting hobby, one that paid.

I didn't think much about it until I received another call from Doug Barnes a few months later. They were shooting *I Married the Klondike*, a series based on the life of Pierre Berton's mother. He asked me if I would like to show up as an extra. Again it sounded like fun, and because it was a period piece I would have to go down for costuming. Since it was for a mini-series I was required for several days.

I must admit it was intriguing to see how a production was made behind the scenes. In the case of the setting for *Klondike*, the street scene was shot through a glass frame that had the upper façade of the buildings. Not having to construct the whole building saved a lot of money. I found that the people who were the background actors were really nice people.

Shooting movies or television shows entailed a lot of waiting for a few minutes of filming. There was also a lot of waiting for the scene or scenes that involved you. That left a lot of time for chatting with your fellow actors. The extras were a mix of people. Some were trying to make a serious career and working for a break for a real speaking role. Others liked just being an extra. There were a few who were filling in their days. And there were a few like me, a curious sojourner.

I was amused when I saw the Ricky Gervais series *Extras*, to see how accurate it was. The reality is that it is a very competitive and disheartening profession with a lot of rejection. I enjoyed it because it was an interesting hobby for which I got paid. I got to meet nice people and see productions from a perspective that was not generally available. While chatting to one of my colleagues during one of the many breaks between shooting, he suggested that I get an agent and gave me the name of his agent to contact. After thinking about it for a week I called the agent. The agent's name was Clibby Verrian and the agency was Face and Places.

Clibby's office was in Scarborough and I went down to meet her. We chatted for about an hour, and I signed up with her for a year to see whether or not it worked out. That was the start of a 10-year relationship.

Anyone who has seen *Tootsie* has seen what the life of an actor is like. The actor goes to innumerable auditions and gets a lot of rejection. Like Dustin Hoffman, you are too short or too tall or too ethnic or not ethnic enough. When you walk in the door, the director knows whether or not he wants you and you can only lose the role by opening your mouth. I honestly don't know how actors can endure the negativity, except that they have to start with a lot of optimism and self-confidence.

There are so many talented and well-trained actors and so few roles, and fewer good roles, that many will take work as extras just to network and keep in the business. I had no training, but I think that Clibby saw the potential for character acting.

Shortly after I had signed with Clibby, she called me to go down for an audition for a new movie that David Cronenberg was directing. David Cronenberg was the wunderkind of Canadian movies. He had a reputation for the creative, macabre and offbeat with his recent productions of *Scanners* and *The Brood*. I didn't know much more about him. I was dabbling in the acting world and I never really followed the acting scene. I just viewed this as an interesting hobby that paid me.

The audition was in some building on Eastern Avenue in Toronto. As usual I was early so was just hanging around at the door to the building when a young fellow walked up. He was wearing a leather jacket and carrying a bag over his shoulder. He saw me and started chatting with me. He seemed like a nice guy and he asked me what I was doing there. I told him that I was here for an audition and that I didn't really do any acting but it seemed interesting.

He said that he was going up as well and we talked and I went up with him. When the elevator stopped and we got out, the young lady at the desk looked up and said, "Hi, Boss!" I knew she wasn't talking to me.

He turned to me and said, "I'm David Cronenberg. Come in and we can chat."

That was supposed to be my first audition, but I got the job without reading for it. I knew it wouldn't always be that easy.

When I got home I called Clibby and told her what had happened. There was a stunned silence and then she congratulated me. The movie was *Videodrome* starring James Woods, Sonja Smits and Debbie Harry. *Videodrome* was to achieve cult status and would later be referenced in many movies, television shows and music.

The first day of shooting I was in took place at the Selby Hotel on Sherbourne Street in Toronto. In the scene were James Woods, Harvey Chao and me. When I got to the location, James Woods walked up to me, shook my hand and said, "Hi, I'm Jimmy." Since I didn't really follow movies and actors, I didn't know who James Woods was but I recognized his name and knew that he was one of the stars. He was a really nice guy who was respected by all of the production staff.

The scene was fairly straightforward and the shooting was quickly done. Naturally I played the heavy, and that seemed to be the beginning of my career playing the bad guy. This would be an easy transition from my role as a hockey goon.

After *Videodrome* I had a number of roles as an extra and one recurring job as a special business extra. This meant that they needed you for every episode for a series so that there was continuity. Ironically, I played a member of the newspaper staff where Louie Del Grande worked in the CBC series *Seeing Things*. This was an interesting job in that you were paid for a full day's filming even if you were not in any scenes and just went home. The Consumers' Gas Building in North York was transformed every weekend into a newspaper building.

My next principal performer job was for John Byner's comedy show, *Bizarre*. The role for was a Japanese waiter. I remember the audition because the director wanted someone with a Japanese accent. So that we didn't have accents, my family did not speak Japanese in the house when I was growing up. I didn't know how to speak with a Japanese accent. By chance the night before the audition I was watching Dick Cavett on television and he was doing his impression of Sessue Hayakawa in *The Bridge on the River*

*Kwai*. So I practised my Japanese accent based on Dick Cavett's impression of Sessue Hayakawa.

When I did my over-the-top Japanese accent for the audition, apparently the director liked it, which made sense because it was a comedy show. The format for *Bizarre* was very different from television jobs that I had been in. There was a rehearsal and then a few days later it was shot in front of a live audience. That was a lot more fun than shooting a scene just for the camera.

The normal cast of *Bizarre* consisted of well-known Canadian actors like Billy Van, Jack Duffy, Jane Eastwood and Steve Weston. The director of the show was Bob Einstein, otherwise known as Super Dave Osborne. His younger brother is actor Albert Brooks, who changed his surname for obvious reasons.

It was intriguing to observe these real pros at work. Acting in front of a live audience was exciting. I must have made a good impression because I was asked to do another *Bizarre* skit a couple of weeks later, no audition required. I would play a karate instructor and kick actor Tom Harvey through a wall.

The next call I got from Clibby was for an audition for *SCTV*. The role was for an Asian gangster. This seemed to be right up my alley. The audition went well. The skit was "The Bowery Boys in the Band" and the guest star was Robin Williams. I had to do more physical work and this time it called for me to get into a fight with Robin Williams.

It was a thrill working with Canadian stars like John Candy, Martin Short, Joe Flaherty and Eugene Levy. For *Bizarre* I had rehearsals, but when I showed up for *SCTV*, I was handed a script and told I had 10 minutes before we shot the scene. The best part of doing *SCTV* was when the cameras stopped shooting. Robin Williams and John Candy kept improvising. It was exciting to watch genius at work. Of course when we shot the fight scene, Robin Williams won and "hit" me so hard that my hat flew off my head.

A few months later I was called back for another job on *SCTV* starring Betty Thomas called "South Sea Sinner."

Years later, after my time in politics, I was attending a gaming conference. The organizer of the conference had engaged Marty Short to entertain, and he wanted to interview someone in his persona as Jiminy Glick. I was asked to be the victim. Marty wanted to speak to me an hour before the skit. When I showed up he looked at me and said, "Bowery Boys in the Band and South Seas sketch."

That was amazing, I thought to myself, because that information was not available on the internet at the time. When the act started it was impossible to keep a straight face. What a talent!

In between the two *SCTV* jobs, I was able to successfully get my first commercial. Clibby sent me down to Hayhurst Advertising to audition for an American Motors commercial. Commercial work, I was to discover, paid very well. You were paid for the original shooting of the commercial and then every time it was shown you would earn a residual. The commercial would contain my voice only for most of the commercial followed by the surprise that I was not white, but Asian. Apparently I got the commercial based on my voice.

During the interview I was asked if I could speak French, and to demonstrate. My French was good enough for the agency to use me for both the English and the French version of the commercial.

On the day that the commercial was shot, I learned the difference between being an actor with a bit role and the main performer. The food provided for the day was first rate and so was the treatment. The commercial was titled "Abacus."

After completion of the commercial, Clibby excitedly advised me that I now qualified to join ACTRA. ACTRA (Alliance of Canadian Cinema, Television and Radio Artists) is the actor's union. This was good news in that it was a lot easier to get auditions and parts if you were a member of ACTRA.

To qualify for ACTRA, you needed to have six speaking parts in an 18-month period. Typically, the irony is that in order to get good roles you need to belong to ACTRA and in order to join ACTRA you need good roles. It was logical move, so I joined ACTRA.

The only other interesting role that I got was in another commercial for a company called Money's Mushrooms. Money's Mushrooms was like the Sunkist for mushrooms and marketed mainly in western Canada and the United States. I was to play a monk. The first visit was for makeup to measure my head for a bald prosthesis. The prosthesis was to be made in New York and flown back for a fitting. After my second visit and the fitting I was given the date for the shooting of the commercial.

When I told Elaine that I was to play a monk in a commercial, she looked at me curiously and asked why they would pick me to play a monk. When I asked her why, she said that I did not look remotely like Friar Tuck. I answered that I was playing a Buddhist monk.

The commercial was pretty straightforward. There were three monks and we were chanting "Mmmmm" until the tag line "mmm-mmarvelous!" I arrived two hours early because I was told it would take about an hour and a half to apply the bald prosthesis. During the shooting of the commercial under the bright, hot lights it was necessary to keep fans blowing to keep me from sweating under the bald prosthesis otherwise the sweat could cause creasing. The shooting of the commercial went very smoothly.

After I removed the prosthesis and was about to leave the director approached me and asked me if I could use chopsticks. I said I grew up using chopsticks and asked him why. He told me that the hand model didn't show up for the close-ups of chopsticks holding the mushrooms and asked me to do the job.

In fairness, I pointed out that my hands had been scarred from various things, including punching out teeth while playing hockey. He told me that makeup would take care of that. So, like George Costanza from *Seinfeld*, I became a hand model.

Eventually my law practice became too busy for my hobby in acting, and although it had brought me much enjoyment, my acting career ended.

# CHAPTER TEN

# MARKHAM, NEW BEGINNINGS

I never had any intention of getting involved in politics. What I did have an interest in was volunteering in my community.

After we got married, Elaine and I had to decide the best place to live and raise a family. We had the choices narrowed down to two communities — Burlington and Markham. Both communities seemed like nice places to work and raise a family. I was more familiar with Markham because I grew up in Agincourt. We used to play hockey games at the Crosby Arena in the days when the players' bench had two rows of seats. The first movie that I had ever seen was in 1963 and it was *The Three Stooges in Orbit*, screened at the old Roxy Theatre on Main Street.

One Sunday we took a drive to Markham to look around. By chance the Family Trust Real Estate Office was open for the first time on a Sunday. We told the agent on duty generally what we were looking for and our price range. Soon we were off to look at homes. Most of the houses were not what we were looking for. We didn't want a modern house, but rather one with some character.

The agent then mentioned that a house had just been listed and might be of interest. It was a century home on Main Street North.

When we drove up, I could see that the house had character. It was a two-and-a-half-storey home with a wraparound porch. As we inspected the house, we could see that it was very interesting. The décor definitely was not to our taste. Almost all the floors were covered in either red or orange shag rugs. The walls were plastered with red flocked wallpaper. After we were back in our own car, Elaine said that it looked like it was decorated in early bordello and that she expected to see Miss Kitty from *Gunsmoke* walk down the staircase.

There were other interesting features. The house had two separate basement rooms. One was the usual basement you expected, with a workshop and laundry room and storage. The other room had a trap door that was covered in shag rug so when it was dropped it blended in with the rest of the rug and was hard to see. The agent explained that the owner occasionally had poker games and the trap door provided security.

There were some really nice features. The house still had all the original stained-glass windows, woodwork and panelling and sculptured tin walls and ceiling in the living room. The house also had one of the only dumbwaiters in town, but unfortunately it had been converted to accommodate the central air and vacuum.

The second floor had a balcony off the main hall and a sun porch off one of the rooms. The attic had stairs leading up and had the potential to be finished.

There were a couple of strange things that jumped out at us. Almost every room had a bar. The upstairs bathroom had been redone to combine the existing bathroom and one of the bedrooms to make a very large bathroom. When I opened what I thought was a linen closet, I discovered that the bathroom had a built-in refrigerator that was full of small champagne bottles.

The property was fairly large, almost half an acre. I didn't think that the house was in our price range by a country mile. Even with my limited ability to visualize its potential, I could see the possibilities. The logistics of buying the house seemed impossible to achieve, however. Not only was our budget limited, but interest rates for a first mortgage at the time were running between 18 and 21 percent.

As we drove home, I commented to Elaine that I really liked the house but it was priced way over our budget. She turned to me and said, "You're a lawyer. Why don't you write up an offer for what we could afford and give it to the agent?"

It was a really smart idea, but I thought that if we were to fit the price of the house into our budget, my offer might be a little insulting. Nonetheless I wrote up an offer for $60,000 below the listing price and for a take-back mortgage at nine percent. I also wrote up the offer under Elaine's name. I had the offer sent over to the agent and didn't really think much about it, basically because I thought that this wasn't even a Hail Mary pass.

That afternoon I was shocked when the agent called me back and advised me that my offer had been accepted. Apparently the house had been listed because the owner had gone on holiday and met a man who asked her to marry him and move to the States and she was in a hurry.

I called Elaine up and said, "Guess what? You just bought a house."

That was how we moved to Markham.

More than 30 years ago Markham was a much smaller community than it is today. Markham was separated from Scarborough by a greenbelt. You basically knew who lived there and who was a stranger. It was a great community and we had everything that you ever wanted. We had a small IGA and a hardware store. We had a drugstore. Lloyd Barthau's jewellery store was a mainstay. I bought my insurance from Carson and Weeks. There was a shoe store, a men's clothing store and a women's dress store. In those days, you knew all of your neighbours and no one locked their doors.

Markham was a good place to raise a family. When I was in politics and had to produce an official biography, our family did not appear in any of them. Elaine would prefer that this continue and I will respect her wish to maintain the privacy of our family. I did end up doing all the normal things. When one of the kids played hockey and softball, I coached hockey and softball. When one of them competed in equestrian sports or figure skating or competitive swimming, that became our interest as well.

I must mention that in 2003, when both the party and I went down in defeat and I had to make a speech to my supporters, my daughter Jacquie stood beside me. She was always there no matter what, but in this particular time of need she never faltered.

I also do need to mention my grandson, Ethan. There are few people who get my jokes. Ethan does. He is a very good-hearted kid and luckily is a gifted student. He once asked me when he was eight years old if I would vote for him if he wanted to be prime minister one day. I told him I would run his campaign.

I have always hated driving to work so we decided to open a law firm on Main Street North, just down the road from the house. This was a big risk because in Markham, I had no clients and no staff and I had to look for a location. There were two long-time, old family law firms on Main Street North: Mingay and Associates and Cattanach, Hindson.

Markham was like a lot of small towns. If you hadn't lived there for 10 generations, you were a newcomer. I knew that it might be a challenge to establish myself in town.

One funny way of identifying how long someone has lived in Markham is by how they refer to the municipality. If you call it a town, you moved here in the '70s, '80s or '90s. If you call Markham a city, you came after 2000. If you say township, you have been here since the '60s, and if you say village, you are a real old-timer.

When I started looking for office space, I found that Carson and Weeks had some space on the second floor of their building that I would be sharing with the Pilot Insurance accident adjusters' office. I gratefully took the space.

Since I had no office furniture and equipment, I took advantage of used furnishings. Since I had no money and no staff, Auntie Haru volunteered to work for me as my receptionist and secretary for free. It had been years since Auntie Haru had worked, but when she was younger she had good typing skills and shorthand. Every day Uncle Tosh drove Auntie Haru to work and picked her up. Auntie Haru and Uncle Tosh were already my favourite aunt and uncle, but I couldn't have done this without them.

Those first days of opening my law office were long and boring. No clients meant no work and therefore no income. We didn't really know anyone in Markham. After a while a few people started to drop by, probably more from curiosity than anything else. Then I started to get some clients. I also got a few clients from the Japanese Canadian community.

I had always been a great supporter of volunteerism since I was young. I coached hockey and softball but I wanted to do more. One day my next-door neighbour, George Crompton, mentioned to me that a few of the guys were in the process of forming a branch of the Optimist Club in Markham and asked if I wanted to come to the organizing meeting.

The Optimist Club meeting was great. I met a bunch of new friends and got a chance to make a difference. I eventually served as the club president and lieutenant governor for the Optimist Club. One of the accomplishments that I felt proud of was an innovation that my friend Dave Hunt and I introduced to the annual speech contest for youth that the Optimist Clubs sponsored. We opened the contest to children who were deaf and could use sign language as well.

Recently a friend, Anne Ashley, a teacher and a volunteer at the Japanese Canadian Cultural Centre, told me that she had attended the speech contest with some of her deaf students and how much that it meant to them that they could compete with hearing children.

Eventually, the practice grew and it became a little too much for Auntie Haru. It was then my sister, Lynne, replaced Haru. She was a godsend. She basically managed the office and took care of the toughest transactions as my assistant. Lynne knew everyone and besides being really intelligent, treated all my clients as if they were special. In those days I could not have managed the office without her skills and her diplomatic relationship with my clients.

Soon after my sister began working with me, I met a young lawyer, Al Parker, who was looking for a place to practise law. When I met Al, I instantly liked and trusted him. It wasn't much later that Al joined me as my partner, and the years with Al were fun and happy. Al was a great guy. We sponsored and coached softball together. I joined the Optimist Club and Al joined the Rotary Club. We volunteered at the Markham Fair and the Markham Festival. I sat on the Markham BIA. If anyone wanted our help, we helped.

Al and I shared the same view of life. We both felt that it was our responsibility to contribute to our community and to give back. Any local non-profit organization that asked for our help, we gave it. In Markham we incorporated scores of non-profit sports groups, charitable organizations and ratepayers groups for free.

In the early '80s the Markham BIA decided to have a Festival of Lights to kick off the Christmas holidays. Al and I helped to organize the event. We dressed up in period costumes for an old-time Christmas, and when the street closed for the event we gave out hot cider and shortbread cookies that Elaine baked.

When the businesses on Main Street wanted to put on an event in the summer, we also helped to organize the Markham Festival, with vendors, entertainment, rides and demonstrations. The Festival continues today as the Markham Jazz Festival. When the Rotary Club or the Optimist Club needed someone to flip burgers at the Markham Fair, we were there.

Al and I did all these things because we wanted to and we had a lot of fun doing it. We didn't do it to bring in business, but we were gratified when people started to come in and give us their business.

It was at this point I realized that in business it actually is better to give than receive. When this is your attitude, somehow mysteriously the returns are multifold. Good karma multiplies.

Al and I never had even one legal aid file, but we knew who in our community needed help. We did a lot of pro bono work. In many cases, people who did need our help were too proud to accept free work from us and insisted that somehow they compensate us. We did work for a lot of strange things — a basket of corn, strawberries and in many cases homemade cookies.

Elaine once said that we would never be really rich because I gave away too much for free.

Once when we were shopping at the local IGA on Main Street I bumped into an elderly lady who lived in subsidized housing and I knew her sole income was from her Old Age pension.

She hailed me in the aisle. "Mr. Tsubouchi! I need a will and a power of attorney. Can you tell me what you charge for this?"

At the time, the going rate was $150 for the will and power of attorney, but I knew that she didn't have much money.

"I'll do it for you without any charge," I offered.

"No, no, no," she said. "I need to pay my way."

I asked her, "How does five dollars sound?"

"That sounds fair," she answered.

She made an appointment to see me on Monday and we prepared and signed her to her will and power of attorney.

The next Saturday while shopping at the IGA, I heard my new client hail me again, "Mr. Tsubouchi, you did such a good job, I recommended you to everyone in my building and told them what your rate was."

I ended up doing 30 wills and powers of attorney at the well-paid rate of five dollars per person.

Years later when I ran for Markham Council and later for MPP, everyone in the building volunteered for me.

Those were our halcyon days. We weren't making a lot of money but we were doing alright, and more important, we felt good about what we were doing and our place in our community. When I walked down the street I felt like I belonged.

We built the practice together. At one point we had nine lawyers and two locations operating.

In 1987, I was asked to get involved with a ratepayers' group that was fighting against industrial development on the north side of 16th Avenue on the other side of the road from their subdivision. The issue made sense to me and soon I was one of the leaders of the group. Fortunately, this was one of the times that the council did the logical things and decided to deny the industrial development and allow residential instead. Although this was better for the ratepayers, it opened a whole new set of concerns.

As 1988 arrived, I was approached by several people and asked if I might consider running for council. The incumbent Ward 5 councillor, Gord Landon, had decided to run for Regional Council and that left the seat vacant. I was flattered but had never considered running for politics before. I did think that I could do a good job but I needed to consider the impact on my business and family.

The person whose opinion I asked was Elaine. My question was simple: should I run for council? Elaine thought about it for a while and then said that I could do a better job than most of the members of council and if I wanted to try, she would fully support me. I appreciated the confidence she had in me, but that then led to the next question.

Ward 5 was an area that contained the old village of Markham. Markham today is the most ethnically diverse community in Canada. This was definitely not the case then. The area was a fairly established part of Markham and the ethnicity was primarily white and British. The obvious question then was, would the residents of Markham vote for a visible minority council candidate?

There were already three candidates for the vacant position, including one of the current hydro commissioners (an elected position), Don McNabb; a ratepayers' president, Donna Shaw; and a popular community volunteer, Roy McCutcheon, all of whom were white.

Elaine looked at me and said, "First of all, you were born here and you sound like it. Second, people have a hard time figuring out what you are anyway. And last, I don't think it would make any difference."

The next person I needed to talk to was Al Parker. As usual, Al was supportive and enthusiastic. He thought it was a good idea. He said, "There's no downside. If you run and lose, look at the profile that we will have for the law firm."

Having made the decision to run for the Ward 5 seat, I needed a campaign manager. I had some experience in political campaigns. I had volunteered on a number of PC campaigns. I had also run my friend Al Rayner's campaign for Ward 4 councillor in the previous election. I decided to call a friend and local volunteer, Linda Paterson. Linda had been active in many organizations like the Markham Fair and was a long-time Markham resident. To my delight, she agreed.

I had decided to pay for my campaign entirely without donations. I knew that if I had chosen to accept them, I could have easily raised more than enough money to pay for the campaign, as one of the things I had done was raise money for Don Cousens, the local MPP. The usual campaign donors were the developers. Since the job of a councillor is about 85 percent development issues, I did not feel comfortable accepting donations from the developers. I do not think that someone could influence a councillor with a donation of $200, but I do believe it presents a perceived conflict of interest to the public.

Campaign donations are publicly disclosed. When a development application going through the process comes to a public meeting where the application is being vigorously opposed by a ratepayers' group, you do not want the fairness of the process to be an issue. The law allows these donations. It is time for the law to be changed to a system similar to the federal one, where no corporate or union donations are allowed. Only personal donations should be allowed, and with limitations on the amount.

Following my decision not to accept campaign donations, I made a public announcement that I would not accept donations from anyone and specifically from developers. The day after my announcement, curiously enough, I started receiving cheques from developers for donations. We photocopied the cheques and returned them to the developers along with a letter reiterating my position. I wanted them to clearly understand that I was serious. We would run a lean campaign that I would fund out of my pocket. On the positive side, accepting no donations made reporting and accounting a lot simpler.

The basic logistics of any campaign may seem simple on paper, but when a relatively inexperienced team is reviewing the decisions, the issues feel a lot more complex. The first part is people. We were few but committed. Our canvassing team would be Elaine and me along with Al Parker, Linda Paterson and Marc Bossi. Al Rayner would run our sign team. Along the way different people volunteered for various jobs.

The first major decision would be what would the signs look like? There were several sign decisions: do you put the candidate's face on it? What colour is it? How big? How many? Where do you put them?

As I had never run for any office before, we decided to put my face on the signs. Putting your face on your sign was not the norm back in 1988. In Markham, there was rarely a change in council. Only when a sitting member of council decided not to run was that considered an opportunity. This is more or less still true today. Unless a member of council gives the public reason to vote him out, rarely is someone voted in. Since the sitting members of council were well known in the community, none of them put their faces on the signs.

The next decision is, what colour do you use? In 1988, most councils did not have party affiliations, with the exception of the City of Toronto and their NDP caucus. In Markham at that time the town had been consistently represented both federally and provincially by the Progressive Conservative Party. Although I had been volunteering with the local PC parties and sat on the local riding executive, I decided to use a neutral colour. My signs would be green. The message would be simple: Vote for Dave Tsubouchi for Ward 5 Councillor.

Our other innovation for the 1988 election came with the size of some of the signs. Campaigns for ward councillor all used lawn signs about the same size. The campaigns would use these lawn signs as road signs as well. Candidates for mayor and a few for regional councillor would use larger road signs. I decided to use large road signs with my photo on them. I thought that the facial recognition would be good since I was a political unknown. The argument against putting my face on the signs was that some time during the campaign somebody would deface my signs and therefore my face. I agreed but I told everyone that we would cross that bridge if and when we came to it.

Our expenses would be fairly low. There would be no campaign office. I am still convinced that the best tool for winning a campaign is for the candidate to knock on doors. We were not going to use a lot of advertising, so had to go door to door. As I have learned later, most campaigns will start canvassing in September after Labour Day. We didn't know any better so we started knocking on doors in March.

Normally I liked to have our canvassing team consisting of Elaine with Linda Paterson or another volunteer on one side of the street and me on the other with Marc or Al. Many times it was Elaine on one side of the street and me on the other. We knocked on doors in daylight and darkness, wind and rain. Despite the sometimes bad weather, it was probably the most interesting campaign I had. I had a chance to listen to people, their concerns, worries and hopes for the town. I was offering a blank canvas for them to write on.

One advantage with municipal politics is that the buck stops with you. There is no obligation to party policies or strategy. It also requires more courage, because you cannot hide behind party policies or strategy. I would listen and use people's comments to think about what might be in the best interests of the town. I was also determined that anything that I committed to, I would carry through to the best of my abilities.

People were very grateful that we stopped to listen and meet them. Many were surprised that someone actually knocked on their doors. The most frequent comment we received was that our visit was the first time a candidate had actually come to their house. The biggest challenge was that many people invited me to come in for a cup of tea and chat. Most times I declined, as time was a factor.

One evening when Elaine and I were alone on a canvas, I heard her shouting at me from down the road to come over to where she was. When I got there, she turned to the man at the door and said, "There he is," and pointed at me. Apparently she had told him that I was canvassing up the road and he didn't believe her that I was actually knocking on doors on his street. He took a lawn sign.

Even with our commitment and enthusiasm, canvassing is hard work. Two days before Election Day, I turned to Elaine and told her that I was tired and had had it. Elaine and I had personally knocked on every door in Ward 5 except for one street. I had driven down the street. Every lawn had a sign for Donna Shaw, one of my opponents and the president of the local ratepayers' association. She also lived on that street. Elaine said we had to canvas that last street. I told her that I just didn't have the energy to knock on one more door. She then told me that she had taken a phone call that day. She said that a woman with a very distinctive voice had called and said that she hadn't heard from our campaign and that she was very disappointed. Elaine knew this woman must be from the one street we had skipped, and told her that we were going to be canvassing on her street that day. We headed out.

It was a small street, so we decided to walk together as Elaine thought that she could recognize the distinctive voice. When we knocked on the last door, which was next door to where Donna Shaw lived, and a lady came to the door and said hello, Elaine elbowed me in the ribs. This was apparently our mystery caller. We had a nice chat.

We felt good that we had finished what we had set out to do and had knocked on every door. When the results came in, I noted that we had a large majority of votes in the poll for the last street that we canvassed.

During the election it was impossible to catch everyone at home. When no one was at home I would write a note on my campaign literature, "Sorry I missed you, Dave." One day Elaine received a very angry call from a lady. She was angry because she had received my campaign literature and she said that someone had written insulting remarks on my pamphlet. Elaine asked what had been written on the literature. The lady said that someone was making fun of my Japanese heritage and had written "Solly, I missed you." Elaine had laughed politely and explained that no one had defaced our literature, but that I had written the note and I had very bad handwriting because I was always in a hurry.

One day the inevitable happened, and somebody defaced one of my signs. I had received at least a dozen calls telling me someone had drawn devil horns on my head. Marc Bossi wanted to go out and replace the sign immediately. I told him to wait a couple of days, because it was getting a lot of attention.

The campaign had run smoothly. The debates were civil and I thought that I had performed well. We had done what we could. Now all that there was left to do was wait.

Waiting for the returns is always the most difficult thing. We watched the returns on the local cable station. After about an hour the station declared me the winner. I could feel one weight being lifted off my shoulders and another replacing it. I wanted to be a good councillor. That meant being truly accountable and doing the right thing.

# CHAPTER ELEVEN

# MARKHAM COUNCIL:
# FROM A TOWN TO A CITY

The 1988 municipal election brought four new councillors to the Markham Council. This was a big change from the usual status quo. The new councillors were Bill Fisch, Jim Jones, Ken Dunphy and me. Bill Fisch was a lawyer who had graduated from Osgoode Hall the year before I did. Jim Jones worked for IBM and Ken Dunphy owned his own trucking company. We all seemed to share the same view of the world needing more accountability.

We joined a council of veterans of many years of service. Tony Roman was a longstanding mayor who had returned to be mayor after stints of being the Regional chairman and the member of Parliament (MP) for York North. The regional councillors were Ron Moran, Fred Cox, Gord Landon and Frank Scarpitti. The returning ward councillors were Bob Sherwood and Doreen Quirk of Thornhill, Tom Newell, who shared Markham Village with me, and Alex Chiu of Milliken.

Frank Scarpitti, who was the youngest member of council, had a natural affinity with the new councillors, all of whom were a lot younger than the existing members. We wanted to involve our ratepayers in the decision-making process, where the older members wanted to keep making the decisions, because they "were paid to make the decisions." There was a lot of push back from the senior members of council because they "knew better," and most of our inexperienced suggestions were dismissed out of hand.

In the year before the election, all of the numerous ratepayers' group in Markham had joined together to form the Federation of Ratepayers of Markham (FORM) because they felt they weren't getting the chance to have any input in the planning projects that were making an impact on their areas of town. The relationship with council had become hostile and carried great distrust on both sides of the issue. The comments of FORM and the various ratepayers' presidents in the local paper were highly critical of council.

One of my pledges in the election campaign was to work with the ratepayers' groups to make sure their voices were heard. I had also explained that I might not agree with them on all the issues, but that the process should not be the problem. A number of the ratepayers' presidents had endorsed me. My first order of business was to set up a meeting with FORM.

I agreed to occasionally meet with D'Arcy Pigott, the chairman of FORM, and I committed to meet with the presidents of the ratepayers' groups in Ward 5 once a month. We would exchange information and they would provide me with their perspective on matters.

The real shortcoming of the planning process is that a developer and his planners submit a development plan to the municipality. They work with the municipality's planners until both sides are satisfied that the plan meets the standards and plans of the municipality. Then a public meeting is held for input from the public. By this time, unfortunately, the die has been cast. Even if the ratepayers raise an issue, if the council decides not to consider it, there is almost no hope for the ratepayers to challenge the decision. Even if they were able to raise the money to challenge the decision at the Ontario Municipal Board, they would be facing a plan that was supported by both the developer and the municipality.

Many issues are incapable of resolution because they are based on entrenched views that no development should proceed. Other issues, like the height or mass of a building, can be mitigated. Many issues have the potential to be resolved, because in the scheme of things they are minor, but they need a chance to be considered.

The first real challenge that Mayor Tony Roman threw at me was a very hostile issue in my ward. A non-profit organization wanted to put a group home for shelterless youth on a residential street. Before the election, an information meeting ended with the police being called because some of the residents were very angry with the idea of a group home on their street. Vitriolic letters to the editor had been written to the local paper. There were allegations that threats had been made.

Tony Roman's only comment to me was "Fix it."

The problem with entrenched points of view is that no one can see the parts of the other side of the argument that are reasonable. If they could, then you could build on what little consensus you had. I decided to elevate the issue beyond the specific case and wanted to see if some principles could be agreed upon. With that in mind, I decided to create a group homes task force to review how group homes of varying kinds could fit within our bylaws. When I ran the idea by Tony and Frank Scarpitti, who was the chair of the Planning Committee, they both agreed.

The next consideration was who to appoint to the task force. The obvious answer was to get the two most vocal anti–group home residents and a representative of the non-profit organization that was applying for the group home for shelterless youth. My reasoning was that if they didn't kill each other after the first two meetings, they would eventually get to see the other side's position without the screaming and threats.

I decided to fill out the rest of the committee with a representative from the school board, a few local volunteer organizations and the Ontario Ministry of Community and Social Services and the Ministry of Corrections. The work plan was to meet every two weeks and provide the task force with every article and bylaw for group homes that I could get my hands on. I reasoned if I worked them like crazy there would be less time for carping.

The first meeting went as I had anticipated. Icy would be an understatement. Some of the other community members tried to act to bridge the awkwardness. The second meeting was frosty but not quite as hostile.

During the third meeting, some discussion of the issues started to happen. The issue no longer became the specific application but finding a solution for the town. Everyone started to see what was considered reasonable in a number of other municipalities. They could see that there were differences in types of group homes and where they were located. They could also see that a municipality had an obligation to all people in their community. Slowly dialogue between the camps started and inklings of respect began to appear.

As discussion started to focus on where various types of group homes should be located and the distance of separation between them so that all neighbourhoods should share the responsibility, it was no longer a question of yes or no but rather how. The group homes that were to be permanent or long-term homes for people with disabilities were dealt with easily. Everyone agreed that they should be in residential areas, so that they could feel a part of the neighbourhood. When statistics were revealed that showed there were many more of these kinds of group homes than the members of the task force were aware of, it reinforced the view that they should be in their neighbourhoods.

There were lengthy discussions about transitional facilities such as interim homes for people leaving correctional facilities. These have been by and large located on arterial roads close to public transit and other infrastructure. The key discussion was about the transitional nature of this kind of home.

After months of meetings and discussions, a consensus started to form. In addition, the residents who had been so opposed to the group home for shelterless youth became more understanding of the home and began to have confidence in the leadership of the non-profit organization.

No one would have thought months before that we could have reached a consensus for recommendations. After months of working together, everyone agreed on the recommendations for our final report. I suggested to Mayor Roman that we have a public information meeting to announce the findings of the task force. After reminding me of the result the previous time an information meeting had been held on group homes, he agreed to allow me to chair such a meeting.

The meeting was held at the local hockey arena and was filled with people. I started the meeting with an explanation of the process and introduced the members of the task force. A town planner did the presentation. This was followed by comments by members of the task force, all of whom indicated their support for the recommendations. The floor was then opened to the public for their comments.

Long line-ups formed behind the three microphones that had been set up. One after another the residents and different organizations spoke. One after another the speakers indicated their appreciation for the job that the task force had done and their support. Every speaker spoke in favour of the recommendations. It was the complete opposite of the previous meeting, which had almost broken out in physical fights.

The recommendations of the task force were presented to council, and council approved the recommendation for a bylaw unanimously. If the story had ended there, it would have been great; however, the Ministry of Corrections, which had a representative sit on the task force, objected to our group homes bylaw. This objection had never been raised during any of our meetings. The Ministry of Corrections wanted to maintain the right to place a halfway house for people being released from prison in the middle of a subdivision. So despite all our work and consensus building, the bylaw was never approved by the province.

The first real clash I had with a developer started out relatively low-key. A school site in my ward was not required by the school board and so was sold back to the developer. The property was located in the middle of a subdivision that had been fully occupied for a few years. The property had been used by the children as a shortcut to the school that had been built. There was also a mature stand of trees on the property.

When land is being rezoned for development, there is a requirement to dedicate five percent of the land for parks. When the whole area was being developed, the five percent park dedication had been taken. In this instance, the neighbours had been using the property as a park and the stand of trees took up about 10 percent of the land. The residents wanted to keep the stand of trees, have a walkway through to the school and assurances that the grading of the new development would not result in the newer area being higher than the surrounding neighbourhood.

Two of these concerns did not seem to be difficult issues. The grading would be a simple and reasonable engineering consideration. The walkway would seem to be a minimal request. The greatest problem would be the trees. This developer had no obligation to give another five percent of the land for parkland, let alone 10 percent.

I met with the developer to try to find a solution that worked for everyone. I understood that the developer was fully in his rights not to do anything with the trees. At the end of the day, it is all about the bottom line. The land was zoned for single detached homes. I suggested to the developer that he could build linked homes that would increase the density and that would give him the leeway to save the trees. He said that he would consider it.

The next day Elaine and I left for a vacation to Hawaii. When we returned a few weeks later I saw that the answering machine was filled to capacity. I then got a call from a friend who suggested I read the local newspaper. The headline read that the developer was threatening to build a funeral home on the site, as it was zoned for institution.

The first thought that occurred to me was that it was silly. The land had been acquired at a considerable cost, and money was to be made by the developer in building homes, not a funeral home. If he wanted to play chicken, so would I.

Eventually, sanity prevailed and the developer decided to build linked homes and the trees were saved. The residents also got their walkway and grading.

A few months later there was a big feature article about this developer in the *Toronto Star*. In the article he bragged about how he always got his way when he developed property in the GTA, except for a small subdivision in Markham. We never knocked heads again.

I found kindred spirits in Frank Scarpitti, Ken Dunphy and Jim Jones. We supported many of the environmental measures that came up before council. The previous council had been at loggerheads with groups such as Save the Rouge Valley and Ten Thousand Trees. When the proposal came up for support for a major tree planting in the Rouge Valley, the old guard wanted to veto the initiative. Frank, Ken, Jimmy and I rallied the votes and got approval. The paper named us the Greenhorn Councillors because we were new and also supported the environmental issues.

One afternoon after meetings at the town, Ken Dunphy asked me, Frank and Jim to see a small forest in his ward that was in danger of being cut down by the developer. It was the middle of winter and there had just been a heavy snowfall. All of us were dressed in suits and dress shoes but Ken convinced us to go with him. Jim Jones brought a video recorder with him. Ken stopped his car off Warden Avenue north of 16th Avenue in the middle of nowhere and told us that we had to walk from there. Ken then traipsed off into the woods. As soon as we stepped onto the land we were ankle deep in snow. I grumbled to Ken that he was ruining my shoes but he just roared out laughing.

We walked for miles. We came to a frozen creek and Jim and I crossed the creek and scrambled up the bank. Frank was next and then started to slip and then went tumbling down the bank. Jim shouted in delight, "I got it all on video."

Finally we came to Ken's trees and started out of the woods. Ken led us out nowhere close to the car, and miles later we were driving back to the town. As much as we grumbled, we had a good laugh and managed to save the trees.

Frank Scarpitti and I became good friends and seemed to work together well and had a lot of fun doing it. We did fundraising together for the United Way by selling doughnuts to the employees of the town. We promoted and ran in the Terry Fox Run. One year for the town's Christmas party, Frank and I dressed up as Santa's elves and during our goofing around delivering the gifts, Frank ripped his pants.

St. Patrick's Church had been doing a fundraising talent show to raise money to send the choir to the Vatican. Frank suggested that we do the "Soul Man" routine as the Blues Brothers. Needless to say, we were a hit.

The way that Markham Council worked in those days under Tony Roman was that despite the division of opinions we stuck to the issues and when we conducted our council meetings in public we somehow found consensus. I credit the style and leadership of Tony Roman.

Tony Roman was a great leader. I remember him explaining to me why he always made sure that all members of council were recognized at any event he attended. He told me, "Dave, when there's credit to be given, share the credit. When it's bad news, I have broad shoulders." I always remembered that advice.

We had a real camaraderie. Often after council meetings we would go to the Councillors' Lounge and play euchre. Tony Roman always wanted me to be his partner. The other side would be a mix of Ken Dunphy, Jim Jones, Frank Scarpitti or Ron Moran. The others would gather and we would have a soft drink or coffee and discuss the results of the meeting. It was at times like this that we found common ground.

I really respected Tony and valued his friendship. I ended up being with Tony a lot for lunch or dinner. Whenever the bill came, Tony would reach and pat his coat pocket as if to say he forgot his wallet. As generous as he was, I cannot recall a time when I did not pay. One evening Tony and his wife, Elsie, were at dinner with Elaine and me at the School of Fine Dining, one of my favourite spots to eat in Markham. When the bill came and Tony started his pat-his-coat routine, Elsie glared at Tony and said, "Tony, pay the bill."

Tony looked sheepish and reached in and pulled out his wallet. Nick Zarafonitis, the owner of the restaurant, walked over and grabbed the bill and said, "Mr. Roman, the dinner is my treat." Tony had gotten away with it again.

The only time that I ever locked horns with Tony Roman came as a result of an initiative that I was driving. During my first term, I was appointed the chair of the Economic Development Committee. I was fortunate to have working with me Mario Belvedere, the Director of Economic Development for the town. Mario is a ball of fire. He is innovative and very bright. Together we decided that instead of being twin cities with other international cities, we would rebrand the pairings as economic alliances. We would look to create relationships with cities that would complement our industrial profile. We created a committee that was composed of the Town of Markham, the Markham Board of Trade and the York Technology Association. We would together determine the strategy that would benefit the town.

This initiative would inevitably lead to trade missions to other cities in other countries. I wanted to limit the political participation so it would not be seen as a junket by the public. By having active partners in the Board of Trade and the York Tech Association, there would be a presumption of business. I wanted the process to be as transparent as possible.

One of the first trips was to be to China. When that was known, one of the regional councillors indicated to Tony that he wanted to be part of the delegation. Compounding the problem was the fact that he wanted to take his wife at the cost of the town.

I told Tony that this regional councillor was not even on the Economic Alliance Committee and that there was no way that the town should pay for his wife to come. I don't know if Tony thought I was kidding, but he just laughed and said that he would put forward a recommendation that the delegation be increased to include the regional councillor and his wife. I told him that if he did, I would vote against it and remove myself from the delegation because he was going to undo all the work that I had done.

At council, Tony proposed his amendment to the resolution. He then recognized me. I promptly indicated that I would vote against the amendment and resigned from the delegation. The amendment passed. The delegation went minus me, but after the council meeting, Tony told me that next time I said something like that in advance, he would believe me.

On the topic of expenses, Rob Ford, who is the mayor of Toronto as I write this, has incurred no public expenses throughout his career as a municipal politician. He also takes a lot of heat from his fellow councillors because he criticizes them for their expenses. I am in favour of politicians charging reasonable expenses. I would prefer that if they went to lunch with someone who might be dealing with the municipality on a development or some other type of business, that they pay for themselves rather than be "treated." I would also prefer that politicians continue to inform themselves on better process and best practices for the municipality through education opportunities.

In my six years as a municipal councillor, I had in total $35 of expenses, and that was for membership in the Federation of Canadian Municipalities in my first year. As in the City of Toronto, in Markham expenses of politicians are published once a year. Unlike Rob Ford, I did not criticize my colleagues. When asked by the media, I always responded by saying that I did it because it was my choice and, to my knowledge, my colleagues were responsible, but they needed to ask them.

In 2012 there is considerable discussion going on about making the Rouge Valley into a national park. Generally most people and politicians are in favour of the idea. After all, the issue is a mother-hood one. Politicians and environmental activists are all elbowing each other out of the way, trying to take credit for protecting one of the largest natural urban parks in Canada.

Early in 1990, the Bob Rae provincial government created the Rouge Park Advisory Committee to make recommendations on all aspects of the park, including allowable uses, setbacks, access, acquisitions, adjacent uses, official status and public policy. An intense schedule was established for meetings, public consultation and liaising with municipal and non-profit stakeholders.

A merry bunch of appointees who represented municipal, provincial and federal government, environmental groups, First Nations, community groups and organizations were tasked with the job. The committee was chaired by Jim French and the members included Marci Burgess (Chiefs of Ontario), Glenn De Baermaeker (Coalition of Scarborough Community Associations), Sandy Gage (Federation of Ontario Naturalists), Art Holder (regional director, Ministry of Natural Resources), Bill McLean (general manager of the Metropolitan Toronto and Region Conservation Authority), Stephen Marshall (Save the Rouge Valley System Inc.), Katherine Murray, Bob Sanders (Scarborough councillor), Andre Scheiman (Architectural Conservancy of Ontario), Geoffrey Sutherland (Ontario Archaeological Society), Joyce Trimmer (mayor of Scarborough), Calvin White (general manager of the Metropolitan Toronto Zoo) and two Conservatives, my friend Pauline Browes, MP Scarborough Centre, and me. A significant alternate member was Edith Montgomery, Scarborough councillor.

Conservatives never get credit for pushing the environmental issues, but Pauline and I did more than our share of pushing for the Rouge Park.

As our review of the issues continued, we became a repository for any issue that arose within or affecting the Rouge Park. One week we dealt with a nest of blue herons and the next we dealt with sight lines. Development projects were placed before us.

After months of deliberation, listening and drafting, a report was presented to the Ontario government with our recommendations to preserve this natural treasure for future generations. The creation of the Rouge Park was a direct result of our efforts. The role the committee played will probably be lost on the dusty shelves of lesser-known historical facts. While others continue to bask in the glory of the Rouge Park, these are the people who did something about it.

Years later when I was the Chair of Management Board for the Province, I was approached by a small group of environmentalists and community activists headed by Tupper Wheatley of the Milne Park Community Association. A sensitive part of the environmentally sensitive lands was being considered for sale to a fast food operation. They asked if anything could be done. A few weeks later, with no fanfare, a new piece of the Rouge Park had been added.

My partner Al Parker fully supported my campaign when I ran for council. One day I went away on a business trip and I returned to the awful news that Al had been diagnosed with leukemia. I thought that he might have months or longer to put things in order, but as it turned out he had acute leukemia and only a handful of days later he passed away.

Life was never the same. Al was 100 percent trustworthy. He had been the only partner that I ever had and had given me a false impression that everyone would act either honourably or honestly.

My first term as a councillor was a great learning experience and I had made some trustworthy friends. As 1991 rolled around, I started to think about campaigning for a second term. I had enjoyed sitting on council and believed that I had created good relationships with my residents. Being an incumbent gives a great advantage to a municipal politician. You have a huge edge in public recognition. Again I decided to fund my own campaign and that we would have a small campaign team. I had worked closely with the ratepayers' groups, and many of them volunteered to help me.

I put together a number of the news articles about me and made a brochure. It consisted of editorial comments and statements about what I had done. When spring came, Elaine and I started knocking on doors.

In July, I purchased a foursome in the Markham Board of Trade golf tournament that was to take place at Glen Cedars Golf Course in Markham. On the day of the tournament, I was playing like a scene in *Caddyshack*. During the game I had hit three flagsticks and on the closest-to-the-pin hole had driven the ball within six inches of the cup. The par three hole for the hole-in-one prize was next to the one where I almost sunk my drive. They were both about the same distance. On the closest-to-the-pin hole I had used a seven iron. My friend, Carmen Salerno asked me what club I was going to use. I answered, "My six iron."

My golf partners looked at me like I was crazy.

Mario Belvedere asked, "You almost sunk the other shot with a seven iron, why would you use a six?"

I answered, "I hit it as hard as I could and I was still short. I'm going to take a little off my shot."

They all looked at me like I was crazy and told me to go ahead. By this time we had two other foursomes on our hole and three foursomes on the other par three tee box watching me.

I took the shot and watched the ball bounce on the green, once, twice and then it disappeared. Mario started jumping and shouting that it went in. I was still looking at the green, puzzled. Then the people by the hole yelled that I had got a hole in one. The prize was $12,000.

We had two more holes to play and I bogied both of the holes. I had a good round and shot a 77. Not that I really want to complain, but if I hadn't bogied the last two holes and had shot a 75, I would have won the tournament too.

Unfortunately I had forgotten to tell Elaine that I was going to be golfing in the Markham Board of Trade Golf Tournament. I had planned to leave after golfing and skip the dinner and still be on time for a dinner I was supposed to be at with Elaine. Caught up in the excitement, I forgot to call her. After the cheque presentation, I called Elaine to let her know why I was really late. By this time she was steaming and either didn't hear me when I told her that I had won the hole-in-one prize or she didn't believe me.

The organizers were good enough to give me the fake cheque I had received to take with me. When I arrived at the dinner I knew I was in trouble, but when I showed her the fake cheque she believed me and I knew that I had just bought a little goodwill. I decided that I would make a large donation to Participation House, a local organization that assisted young people with disabilities.

We started knocking on doors in the early spring again. As time passed and we continued to work on the campaign, I had not heard any rumours about possible opponents in the election. There are not many political races that are uncontested, so my optimism was balanced by realism. When the cutoff date arrived, I visited the Clerk's office to see who had registered at the last minute to run against me. I arrived to see most of my fellow council members, who were there for the same reason. Everyone started to congratulate me. No one had registered to run against me. I was one of only a handful of people who had been acclaimed in the GTA.

My second term started with Mayor Tony Roman asking me to be the chairman of the Planning and Development Committee. Tony liked the idea that I had been able to create good relations and communications with the various ratepayers' groups in town. I continued my monthly meetings with the ratepayers' groups. My meetings were open to my fellow councillors to attend, and Frank Scarpitti, Jim Jones and Ken Dunphy took advantage of the opportunity. I am pleased to say that during this term we didn't have any appeals to the Ontario Municipal Board. We were able to work out all the issues. As a result of being listened to, FORM voluntarily disbanded.

Mayor Tony Roman had been an athlete when he was younger. A fact that was not well known to the public was that he had been stricken with multiple sclerosis, a very debilitating disease. He had been slowly losing the feeling in his legs. His disability started to become visible. At first he used canes and then he slowly lost the ability to walk. It was excruciating to watch.

During the earlier days of his fight with MS, I was able to persuade him to stop driving. Eventually he lost the fight and succumbed.

Tony was more than just the mayor to all of us. To me, he had been a mentor. Years later, Elsie Roman, Tony's wife, told me that Tony had hoped that I would be mayor one day after him.

After Tony died there was a lot of maneuvering. Council decided to appoint someone to replace Tony Roman as mayor for the remainder of the term. The natural replacement would be one of the regional councillors. After the appointment of the mayor, one of the ward councillors would have to be appointed to fill the vacant regional councillor position. Following a lot of deal making, Frank Scarpitti was appointed to fill in as mayor and Ken Dunphy was appointed to be the new regional councillor.

I liked Frank's style. He would have an open and transparent government. Frank was also a good listener. Frank's only short-coming was his habit of being consistently late for everything. It wasn't a case of discourtesy, but he got so wrapped up in what he was doing he lost track of time. I will take integrity over prompt-ness all the time.

The rest of the term proceeded in a fairly uneventful way, which in politics was good news. As the term was winding down, our local MPP, Don Cousens, advised me that he was not going to run for re-election and would instead run for mayor of Markham. He sug-gested that I consider running for the provincial nomination. The reality was that Don Cousens was tired of being a backbencher in the Opposition. Don had had a very brief posting as the Minister of Corrections for one month before the Miller Conservative gov-ernment fell, but his last 10 years were as a backbench opposition member.

Mike Harris had become the leader of the party in 1990. Don Cousens was never close to Mike Harris. The party was floundering in last place behind the NDP and the Liberals. The PC Party was having difficulty raising money. It's no wonder that Don Cousens wanted to jump ship.

When I was considering whether to run for the nomination, we assumed that because of the state of politics at the time, if elected I would likely be a backbencher in opposition. As the sitting mem-ber of provincial parliament and a backbencher for most of his career, Don Cousens was able to maintain his job with a technology company. Backbench MPPs were paid around $80,000 per annum.

Between the two jobs, Don was able to maintain a good lifestyle.

The likely scenario for me would be to continue to run my law practice and juggle the schedule for the commitment at Queen's Park much as I did with my council obligations. It had taken years to build up my law practice and I didn't want to give up on the fruits of my labour. If the events transpired in this way, it would have very little impact on my income and quality of life.

After talking with Don Cousens, I believed that I could accommodate the time commitments. Based on this scenario I decided to run for the nomination for Markham. This decision led to a number of other preliminary decisions. The first decision was an ethical one. There was a municipal election in the fall of 1994. Incumbent municipal politicians are rarely unseated unless there is either scandalous behaviour or gross incompetence. Municipal politicians are very sought after and recruited to run provincially or federally because they already have experience, are well known and have a campaign team. They are less risky because they have a track record.

Most municipal politicians, with the exception of those in the City of Toronto, which has a strong NDP caucus, are agnostic and opportunistic on party politics. This means that many municipal politicians are sought after by all parties.

Municipal politicians are also risk averse. The rules of running for political office are lopsided. While a federal or provincial politician cannot run for another office unless he or she resigns from office, municipal politicians can retain their current office and run for MPP (provincial) or MP (federal) and, if unsuccessful, return to their position as a mayor or councillor. This meant that most municipal politicians would run in the fall of 1994 even if they intended to run in the provincial election in 1995.

In 1991, I had been acclaimed as councillor for Ward 5 in Markham. I had not heard of anyone who had intended to challenge me. Somehow it did not feel right to run for one office when I fully intended to pursue running for the nomination. I declared publicly that I would not be seeking re-election for councillor for

Ward 5 and that I would be seeking the nomination to run for the PC Party for Markham.

This had the effect of a lot of people deciding to run for my soon-to-be vacated position, all of whom wanted my endorsement for their campaigns. I felt good about my decision. It was important to be committed. As it turned out, I was one of only a handful of sitting municipal politicians in Ontario who did not try to have their cake and eat it too.

The second decision was to put together a nomination campaign team. The Markham PC Association had put together a nomination committee, and, technically, members of the nomination committee were not allowed to be partisan during the process. There were a number of volunteers I came to know through the many campaigns in which we worked together. I thought immediately of Marjorie Nielsen. Marjorie was a long-time Progressive Conservative member and volunteer both for the provincial and federal parties. I called Marjorie and she immediately agreed to be one of my key organizers.

When we got together for coffee, Marjorie suggested that we ask D'Arcy Pigott and Kerry Bristow to help us. I knew D'Arcy as the past president of FORM and Kerry as a youth volunteer for Don Cousens. We then broadened the committee by adding many of my contacts with key organizations around town with the Markham Fair, the Rotary Club, the Lions Club, the Optimist Club, the Italian bocce club, the Greek Orthodox Church, the Chinese Cultural Centre and Markham sports teams. Another very important volunteer was Richard Van Seters, who was a key organizer for the Reform Party. A lot of my other friends came and volunteered, like Dave Forfar, my old high school buddy.

Nomination races were challenging, in that money donated to a nomination campaign is not eligible for a tax deduction. The greater challenge is that you are trying to get people to buy a membership for the PC Party and support you by attending a nomination meeting. Some candidates will pay the membership fee but we did not, as someone didn't just need to buy a membership, but they had to come out and vote. That required commitment. I also decided not to take any donations for the nomination campaign, but rather to pay for it myself.

We decided that we would need some kind of brochure and signs that we could use, both for the lead-up to the nomination meeting and also for our supporters to hold at the crucial meeting. There were many opportunities to get out in the public. We participated in the Unionville Festival parade with our signs and supporters and held a picnic. More important were the opportunities to speak to service clubs, sports clubs and organizations.

Our campaign went well and we were having a good deal of success in signing up new members.

The nomination committee seemed be going out of its way to get someone to run against me for the nomination. I thought that I was well placed to win both the nomination and the election. Eventually the nomination committee got two candidates. One was a party member who ran for the nomination anywhere that he could without any success and who did not even live in the riding. The other had been a card-carrying Liberal until a month before she decided to run against me for the nomination. Neither of them had any credibility, experience or public recognition.

The candidate debate took place at Brother Andre Catholic School and the gym was packed. In our opinion, it was no contest. Neither of the other candidates had knowledge of local issues or PC Party policies.

On the night of the nomination meeting, which was held at the same school, the parking lot was packed. There was one problem, for me, at least. The nomination was being held on the same night as the opening of the Markham Fair, and many of the volunteers for the Markham Fair could not be at the nomination meeting. This affected only my campaign.

When I looked into the gym, I could see that there were more than a thousand people in attendance. When I took a closer look and walked around I saw that most of them were wearing Dave Tsubouchi stickers or were holding my signs.

Each candidate was given time for a demonstration and speech. Kerry had organized my youth supporters for a march in with music and signs. I then gave my speech.

The election was over on the first ballot. Of the thousand or so people, only a handful were not my supporters. I was now the Mike Harris candidate for the next provincial campaign.

# CHAPTER TWELVE

# THE COMMON SENSE REVOLUTION AND THE 69-CENT TUNA SKIRMISH

The Ontario provincial election of 1995 has been well documented and commented on. Mike Harris and the PC Party started in third place with no hope of winning. People were sick of Bob Rae and his tax-and-spend policies. People were out of work. Taxes were stifling businesses and people were having a difficult time just surviving. Bob Rae was spoofed as man of the year in Buffalo because Ontario jobs were going there. The Liberals were riding high in the polls and their leader, Lyn McLeod, was being touted as the premier elect.

No one paid attention to Mike Harris. There was no media attention, and as a result very little attention was paid to the PC campaign or platform even though it had been released a year ahead of the election. Mike Harris was running as the "Tax Fighter."

The name of the platform was the Common Sense Revolution, and it had been developed through a large-scale, grass-roots consultative process throughout the province. There was great campaign discipline. The messaging was to be uniform and clear: tax cuts equals jobs. That was the mantra. All candidates and local campaigns needed to believe and embrace the concept. Freelancing on this issue was not tolerated.

My first experience with a candidate school took place in early 1995. I remember Peter Van Loan, the president of the PC Party of Ontario, and Guy Giorno both being there. One of my colleagues at dinner stated that as the local candidate, he needed to develop his own message and that he would pick and choose the parts of the party's platform to use. He was severely chastised and properly converted to a believer.

As in most campaigns, there is usually some significant turning point. Many times it is an error, the wrong wording or timing. Less often it is a significant moment during the televised leaders' debate.

In the 1995 campaign, it was Lyn McLeod's comment that the definition of domestic violence included verbal abuse. The next day the *Toronto Sun's* headlines read, "Shout at spouse, lose your house." Lyn McLeod's popularity and the Liberal Party started to plummet. Ironically, years later, Attorney General Jim Flaherty introduced Bill 117, the act on domestic violence that would apply to verbal abuse.

As the Liberal Party began to crash, both the Liberals and NDP started to take notice of Mike Harris and the PC Party. He had had been playing the role of the tortoise and had sneaked by the assumed hares of the race.

By the time the media started to take notice and pick apart the Common Sense Revolution they also realized that the writing was on the wall. Everyone assumed that promises made during elections were just fluff. No one counted on Mike Harris actually doing what he said he would do. No one expects a politician to keep his or her promises.

The 1995 campaign kicked off in Markham at Patriot Computers, a company that was run by brothers Mark and John Durst. I waited outside for Mike Harris and the Common Sense Revolution bus to arrive. I didn't really know him that well. I had chatted with him at conventions and what I saw of him I liked.

Mike Harris arrived accompanied by a throng of media. I greeted him and introduced him to the Durst brothers. The tour was my first with the leader. We met employees and saw the company's operation. We then visited a family in Markham and they would indicate how a personal tax cut would benefit an ordinary family. Tax cuts equals jobs.

What I could see about Mike Harris is that he genuinely wanted to assist ordinary families in Ontario. I could also see how well he connected with the working guy. He didn't talk down to them. He spoke the same language. He didn't think he was better or smarter than them. He believed that he was in a position to help them.

Mike Harris returned a little later in the campaign to officially open my campaign headquarters and to do some campaigning on Main Street with me. He is great with people. I took him over to Goodies Restaurant at Markville Mall, where he chatted and met with customers and Frank Ampatzis, the owner. We then went to Main Street and visited the businesses. We stopped in to see Ross Rennie at Markham Hardware and Greg Weeks at Carson and Weeks Insurance. Mike Harris was a smashing success.

My opponents in Markham were Khaled Usman, a long-time Liberal organizer and resident, and Mike Tang for the NDP, who did not live in Markham. Pat Redmond ran for the Family Coalition Party. When the campaign started, I felt that I could win the local election, just as Don Cousens had done for years. Neither of my main opponents had any experience in the public forum.

When the campaign started I decided that I would place my key organizers from the nomination campaign in the leadership positions of the election campaign. I had inherited the executive team from Don Cousens, but I wanted people who were loyal to me, and that was not necessarily Don Cousens's people. Jim Anderson would be the campaign manager and D'Arcy, Marjorie and Kerry would take key roles.

The great advantage of a nomination race is that we had tons of new volunteers.

My family members were great supporters. Elaine was everywhere and did everything from making sandwiches for volunteers, putting up signs, canvassing and volunteering on the phones. Jacquie canvassed after school. My mother, sister and Auntie Haru worked the phones while my dad came out to canvas and Uncle Tosh generally helped. My cousin George, his wife, Susan, and their whole family helped.

There were a number of debates. One of the two important debates was sponsored by the *Markham Economist & Sun* and the Markham Board of Trade. The other was the televised debate on Shaw Cable. There were all kinds of smaller debates and some conflicted with other commitments. Both of the main debates went well.

Early in the campaign I had agreed to speak to a class on politics at Father McGivney Catholic High School. Later in the campaign a debate was scheduled for Markville High School on the same day and same time. I felt that it would be unfair if I were to cancel the time at Father McGivney so I gave my regrets to Markville High School but I made sure that they knew why I wasn't going to be there. I also notified both the local paper and cable television.

The newspaper coverage was interesting. They interviewed the students after the debate as to who they would vote for. Even though I was not there, I was overwhelmingly chosen.

I never really knew Mike Tang of the NDP because he was never a factor in the election. I have been involved in many political campaigns. Over the years, some of my opponents had no ethics and had dirty campaigns. There is no room in elections for people who demonstrate a lack of integrity. If they conduct themselves like that during a campaign, you can assume that the unethical behaviour will continue.

There is such a thing as a campaign that is tough but fair. I found this to be case with my Liberal opponent, Khaled Usman. During the campaign we both gained a respect for each other. As time passed we became friends. When I was raising money to assist the Japanese people as a result of the 2011 earthquake and tsunami, after Frank Scarpitti and Ralph Capocci, one of the first people to offer to help was Khaled Usman.

As the results started to come in on Election Day — June 8, 1995 — I could see that not only was I going to win handily but we were going to form the government. I ended up winning with the biggest plurality in the province, defeating my closest opponent by more than 26,000 votes and gaining almost twice as many votes as all my opponents together.

The PC Party had won 82 of the 130 seats, giving us a large majority government. That evening brought great elation.

The next day brought a lot of questions. The PC Party had been very successful and elected many talented new members and re-elected many experienced members, many of whom had expectations that they would be in cabinet. There was a lot of pressure being applied by those who felt that they had political debts owed. This had nothing to do with me. I never lobbied to be in cabinet nor did I think that I would be considered. I didn't think that the majority win would change my plans significantly. I knew that if I was a backbencher for the government, there would more responsibility than in Opposition, but I felt I could manage the extra time required.

The newspapers, radio shows and television coverage all speculated who was going to be appointed to what ministry. Most were well-known names. I had not been mentioned in any article or show.

Life would go on without much disruption. I reveled in the realization that I was now the MPP for Markham. I was also the first Japanese Canadian to be elected to a provincial legislature. The days that followed were full of congratulations. Wherever I went in town I was met by a lot of goodwill.

Ignorance is bliss.

I was in the pool swimming and enjoying the beautiful weather when Elaine shouted to me, "You have a phone call from David Lindsay."

I got out of the pool and said hello. I knew that David Lindsay was one of Mike Harris's closest advisers and wondered why he was calling me.

David Lindsay congratulated me on my victory and advised me that I would be receiving a call from the premier shortly and that he would be offering me a position.

When the call ended I told Elaine about the call. What did he mean by "offering me a position"?

Fifteen minutes later, the phone rang. It was Mike Harris. He congratulated me on my victory and welcomed me to the team. He then asked me to become the Minister of Community and Social Services. He said that it would have some of the heaviest lifting for the new government.

I don't think that I appreciated exactly what he meant. I hadn't considered the possibility of being appointed to cabinet. I didn't really know what the responsibilities of an MPP were, let alone the responsibilities of a cabinet minister. I knew what our platform called for, but I really had not given a lot of thought to how this would be implemented. I also remember my father once telling me never to refuse an opportunity.

I told Mike Harris that I would be honoured and thanked him.

I was stunned by the conversation. The art of selecting a new cabinet in a newly elected government is shaped by a combination of geography, ethnicity, gender and political debts. It has less to do with skill and experience. The new cabinet will be a reflection of the new direction of the party. Who is selected will enable the best spin. These factors require that a certain number of rookie cabinet ministers be selected. There will also have to be some seasoned pros to take the toughest jobs. Ethnic people or visible minorities will be helpful to the public image of the party. Balance will require there to be as many women as you can muster. The urban versus the rural and city versus the suburbs issues must be addressed. The most important factor is how close you are to the premier.

There are better determinants of how valuable particular cabinet ministers are: when they were appointed to cabinet, and how long they lasted.

To assess the talent level of cabinet ministers, you need only see when the person was elevated to cabinet. People I viewed as very

Grandfather Chozo Takahashi. I never met him, as he died while being transported to POW Camp 101.

Grandmother Suga Takahashi. She had an iron will and raised her children by herself after the government took everything away after World War II.

With my brother, Dan.

Me at age 13, off to play shinny.

With my friend, Jimmy Chaney, on the way to Cubs.

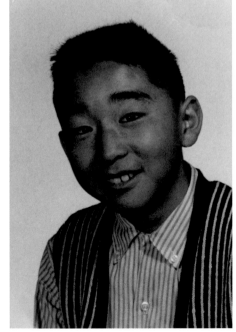

In Grade 9 with my uncool brush cut.

Grandmother Tsubouchi and my sister, Lynne, when my mother was in the hospital.

Christmas 1955: Mom and Dad, Dan and me.

From left to right: Dad and Mom, Uncle Tosh and Auntie Haru, Auntie Kay.

On my way to my high school prom, feeling pretty cool in my rented tux.

Playing guitar was a lot cooler than the clarinet.

At the school band picnic with friends.

My mustache and long hair days at
Osgoode Hall Law School.

Our version of Team Canada 1972 — we won the championship.

With Linda Franklin and Bruce Walker, celebrating the passing
of the VQA Act.

The Tsubouchi men — me, Dad, and Dan in 1996.

At Assumption University, receiving my honourary doctorate with Chancellor Aris Kaplanis and Ted Manziaris.

Deer Lake reserve with my friend Goyce Kakegamic (in sunglasses), Deputy Chief of the Nishnawbe Aski Nation.

Mom in front of my campaign headquarters in 1995 in Markham.

Launching the 1995 Common Sense Revolution Campaign.

At the Molson Indy with David Cronenberg in 1998.

Launching the 1999 campaign with Mike Harris at Patriot Computers.

With my friend Danny (third from left) in Cambodia.

With Dad at the POW Camp 101 reunion.

Deputy Minister Terry Smith presents me with the "headline": "Tsubouchi Saves First Parliament."

talented politicians and intelligent people were appointed in the second and third cabinet shuffles. Examples are Janet Ecker, Jim Flaherty, John Baird and Tony Clement. All of these people were able to spend some time as parliamentary assistants and were given specific tasks that measured their potential. They were also able to observe how to become and act like a capable minister. All of them became capable ministers and went on to do some very important things for the province, and Jim, Tony and John became very influential ministers for the Harper government. Their appointments were based entirely on merit and were well deserved.

The second factor is longevity, particularly in the first cabinet of the government. There were only three ministers who served without interruption for the entire two terms of government. A few of my colleagues had to step down for various reasons. Some were not reappointed at times. Others were appointed later. The three cabinet ministers who had survivability were Dianne Cunningham, Elizabeth Witmer and me.

When the time came for the selection of the first cabinet for the new government, everyone who had been in the pre-government caucus expected to get the call to serve in cabinet. In addition, many of the newly elected rookies felt that they had the talent to get the call as well. There was going to be a lot of disappointment, as we had been elected with a large majority, winning 82 of the 130 seats. The angriest reactions would be from the unsuccessful longer-serving caucus members.

I had no expectation nor was I particularly interested in being appointed to cabinet. I had much to learn simply as an elected MPP. If I had known the impact that this decision would have on my life, I might have declined. The best qualities that I used in my municipal government career — candour and honesty — were to prove to be liabilities in communication with the media.

I and many of my colleagues had been called up by the premier. To many the call never came. This would prove a challenge for the premier, keeping the many disgruntled caucus members as one cohesive group so that he could implement the Common Sense Revolution.

The inevitable leaks to the media were from some of the disappointed older caucus members. Some of these caucus members never realized that the media is not your friend. No matter how much inside information you allow them to have, if you are the story of the day there is no time out.

When Mike Harris called to ask me to serve as the Minister of Community and Social Services, I knew that there was going to be some tough slogging but I did not anticipate how much opposition there was going to be. I knew that we had promised to reduce welfare payment rates to 10 percent above the average rates of the other provinces. The promise was not to reduce welfare rates to the lowest or the average, but to 10 percent above the average.

The promise to reduce the welfare rates was accompanied by other commitments. The first of these was that there was to be no reduction of the disability payment rates. The other half of the welfare reforms was to be the institution of workfare. Workfare was intended to provide the job skills training and the life skills training needed to allow someone who was on welfare the opportunity to get a job. In addition, workfare was to provide assistance in employment placement. Mike Harris used to say that it was important for to give people help to find the dignity of a job.

Workfare was designed to engage many non-profit organizations that had already been active in this area to expand their programs and opportunities to train more people. The government was committed to spending substantial resources on these programs. Welfare was going to be directed to people who truly needed help and those who were temporarily unable to work. At the same time, there was a need to crack down on those who abused the welfare system.

This was all set out in the campaign documents of the PC Party. It was no secret. The surprise was that Mike Harris was one of the very rare politicians who did what he said he was going to do.

Because our mandate was reform, after the election, the government had a sense of urgency to "get things done." There were also staff to be hired, policies to be set out and committees to be formed. The one thing that was lacking and ended up creating a problem for many of our ministers, me included, was media training.

The only training we had received was back at candidate training. This had covered general questions that were directed to the candidates during the election period. It did not deal with standing in front of 20 members of the press gallery who were tossing grenades at you.

Even more important than actual media training would have been providing us with some intelligence on who was who in the press gallery. Most of us were not familiar with the views and slants of the press gallery or their newspaper, television network or radio station. This later proved critical.

Even those of us who had held office in municipal government had no experience with reporters who had basically already written the story that they wanted before the interview. Some were better than others. Some had ethics. Others had none. When I talk about ethics in the media, I think that someone who at least allows you to put forward your point of view honestly has ethics. Those who make up facts do not. Tough reporting is ethical as long as it is honest.

The unfortunate timing for me was that the welfare reforms were the first out of the gate without any other reforms to give ground cover. This was the first important action by a new, unproven government. Every reporter was out for a story.

Despite my years of municipal service, I was very green at the higher level political tactics needed to drive a message. The truth takes a backseat to driving the message. In municipal politics, the truth should trump all and the buck stops at the individual, as there is no party or policy to hide behind. If someone asked you if it was a good idea to build a high-rise next to his house the answer was simple: "No."

In provincial politics, no one is interested in the truth, especially the media. An honest answer is mocked because the political skill of messaging is king. I learned to be circumspect with the media a little later.

There was reporter who had worked at the *Toronto Sun* and was particularly disliked. Despite the fact that he worked at a right-leaning paper, he looked for opportunities to create controversy and embarrassment for the government. The inexperience of our government had him salivating at the many possibilities for creating havoc.

Years later, I became philosophical as a consequence of dealing with the media. My view was simple. If I screwed up in my actions or in how I had conveyed the motives of the government, then it was my fault and the negative consequences were warranted. I expected no leeway and certainly no mercy from the media. What I did expect was fairness in reporting. Fairness would include truthful reporting and no fabrications. It was a little too much to expect a balanced story, but it would be reasonable to expect an opportunity to give a different point of view from the one that was going to appear in the story. Most of the reporters could be very tough interviewers but they were decent people. They did not resort to trickery, unfounded inferences or lying. Unfortunately there were a few who stooped to less reputable tactics.

In the first year of our government, that was this reporter. I learned the hard way. After a meeting I had at the legislature, I was walking back to my office at the Ministry of Community and Social Services when he was lurking about and he approached me to ask some questions.

One of the cardinal rules that a rookie cabinet minister should always obey is never go anywhere without your communications assistant. Both my CA and I were inexperienced at doing the government thing. Neither she nor I had thought I would have needed her with me. Other more experienced CAs that I had later would never let me out of their sight, even when I gained polish and experience. One of the most important functions of a CA is to record everything so that we had a verbatim recording of what I had said. At the very least, if I said anything inaccurate or inappropriate, we would know what the damage control would entail. It would also help to keep the reporter to the truth, at least most of the time. In politics there is no such thing as off the record.

He asked me if people would be moving to British Columbia because their welfare rates were higher than Ontario's. I knew that he was up to something. I didn't want to respond with a cause-and-effect answer and I didn't want to answer a hypothetical question. I said that I wasn't about to answer a hypothetical question. I walked down the stairs and out to Wellesley Street, where he continued to follow me and ask the same question over and over again. Finally, just to get rid of him, I said, "The weather's nicer in B.C." The next day the *Toronto Sun's* headline read that I told people on welfare to move to British Columbia because the weather was better.

I was upset because I had not connected welfare and the weather in B.C. In fact I had deliberately tried to avoid not only that statement but any other speculation, if for no other reason than that there was no proof that people were going to move to B.C. for welfare reasons. I had not said what the reporter had implied I said. I had discovered that this was his normal way of reporting. There was no point in calling him. It was at that point that the Office of the Premier's let us know what his reputation was.

I picked up the phone and called Paul Godfrey, the publisher of the *Toronto Sun,* and explained to him what had happened. Paul was a decent person and believed me; unfortunately, I did not have a tape of the interview and could not demand a retraction. Paul offered to have an article written on a different positive aspect of my life. It was a nice offer but the damage had been done. This reporter had gotten away with it, and I had the makings of a poor reputation for communicating.

This particular reporter continued to look for opportunities to attack decent people with innuendo and his poison pen. He would jump at any chance to criticize two very good men, Al Palladini and John Snobelen. Of the three of us, John Snobelen had the most polish at the provincial level. He is a very intelligent person who is always underestimated because of his "Aw, shucks" cowboy attitude. John's problem was saying that the way to force reform is by creating a crisis. His statement was recorded and used by both the media and the teachers' unions to embarrass him.

John had the onerous task of trying to create higher standards and results for the students of Ontario. His task was one of the most difficult, as the teachers' unions in Ontario resisted almost all change regardless of the government in power. John was also given the job of increasing accountability to parents and teachers by creating a College of Teachers and at the same time holding back the unions' demands during collective bargaining to achieve a balanced budget for the province. Two areas where the unions held power that they would be unwilling to give up without a fight were salaries and public accountability.

It was never a strategy of the Harris government to "get" the teachers. If there had been such a strategy, I and many of my colleagues would never have run for the PC Party. I didn't see what the problem was for increased accountability to students, their parents and the public. We had a responsibility to ensure that our students were equipped with the best public education possible. We also had a responsibility to ensure that taxpayers' dollars were being spent wisely. Those of us in the government owed much of our success to the great and caring teachers in our lives.

No one had anticipated the animosity that came from the unions. There had never been a war against teachers, but the unions had declared war on us and their number one target was John Snobelen. The "create a crisis" speech became a rallying call and John's lack of a higher formal education became part of the criticism against him for his "lack of understanding." No teacher was allowed to deviate from the union stance. During the election of 1999, when the teachers' union waged a campaign against us with signs and advertising almost on a level with the opposition parties, I was told by many teachers when I knocked on their doors that they had been forced to put up a sign but that they did not support the strategy of their unions. Many were afraid to voice a different opinion.

Unfortunately, John Snobelen, after accomplishing most of the real difficult reforms and becoming the target of the unions and media, was given a number of other cabinet posts that were far beneath his talent and intelligence and in many cases were not that relevant. He continued to be harassed by the media to the extent that one of the newspapers published a photograph of him on vacation with an attractive woman while they were in their swimsuits. John eventually became disgruntled and the PC Party lost a very strategic and creative thinker.

Al Palladini was one of the most generous and likable human beings that I had ever met. Before entering politics, Al had been the owner of Pinetree Lincoln Ford, one of the most successful car dealerships in Canada. His radio ads were ubiquitous. One of the stunts that the company put on every year was an endurance contest in which Al gave away a new car to the person who lasted the longest while standing and keeping a hand on the car. Al was a master of marketing and a self-made man. Al had a forthright honesty that made him a target of this reporter.

Al also had a wonderful sense of humour, but he didn't realize that the media did not have a sense of humour, nor did it understand irony. He would answer a question with candour and honesty. The reporter tried constantly to portray Al as an unsophisticated immigrant. Any answer that Al gave was treated with derision. Once when asked how he would get downtown during a bad snowstorm, Al humorously said that he would hitch his huskies to a sled and mush his way down. The media report tried to show him as inept and unsympathetic to the public.

Even though Al had little formal education, he was a very smart and successful businessman. Unlike John, who had been tasked with a difficult portfolio, Al was the Minister of Transportation, so eventually people like this reporter left Al alone to move on to bigger issues of the day. Al was allowed to get increasingly better and got more suitable cabinet postings. Industry and Trade was a perfect ministry for the super salesman of the province.

The height of unfair reporting was the treatment of Al Palladini's marital problems and separation. Al resigned from cabinet to deal with this very acrimonious and difficult situation. Al died one day in March 2001 on a golf course in Mexico doing what he liked to do. The legislature was never the same without him. He was one of the really good guys.

Many of the media disasters our party faced might have been averted with media training and experienced staff. I had not helped out my own situation. Two other incidents point out my own naïveté. The first was my fault entirely and the second was not. All of the new cabinet ministers had relied on a pre-approved list of potential staff to hire from. Most of us had no idea of the kind of experience that we were looking for or the skill sets required. The result was that most of us were learning on the job. This experience was not so onerous if you had a junior ministry or one that did not need a lot of the heavy lifting of reform priorities. Unfortunately for me, I had the second-largest line ministry and the only reform measures scheduled for the fall sittings of the legislature.

A little bit of experienced staff advice would have likely pre-vented my shopping list communication gaffe, but ultimately it was my mistake. I would have been told that you cannot relate personal experience to government policy. I would also have been told that no one could believe that a lawyer from Markham, Ontario, who drove a Corvette could understand anything about being needy. The problem I personally had was that although I strongly believed that people needed to take responsibility for their own lives, I also believed that there were people who could not do so for various reasons and that everybody's circumstances were different. I also knew what it was to struggle. No one really appreciated what my background was, nor did I feel that I needed to tell anyone.

I had come to understand how hard my parents had worked to get ahead and the sacrifices that they had made to make life better for us. I also understood how hard they tried to make us see that we were no different from anyone else. I had seen my mother mending clothes late into the night. I never saw my father because he was always working.

My father vowed after the government had put him and his family into incarceration that he would never take a penny from the government. As a child I knew from time to time how difficult the struggle was to survive, but both my mother and my father had strength of character and the spirit to keep going. They did the best they could for their children. Our lives were lived without luxury but we were happy.

In a way, my own life created more problems for me in my new role than if I had lived a privileged life. Everyone in my family worked hard against the odds to make something of our lives. My father and mother taught us that by their actions. We did not know how to do anything other than to work hard and keep going. At times, of course, we had failed along the way, but we always got back up and kept going. We didn't know how to give up.

We had to work harder than most ordinary Canadians because we lived on the fringes of acceptability. We were acceptable, sort of, because we spoke English with no accents. We tried to fit in. Fortunately all of us were gifted students and athletes, but we also worked harder at that than anyone else. Even still, no one would have ever invited me when I was young to the Granite Club or the Royal Canadian Yacht Club other than as a server.

Every day of our lives was a fight to be accepted and to survive.

When told by the poverty advocates how difficult it would be to survive on the reduced welfare payments, I asked one of my staff to get the Health Canada food guide and we put together a possible shopping list within the welfare payment that met the dietary needs. Stupidly, I was trying to be helpful. But to the anti-poverty groups, it was not about whether it worked — it was about the politics.

When I referred to this research during Question Period, all heck broke loose. The Opposition and the media demanded that I release the shopping list and we did. The response was all out of kilter, but the main thrust was that I was callous and did not understand the issues of poverty. What I didn't understand was how to communicate properly. I learned a valuable lesson in messaging in politics. The truth does not matter, only the spin. I should have remembered the lesson from high school politics, that it's not what you say, but how you say it. It continues to bother me to this day that honesty and sincerity are often mocked in the cynical world of politics. As I gained experience and expertise in spin, I never really agreed with it.

The other incident that caused me trouble was not my fault, but it also taught me two valuable lessons. The change in welfare payment rates, which were to be reduced to 10 percent above the average of the other provinces, was not supposed to affect the rate paid under the disability payments. The issues were to be separate and the regulations were prepared by legislative counsel. The normal process for a change in regulations was for the regulations to be drafted by lawyers who worked for the government, normally in the Ministry of the Attorney General. The draft regulations were reviewed by the ministry officials and lawyers and by the Office of the Premier (the premier's office). The regulations were then presented to the Cabinet Committee for Legislation and Regulations, where they were again reviewed and, once approved, reviewed again by the lawyers. Then then the agenda of the Legislation and Regulation Committee was put on the cabinet agenda. Once approved by cabinet, the regulations were made public in the *Ontario Gazette*.

The role of the minister is to deal with the policy being affected by the regulation. The role of the minister is not to act as the lawyer for the ministry. The regulation that provided the new rates for welfare had unfortunately incorrectly applied that rate to the disability payments. The legislative counsel had made an error and the Legislation and Regulations Committee had not caught the error, so it had been approved and gazetted.

The error had been found by the opposition parties and became the issue of the day. When it was discovered, my staff and I met with the premier's office at a meeting held by the premier's staff member, who was running communications for the premier. It was acknowledged that the error had nothing to do with me and that both legislative counsel and the Legs and Regs Committee had blown the regulation. He suggested that I do a mea culpa at the next session of the legislature and apologize for the error. Since I had been in the role for less than a year and had inexperienced staff, we agreed to comply with his edict so the blame could rest on just me and not the government.

The next day I stood and read a prepared statement and took responsibility for the mistake. Not surprisingly, I was lambasted for the mistake and accused of incompetence despite the fact that no minister ever sat down and drafted regulations for their ministry and even though there was a logical explanation for the error. I concluded later on that because I was a newcomer it was easier to lay the blame than fault others who both knew the Premier's communication assistant better and had more seniority and political clout than I did.

The two people who showed class and loyalty during this incident were Mike Harris and Norm Sterling. Mike Harris knew that it was not my mistake and never wavered in his support for me. Norm Sterling was the chair of the Legislation and Regulation Committee of Cabinet that reviewed all legislation before it was tabled. Norm apologized to me for his committee missing the error, although it wasn't really the committee's error. The responsibility lay with legislative counsel of the Attorney General's office.

There were two lessons I learned from this. The first was that I was never going to be responsible for anyone else's error again. Every piece of legislation or policy that crossed my desk, I read. I quickly gained a reputation among the civil service of being the most prepared and well-read minister. I then expected all others whom I dealt with to be just as prepared. This included my staff, my ministry officials and all of my colleagues who sat on any committee that I chaired.

The second lesson took a little longer. I was only able to implement this lesson when I gained a little more seniority and influence. The lesson was, don't take crap from the Office of the Premier. After the poor performances, earned and unearned, I made many changes in staff. I hired a new chief of staff, John Guthrie, who brought with him a wealth of experience. I brought in new, smart young staffers, like Derek O'Toole, Troy Ross, Barry O'Brien, Paul Burns, Deb McCain and later Sherri Haigh, Bill Campbell, Sam Eldiriny and Ian Dovey. Most important, when I disagreed with the staffers of the premier's office, I walked over to Mike Harris's office and sat there until he arrived and talked to him about the issue and he agreed with me. Once that happened, his staffers knew that if I disagreed with them, I would go over their heads.

Occasionally the government wanted to frame a new direction with a stunt to get good media play. Some of the stunts were undignified. I started saying no to anything I thought was inappropriate, but there was always another taker. I also gained an aversion to throwing someone under the bus. Unfortunately this view is shared by few people in power.

The most controversial statement that I made was when I suggested that people shop more carefully and perhaps buy something like tuna when it was on sale for 69 cents or buy dented tins in bulk if someone would give you a deal. Both were things I had seen my father do when we had no money. There was a huge amount of furor that arose because of my "hubris."

The media and Opposition were howling for my resignation. All my staff members were in damage control. I decided that the best thing to do was not to go ostrich but to go on television and radio to try to explain the welfare policies. I did radio call-in shows and made television appearances daily. The first radio show that I did, the host, of course, asked about the 69-cent tuna remark. I answered by saying that tuna was one four-letter word that I would never again say in public. The host started laughing and never came back to the comment. I faced my mistake head-on. The media had no interest in the details of my life and our struggles. Truth matters less than spin in politics and the media.

I would also learn later that as an unknown and untried politician, I would be given no slack. Like the POWs at Camp 101, I wore a big red circle on my back for a target. I was inexperienced but I learned quickly.

The first of many consequences of the reforms began. The

number of people on the welfare rolls started to dramatically fall month after month. Coincidentally, the PC Party started to rise in popularity. The correspondence and telephone calls to the ministry were 10 to 1 in support of the welfare reforms. The people who phoned in to the radio call-in shows were overwhelmingly in favour of the reforms. I was able to have a platform across the province to explain in more than a 15-second sound bite the policies, which included a crackdown on welfare fraud, making a condition of teenagers getting welfare that they had to be in school and living under the supervision of adults, and the spouse-in-the-house rule, where if you were living legally common law with someone who had significant income, that income would taken into consideration if you applied for welfare.

The *Queen Mary* had apparently been turned around. Positive articles started to be written on the reforms. Media started to then acknowledge the other part of the reform, and that was the creation of workfare, a program to provide training and opportunities for people on welfare to get real jobs. Workfare was to partner with credible agencies such as the Salvation Army and the YMCA and provide them with funding for training and jobs placement. The intention was to assist with funding these agencies that already had good reputations and could expand their programs and to help people get the "dignity" of a job. The government was also working to extend any health, drug and dental benefits for people on welfare as they attempted to get off welfare to avoid providing a disincentive. Again, the anti-poverty groups that had opposed any welfare reforms frightened many organizations into not participating.

In the years from 1995 to 1999, more than 451,000 people left the welfare rolls. Two independent studies showed that "60 percent of adults leaving welfare did so for employment-related reasons. Others have changed their living arrangements, gone back to school or entered a training program."

Despite the predictions of the media, I survived my first year in cabinet. My survival was based more on the loyalty and faith of

Mike Harris and as a reward for doing some heavy lifting for the government than on the merits of my performance.

When the legislature opened in the fall of 1995 and the lawns of Queen's Park were filled with protesters, I remember turning to Premier Harris and saying there's good news and bad news today. I said the bad news was that we had hundreds of people protesting against the government. He then asked what the possible good news could be. I said, "They can't pronounce Tsubouchi so they are all shouting 'Harris.'"

# CHAPTER THIRTEEN

# MIKE HARRIS, THE LEADER

Most people have a strong opinion of Mike Harris. The majority of the opinions are based on the impressions that people gained from the media or from opposition to government policies. Even those who know Mike Harris have strong opinions. I can speak only about my impressions, which were gained through my relationship with him on a few different levels.

Opinions have varied. If you disagreed with some of his policies, you portrayed him as an unfeeling ogre who would slash spending and government jobs without any remorse. If you worked with him, you saw him as a great leader. The media either loved or hated him, but luckily for them they had a headline and story every day.

I first met Mike Harris early in his mandate as leader of the PC Party of Ontario. He was making a speech at the Firefighters' Club in Markham. He was doing his road show as the "Tax Fighter." My first impression of Mike Harris as a speaker was underwhelming. The party had been decimated by losses under both Frank Miller and Larry Grossman. The leadership race had been able to attract only two candidates: Mike Harris and Dianne Cunningham. There seemed virtually no interest in the message, the party or the leader. Only the long-time party faithful were at the luncheon speech.

Within the year, with a continuous diet of rubber chicken and barbecues, Mike Harris transformed himself into one of the best political speakers I had ever heard. When Mike gave a speech, you believed his sincerity, probably because he was sincere. Mike was affable. This was not surprising to me as I got to know him better. He was a very humble person and never became arrogant or believed that he was more important than the office that he held.

Mike Harris was a man who had grown up in a small town and never lost that small-town quality. He was approachable. He wasn't a snob. You would not be surprised if you walked into a Tim Hortons and saw him sitting there.

Every strong political leader I knew had at least one of two qualities: charisma or affability. Most had a blend of both. Pierre Trudeau had charisma. For years when I was growing up, I thought that he was a giant both in deeds and stature. I was shocked to discover how slight a man he was. When Trudeau entered a room everyone was captivated by his presence.

Former Prime Minister Brian Mulroney is the same. Brian Mulroney is a riveting political speaker and personality. He is charming beyond belief. When you meet him, he also has an affable quality. He never talks down to anyone. It has been my privilege to be with Brian Mulroney on many occasions and I have enjoyed his company and sense of humour.

Joe Clark is affable. He treated everyone with respect no matter what their lot in life was. I would occasionally accompany Joe to Blue Jays games. He would insist that we walk down to the stadium. As we walked along people would come up to him to say hello or to just shake his hand. These were not Bay Street lawyers who were greeting him but the guys who sold hot dogs or people also heading to the ball game, wearing Blue Jays sweaters. Everybody liked Joe Clark.

In the same league of affability is Jean Chrétien. During his long political career, nothing ever stuck to the Teflon man because he could just laugh it off and dismiss anything with a humorous comment. Jean Chrétien can also charm anyone.

Mike Harris is affable but he grew into a person with charisma. I often heard him deliver speeches that I had heard several times before, yet I was still listening to his every word.

In 1995, just after the election had been called, I was asked to campaign with Mike Harris down in Kensington Market. Mike and I were going to be walking down the street and just dropping in to all the stores. There was nothing pre-arranged. There were no safe businesses that had been pre-approved. The party was in last place. We had no choice but to take a few chances.

We had been lucky enough to arrange for some media to join us on our campaigning. We had the Chinese newspaper, *Ming Pao*, and a television cameraman. Mike had with us two volunteers who knew a few people. The rest was up to us.

The first thing I saw when we arrived was a protester holding a sign that proclaimed that socialists were opposed to Mike Harris. I had no experience with protesters and I turned questioningly to Mike Harris, who winked at me and said, "I wish we could pay him to be with us all day."

I asked why.

Mike looked at me and said, "Good advertising. People who support us would not be supporting him."

Unfortunately the protester only stayed with us for about 15 minutes, got tired and left.

I was amazed at the response that we received from ordinary people who had small businesses — grocery stores, coffee shops. They listened closely to Mike and shook his hand. We were welcomed everywhere that we went. I realized then that Mike Harris spoke the same language they did. He struck a common tone with them. I also came to realize that even today, very few politicians stand up for the ordinary working man, people like my father who quietly worked at their jobs, raised their families and paid their taxes.

The best quality that Mike Harris had was his loyalty. As leader of the party, he kept some very strong personalities in line because he was respected by his caucus. When we formed the new government in 1995, most of the caucus who had been re-elected were expecting to get the call to serve in cabinet, regardless of their skill levels. The attitude was they had been there and had the experience and had done their part to get the party elected with a majority.

Somehow Mike Harris was able to keep together as a team a very diverse group of individuals who spanned the conservative political spectrum from left of centre to extreme right and from political newbie to grizzled veteran. A large part of this came from the fact that no matter what your view was of the situation or the party, we all respected Mike Harris. In many cases, it was the little things that he did without planning or intention that earned our loyalty.

At times when there was pressure on the government to get certain legislation passed and the legislative calendar was elapsing, government would pass a motion to go to midnight sittings. That meant that the legislature would run from 10 a.m. to midnight. Needless to say, nobody liked midnight sittings. If a cabinet minister had a speech to give in the evening, he needed to get another cabinet minister to substitute for him. This was when having your colleagues owe you came in handy.

Even when it was not your night to sit on midnight sittings, all members of the caucus were on call in the event there was a quorum call or some unexpected vote. The government was obligated to maintain quorum in the legislature at all time. That meant if there were not 12 members in the House including the Speaker, the bells would ring for five minutes. If quorum was not present after five minutes or sooner, the Speaker would declare the House adjourned until the next day.

Although the opposition parties had no requirement to make sure a quorum was present, opposition members would be present to make sure the government did not pull a fast one as well. The favourite tactic of the Opposition was to wait until there were fewer than 10 government members present and then they would all leave except for one Opposition member, who would request a quorum call.

No real debates occurred during midnight sittings, although that is what they were technically called. Some member would drone on about nonsense while everybody else would answer their correspondence or read notes for the next day. They were there to put in the required "debating" time before the next reading of the bill could occur. Very rarely did anybody show up voluntarily except for Mike Harris. The premier did not have any responsibility for midnight sittings, but occasionally at 10 or 11 p.m. he would be there sitting with all the other unfortunates, chatting with them, asking about them and generally cheering up the troops. That was real leadership.

My first ministry, Community and Social Services, was an overwhelming challenge for me. It was a huge line ministry with the only reform agenda for the first session of the government. I had inexperienced staff and no training. Throughout this difficult time, Mike Harris was nothing but supportive. He once said that I had been doing all the heavy lifting at the start of our government. What I learned about him was his very strong sense of loyalty.

When I was under fire for the regulatory error created by legislative counsel, when everyone wanted to throw me under the bus, Mike Harris continued to support me, even with his staff and outside communications advisers telling him to blame me. He continued to support me despite the braying of the media.

There were times when I was under a continual barrage for our welfare reforms, when Mike Harris would answer some of the attacks by talking about his life. No one expects the premier to do that, but he did. I will never forget his direct honesty and loyalty. I was never asked to resign. I was only told to hang in there and that he appreciated my efforts.

The lesson for me was to not take the situation as the end of the world. I approached the media and didn't run from it. I looked for opportunities to explain our policies and I learned to laugh at myself. The media soon realized that I was not afraid of them and that I would stand there and answer their questions. Eventually the government embarked on other reforms and, like all great storms, it passed.

Although I was never out of cabinet in my career, I also came to greatly respect Mike Harris for his loyalty and his friendship.

Being a cabinet minister is in many ways similar to playing goalie for the Toronto Maple Leafs. If you make a mistake, the opposition scores, the red light goes on and the buzzer sounds. The next day everybody analyzes why you let in the goal. The media always has an opinion even though they themselves have never played the game or paid the price. There is no forgiveness. To paraphrase Tom Hanks's character in A League of Their Own, there is no crying in politics.

Another unfair and untrue characterization of Mike Harris is that he was an unfeeling person who was solely interested in slashing budgets with no consideration for the impact on people. Mike Harris is a decent human being.

What always amused me was how Mike Harris described his decision-making. He loved to say that his gut told him to do something. What he really meant was that he read everything and thought about it and that both his intellect and instinct agreed that this was what he should do. Mike Harris had great political instincts but he also had a very strong sense of right and wrong.

In most discussions at the cabinet table, the attorney general would present a statement that had been given to him by his officials to represent the position of the ministry. He would also have his own opinions. The legal opinions of the Ministry of the Attorney General quite often would state what the legal obligations of the government were or if the government was compliant with its own rules.

I came to realize that many of my colleagues did not understand that this was the lowest standard, the bare minimum, required of government. They didn't seem to understand that we should not be doing what we had to do but rather what we *should* be doing. I saw this reasoning in several incidents that highlighted why governments should be doing the right thing.

In 1998 the issue of compensation for the Dionne Quintuplets arose. The Dionne sisters, who were in their sixties, were looking for some kind of compensation for their treatment at the hands of the Ontario government when they were children. They had been taken from their home and put on display while the government profited by treating them like animals in a zoo, charging tourists admission to stare at them.

As the briefing unfolded, we were told that we had no obligation to the Dionnes because the incident had occurred during the Mitch Hepburn Liberal government. We were also advised that we should hire a very aggressive lawyer and fight any claim.

I had just watched a made-for-TV story about the quintuplets, and I felt sorry for the mistreatment that they had suffered at the hands of unfeeling and exploitive government officials. I knew that this had happened in the 1930s but their situation seemed very unjust. I stated my view. I could see that Mike Harris was swayed by my argument. It was a case of not just doing what we had to do, but doing what we should do. A number of my colleagues seemed to be persuaded as well.

The official position was again put forth that this situation could be dealt with quickly and without much fanfare. I countered with the pragmatic view that it was better to give the Dionnes something at a time when we didn't need to, and get some credit for treating them decently. If we didn't, I said, we would eventually be dragged through the media and forced politically to give them something, and then we would be given a figurative kick in the ass.

Mike Harris was eventually persuaded by the attorney general, much against his better judgment, and we fought these poor elderly women aggressively. Eventually we were dragged to settle the case and were treated as we should have been. This was one of the few times that Mike did not follow his gut.

A similar incident with the opposite result was the handling of the Hepatitis C compensation. Our government had been pushing the federal government to resolve the matter of compensation for those who had been infected by Hepatitis C as a result of tainted blood. Again the attorney general advised us that our government had no obligation, as the responsibility for the issue was the federal government. We were also advised of the cost of the compensation. The problem with the federal offer was that it excluded many victims from the settlement. These people were very ill and many were afraid that any compensation would come too late to do any of the victims any good.

This was very much like the Dionne Quintuplet issue, except with a much greater price tag. Mike Harris, despite the advice of the ministry, followed his gut and did the right thing — not the minimum that we were obligated to do. Ontario broke ranks and agreed to compensate those victims who had been excluded from the federal offer. His decision had nothing to do with any political capital, and only with doing the decent and right thing.

I had the pleasure of seeing the real Mike Harris. He is a good person with a great sense of humour.

Not everyone got to see the relaxed and real Mike Harris. In politics it is all about public image, maintaining discipline and driving a message. There is zero room for error and consequently there is a need to be on one's guard at all times. Humour is rarely appreciated by the media, either on purpose or through ignorance. The media rarely understands metaphor or irony. This hypocritical attitude of the media and the gap between their own skill sets and education and their portrayal of politicians as uncultured boors is never pointed out.

There is not an extensive background of literary knowledge apparent in either the press gallery or politicians. Politicians seem to come either from the school of hard knocks or with a formal education in political science or law. The difference is that politicians rarely pretend to have a background in the arts and culture, nor do they challenge others about their arts pedigree.

The first time that I witnessed this artificial snobbery was when some reporter trying to embarrass Mike Harris on National Book Day asked him to name the last book he had read. I blame his communications person for not being better aware and prepared.

I challenge most people who read an average number of books to name the last book that they read and not have their answer twisted into a funny story for the newspaper. Mike Harris answered *Mr. Silly*, a book that he had read to his son. Of course this led to very derisive headlines and stories the next day.

It is unfortunate that few people got to see Mike Harris's good sense of humour. One day Mike Harris, Ernie Eves, Al Palladini and I were playing a round of golf at King Valley. The best golfer was Ernie. Most people would assume that Mike Harris was the best golfer, but as the premier he rarely had time to play golf. The next would be Mike, then Al Palladini and then me. Typically, to have some fun, Al Palladini said to Mike and Ernie, "Dave and I will take on you guys."

I turned to Al and said, "This is probably not a good idea since it's August and August is cabinet shuffle time."

Typically, Al's response was a hearty laugh.

So the game was afoot. It was an odd game. When I am on my game, I hit a long ball. It has a lot of spin. All day Ernie kept on saying with surprise, "Whose ball is that?" when he saw my ball ahead of his. It was one of those days when Mike and Ernie were a little off their games, and Al and I either birdied or parred every hole. By the time we got to the 17th tee, Al and I were up $50 on Mike and Ernie.

Just as Al was about to tee off, Mike said in jest, "You know I never lost more than $15 from anyone who stayed in my cabinet."

Al sliced the next ball out of bounds and so did I.

Unfortunately for Mike and Ernie, we couldn't lose enough and they ended up paying us $25 each.

The next day at home, the phone rang and Elaine answered the phone. She turned to me and said, "It's Kitty Knight, Mike Harris's assistant and she wants to know if the premier can speak to you."

Then she added, "You're not in a cabinet shuffle are you?"

My only response was a shrug as I took the phone and said, "Hello."

It was Mike Harris. "What are you doing tomorrow?" he asked.

"Actually I am giving a speech for you," I responded. "Why do you ask?"

"I want to win my money back," he said.

I answered, "Tough luck" and hung up.

I turned to Elaine and said, "Looks like I'm not in the shuffle."

A similar incident took place at the National, where Al Palladini was a member. In this case it was Mike Harris, Al Palladini and Chris Hodgson. Al suggested that he and Chris take on Mike and me.

I chuckled at Chris and said, "It's not good to take the premier's money."

Mike Harris turned to me and said with a grin, "It's not good to lose his money either."

It wasn't just the members of his cabinet and caucus who respected Mike Harris. At conventions he was as patient as Bobby Hull is when he signs autographs for everyone. The supporters, young and old, newcomers and old faithful members, would flock to him like he was a superstar. Mike Harris would stay with them patiently, chatting with them or having his photo taken with them. No one was disappointed. I always saw Mike Harris as a very humble person.

I also saw him as a very fair person, both in dealing with people and with policies.

During one cabinet meeting, a very heated debate broke out. I was the Consumer and Commercial Relations Minister and the issue dealt with alcohol. Ernie Eves had a very strong opinion on the issue and started raising his voice at me. I responded in kind. Mike Harris waded into the argument. Then I did the unthinkable: I yelled at Mike Harris.

No one ever yelled at Mike Harris. First of all, it is very discourteous to shout at the premier of Ontario. Second, Mike Harris was a larger-than-life person who intimidated even some of my cabinet colleagues.

I then compounded the unthinkable. I picked up my heavy

cabinet binder and slammed it on the cabinet table. I grabbed my briefcase and left.

Everyone was surprised when I walked back into my office. No sooner had I sat down than my assistant walked into my office and said, "The premier is on the phone and wants to talk to you."

I confess that there were a number of thoughts that ran through my mind. I picked up the phone and said, "Hello."

Mike Harris asked, "You're not still mad at me are you?"

I said, "No. Are you mad at me?"

He said, "No. Good."

That was the end of the conversation and the end of the incident. Mike Harris was not a petty person.

Knowing Mike Harris the way I did, it surprised me from time to time that others were in awe and perhaps a little in fear of him. More than a few times in caucus meetings one of my cabinet colleagues would say that he had a great idea for the premier. To which I would say, why don't you go over there and sit next to him and tell him? My colleague would ask me if I would tell Mike instead.

Everybody I know, regardless of party affiliation, got into politics to make the world a little better. We differ on what that means and how to accomplish it. No matter what you do in politics and for whatever reason, someone is not going to like it. The best compliment that I can say is that someone is a good person. Mike Harris is a good person.

# CHAPTER FOURTEEN

# Bringing Down the House

A crucial part of a politician's success or failure is his or her ability to perform in the legislature. The performance will influence the opinions of many different audiences, all of whom will in turn affect his or her public image. The media closely monitors the daily thrust and parry of Question Period. They will use the statements made in the House as the basis for their daily press scrums. If there are any missteps or new and interesting information revealed, the media will be ready to spin the story.

The opposition parties will try to detect any weaknesses in the various cabinet ministers. If they smell fear, they will be quick to pursue their quarry, both inside the legislature and outside. Bad performances will lead to encores demanded by the Opposition through their Question Period strategy. Politicians will tell you that the level of rancour in the legislature rose when the proceedings became televised.

The televised nature of Question Period has great influence on public perception. Television allows the public to make instantaneous judgments about politicians. Just as television changed the public's perception of the Gulf War, it has a similar effect with respect to politicians.

In communication guru Barry McLoughlin's book, *Communicate with Power*, he comments, "When John F. Kennedy debated Richard Nixon on television in 1960, the majority of viewers were most swayed by the calm, cool, collected appearance of Kennedy. The majority of those who listened on the radio, however, were more impressed by Nixon's performance. The lesson is, though, that non-verbal signals tend to dominate the verbal message." Barry McLoughlin also concludes that your impression comes 55 percent from tone and attitude, 38 percent non-verbal and 7 percent verbal. In a separate study, Barry McLoughlin concludes that what your audience perceives of you is caring (50 percent), honesty and dedication (35 percent) and competence (15 percent).

This tells us that what is important is not what you say but how you say it. Appearances leave the impressions, not the words. This does not free you from accuracy and truthfulness, because a failure to be correct or honest will have other consequences, far worse than leaving a bad impression.

It is helpful to understand what happens before, during and after Question Period on a normal day for a cabinet minister. Question Period is the opportunity for opposition members to ask questions of the government on any topic of their choosing. The length of time spent on Question Period varies from government to government. It can be as short as 30 minutes or as long as one hour in Ontario. The questions and responses are sometimes limited in time to allow more questions to be asked.

Originally in 1995, under Speaker Al McLean, there was no limitation on the length of the questions and the answers. This meant that the Opposition leaders would use the time to give a speech or ramble on and on about the shortcomings of the government. The cabinet ministers in their responses would take as much time as they could to run down the clock. This changed under Speaker Chris Stockwell, who tried to limit both the questions and the responses to one minute each. As much as Stockwell tried to be fair, my measurement of the time allocated to Opposition versus that of the government showed 20 percent more time given to the Opposition.

Some observers among the public thought that the cabinet ministers were supplied the questions in advance of Question Period so that they could prepare. The situation is exactly the opposite. There is no advance notice. In fact, the opposition parties try to catch the government by surprise.

There is a certain amount of anxiety that goes along with Question Period. My colleagues would react to it in a wide variety of ways. Some of them would physically shake with fear. One of them explained to me how she would make sure she leaned against her desk so that she could remain steady on her feet. Some very intelligent and talented people would freeze and give very wooden, ineffective performances.

The only cure for fear is experience. Adjoining to the legislature are two very large rooms — the West Lobby for the Opposition and the East Lobby for the government. These rooms are lounges with coffee and refreshments and comfortable chairs for the members to relax in. Before Question Period every day I used to do either cryptic crossword puzzles or *New York Times* crosswords. I rarely looked at my House Book notes. Many of my colleagues used to comment that I was probably the most relaxed cabinet minister before Question Period. They actually got the cause and effect in reverse: it wasn't that I was so relaxed that I did crossword puzzles; I did crossword puzzles to relax. No matter how long you do Question Period there is always some nervousness.

The typical day for a cabinet minister begins with reading all four major newspapers — the *Toronto Sun*, the *Globe and Mail*, the *National Post* and the *Toronto Star*. You are reading the papers with blinders on, trying to determine which news stories might be of interest to either the media or the opposition members. On the way in to the office, I always listened to CFRB to catch the radio perspective on newsworthy stories.

Once I arrived at the office, I would review the clipping services.

This is the summary and actual stories that have been compiled from across the province that were relevant to the ministry. The clippings would contain the press clippings and also summaries of the television and radio stories from that morning and the day before. They would contain the big stories that were covered by the major media and also the small stories that came from different ridings across the province. The latter is important because often the opposition members would ask questions that were relevant only in their riding. These were often the last questions asked during Question Period.

The next step would be to discuss the issues with both my communications assistant and my legislative assistant. The CA would have attended a meeting first thing in the morning with all the other CAs in government along with the premier's. This meeting would be to anticipate which questions would arise. If the premier was attending Question Period, he would have to be prepared for all questions. If he were not, then either the deputy premier or the Chair of Management Board as acting premier would have to be prepared.

If we determined that it was likely that a question would arise during Question Period and consequently have to be responded to in the media, my legislative assistant would have to prepare a response for my House Book and my CA would have to think about how we would spin the story to the media. Both of these tasks could include the gathering of factual material from the ministry offices or more extensive research.

It would be important to know how to respond to the media before I left the office. Even though the media would have access after Question Period, they were obviously not restricted to that time and could ask questions any time that they saw you. There were two other normal scrum times: before caucus meetings on Tuesday mornings and before cabinet meetings on Wednesday mornings. A large part of the cabinet minister's time before Question Period is taken up by the preparatory work.

Question Period itself is a series of question to the government by both opposition parties and government backbench members. The leader of the Official Opposition is allowed to start off by asking two questions, each of which can have three parts asked separately. The leader of the other opposition party is allowed one such three-part question. Each part question is allowed to be one minute in length. The premier or his substitute can respond to each part with a one-minute response. In theory this should take 18 minutes out of the total 60 minutes of Question Period. The rest of the questions follow a strange rotation, one that includes government backbenchers, of two-part questions. This goes on until after Question Period's 60 minutes have expired.

At the conclusion of Question Period, the cabinet ministers retire to the East Lobby to speak to their CAs and legislative assistants to determine if the media will want to question them. My CA would have circulated among the media already to see if they wanted to talk to me and what about. The inexperienced CAs would not have done this and therefore their ministers would be guessing.

If you are standing up in the House to answer a question and your heart is racing and you can feel the blood pumping in your body and you feel that you can't think, you had better have good notes in your House Book. The House Book is a communication aid for use in the legislature that is prepared by your legislative assistant and contains prepared answers for issues that have been anticipated.

Although facts and background are important, it is far more important to understand that Question Period is not an exercise in answering questions with many facts; it is an opportunity to deliver your message. Many ministers forget this simple fact and instead inundate everyone with reams and reams of facts. Most people will have turned off their ears after one minute of this blather.

A good House Book will allow you to start with a few facts to set the record straight, then indicate the action that you will take and last, deliver your message. An example could be the following:

Opposition Member: Minister, by allowing slot machines at racetracks, aren't you pushing more people into problem gambling and showing that you don't really care?

FIRST, THE FACTS

Minister: When you were the government, you created the biggest expansion into gambling by opening commercial casinos. As you know, gambling already takes place at racetracks but the racing industry is experiencing huge financial problems. It is also an industry that supports around 40,000 jobs, mainly in rural Ontario.

SECOND, THE ACTION

Minister: We are investing five percent of the revenue from the racetrack slots into research, prevention and treatment of problem gambling, which is more than all the other provinces combined.

THIRD, THE MESSAGE

Minister: The Canadian Foundation for Compulsive Gambling has recognized our government for our leadership role in combating gambling addictions. We are also saving thousands of jobs, many of them for people who might otherwise be collecting social assistance.

A good legislative assistant is worth his weight in gold. My best legislative assistants have gone on to take key policy assistant roles. People like Derek O'Toole, Bill Campbell and Troy Ross learned how to get answers quickly and accurately, usually under considerable pressure. The legislative assistant in theory should know almost as much as the minister, especially about the day-to-day issues. The best legislative assistants I had sat in on all ministry briefings.

The penny dropped for me when I realized that I had only one job and that was to deliver a message, not a million facts. When I was armed with the message that I wanted to deliver for the day, the rest was really just filler. My House Book would be opened at the appropriate page and I could select one out of many facts to recite.

The three-part process of facts, action and message accomplishes in three steps what Barry McLoughlin proposes in one step when responding to questions by reporters. He calls this method bridging.

There is one other person who helped me get my sea legs. One day I was talking to my friend Chris Hodgson and was complimenting him on how much his performance during Question Period had improved. I couldn't particularly attribute his improved performance to any one factor. He told me that he had consulted someone who had helped him specifically with Question Period.

Not every politician handles all aspects of communication well. Some are better at giving speeches. Some excel at media scrums, always providing a sound bite at the right time. A few are really good at Question Period. I believed that my forte was giving speeches and I had become comfortable in media scrums. I still thought that I might be able to improve my performance in Question Period.

Through Chris Hodgson, I met with communications expert Holly Sloan. I wasn't sure how she might benefit me, but it appeared that she had boosted Chris Hodgson's performance. John Guthrie, my chief of staff, thought that if I sat down with her and was comfortable with her, she might be able to help.

While Barry McLoughlin was very talented in the message, I found that Holly specialized in non-verbal elements. In other words, she taught the "how," not the "what."

Our first exercise together was to review tapes of my performance in the House. I was then asked to be critical of my performance. I had asked my CA, Ian Dovey, to sit in on the sessions. Ian had been a former television on-camera reporter and knew a thing or two about how to convey a message. We all understood that it was no time for ego if I was to get the benefit of Holly's services.

We also reviewed some tapes of some of my colleagues and opposition leaders and analyzed the good and bad performers. The first thing that I noticed was that I spoke more quickly than I did in a conversation or when I gave a speech. I realized that I was speaking quickly in order to get more facts in, in the one minute I was allowed for a response. I had been giving up more effective presentation in exchange for more words. Was it a good trade? Of course not.

Holly asked me what the difference was between giving a speech (which I was good at) and responding during Question Period. I concluded that I was more comfortable giving a speech. When I gave a speech, I took my time and felt I was in control. It was an attitude. Even if someone had asked me to limit a speech to 10 minutes, I never felt an obligation to do so. When I took my time I could change my intonation. I could give examples to emphasize my points. I was far more interesting.

The penny dropped at this point. Sometimes less was more. A smaller amount of information more effectively conveyed was a better goal. Aside from making the mental leap to speak slower and as if I was giving a speech, there were some physical tricks I could follow to slow myself down.

We reviewed tapes of Mike Harris. After being asked a question, the premier took his time standing up. Often he would pause to do up the button on his suit jacket. And yet he had an intense look on his face like a boxer walking up to get instructions from the referee. This was his windup. When he stood up, you were waiting for his words. You felt that he was going to say something important. When he spoke, his words were measured in the way he spoke.

In contrast, when one of the opposition members was called upon by the Speaker of the House to ask his question, he popped up like toast from a toaster. He was on his feet so quickly it was as if his words had to catch up to him. The audience would feel similarly hurried, so that less attention would be paid.

One of my colleagues who always had a presence when he spoke was Noble Villeneuve. Noble was for our first term of government the Minister of Agriculture. He was equally as effective in English and French. When called upon, Noble would slowly get to his feet. He gave the impression that he was sucking all of the air out of the legislature and he would always start his answer in a booming bass voice, "Speaker!" Noble certainly got your attention.

Holly and Ian would run me through practices of standing up slowly and buttoning up my suit jacket and creating anticipation of my answer. We practised until it felt comfortable and I did it naturally.

The slower approach to standing actually helped me slow down my delivery. The slower and more emphatic my approach, the more I became aware of how quickly some of my colleagues were talking. Most were less effective when they were racing their words. More often than not, when they were trying to squeeze in endless facts, they were cut off mid-thought by the Speaker, leaving the listener hanging on an incomplete sentence. It is better to start strongly and end strongly with less information.

There are exceptions to this rule that slower is better. John Baird, the former Energy Minister, had a consistently fast but effective approach. John was able to switch gears and make effective emphasis at lightning speed. In the midst of this blur he was always able to slip in an interesting sound bite for the media. Performing like the "Flash" is not for most mortals.

To remind myself of my goal, every day when I sat down at my desk in the legislature, I wrote down in big letters on a piece of paper, SLOW DOWN. When I stood up to answer a question, I was reading that piece of paper. Other than Helen Johns who sat beside me, most people including the opposition members thought I was reading a briefing note. I was just reminding myself to slow down.

Speaking too slowly is just as ineffective. In fact, speaking too slowly is probably worse because you begin to irritate the listener. Losing the audience is one thing but having the audience become hostile because of your delivery is disastrous.

There was one opposition member who spoke so slowly and ineffectively, you thought he might have been new to the English language. He wasn't. He was from a long-time old English-speaking Canadian family. He was just a lousy speaker. He spoke so slowly that you wanted to throttle the words out of him. No one ever heckled him, however, because we thought it would be like pulling wings from a fly. He was totally ineffective and defenceless.

The next thing that Holly asked was, "Who are you talking to?" I explained to her that even though an opposition member had asked the question, all questions and responses must be directed through the Speaker of the House. I then explained that at times I was directing my response at the Speaker and at other times I was speaking to the member who had asked the question. The Speaker was located at the end of the legislature and the opposition members were located across from the government.

Holly then asked, "Who is your audience?" Since the proceedings in the legislature were televised, I told her my audience was the viewing taxpayer who was watching from the comfort of home. The conclusion was that I should be speaking to the viewers at home, not to the Speaker, not to the Opposition, not even to my own members. This meant that I had to be conscious of the television cameras and overcome the desire to talk to a live person.

Over the next few days in the legislature I tried to be more conscious of speaking to the television cameras. Although it may have looked awkward in the legislature, when I viewed the results from the tapes, it certainly looked better from a television perspective.

There are many small things that appear on tape that you are not aware you are doing at the time. I noticed that I was continuously shifting from foot to foot. It took a real conscious effort to stop fidgeting, but it looked a lot more presentable and didn't distract from my message.

Advice can come from the most unexpected quarters. Occasionally, I used to chew gum before going into Question Period. One day I forgot to discard the gum. During my eight years as a cabinet minister I usually sat just over the right shoulder of the premier. That meant that whenever the premier answered a question I was on camera.

This particular day I had no questions from the Opposition so I ended up reading some other material for some upcoming meetings. After Question Period, as I was walking through the East Lobby, I was advised that there was a telephone call for me. I picked up the phone and heard my mother on the other side telling me not to chew gum on camera because it didn't look good. This was good advice.

Another piece of familial advice came from Elaine. Most of the more experienced cabinet members, when the question is not directed at them, are engaging in activities other than listening to the question and response. Most are reading other material for upcoming cabinet committee meetings or briefing notes. I was proofreading a speech for that night. One of the pages handed me a note to call home. When I left the legislature to call Elaine, she told me not to sleep while I was sitting behind Mike Harris. I explained to her that I wasn't sleeping but reading. She insisted that I looked like I was sleeping. My comment to her was that I was Asian and maybe when I was looking down to read it appeared that I was sleeping.

When I saw the tapes of Question Period, I realized Elaine was right. It did look like my eyes were closed. From that day on, whenever the question was to the premier or to anyone else with whom I might appear on camera, I made sure I was looking up.

Holly asked me one day if the constant heckling and shouting that occurs in the legislature bothered me. To tell the truth, after years of responding during Question Period, I didn't even hear them anymore. I simply blocked out the noise. This also helped my golf game. You could fire a cannon behind me when I putt and I wouldn't flinch.

Speaking of golf games, my friend and golf buddy Dan Newman was barely over the elation of being appointed to cabinet when he had one of the greatest issues of our government thrust upon him. Dan had just been appointed to what was normally a junior cabinet portfolio, Environment, when the Walkerton tragedy occurred.

Although Dan had not been the minister for the period of time that was reviewed leading up to the tragedy, under ministerial responsibility he was charged with accounting for it. For a very long period of time, Dan had to answer every Opposition question during Question Period for months. To his credit he did it with professionalism and empathy.

Heckling in the legislature is a tradition. Although the rules of the legislature or Parliament prohibit heckling, it is an accepted occurrence and unless the heckler gets too personal or says that another member is lying, it goes on. Some hecklers are actually amusing but most are simply rude. It is no wonder that classes of schoolchildren scratch their heads after seeing some of the disgraceful behaviour that occurs in the legislature.

You cannot let yourself be distracted because it will take you off your message. At times this is hard because some members have lungs of leather and can project like a bullhorn. The noise from the opposition hecklers is compounded at times by some of your colleagues who are trying to be helpful by yelling back at the Opposition. Unfortunately they are just adding to the noise.

There are times during Question Period when a question is asked and the minister has a great zinger. Perhaps it is a contrary quote by the member asking the question. Or perhaps the member is using incorrect information and the minister has the definitive proof. For example, an opposition member once asked me a question about the appropriateness of a cabinet minister's photograph appearing on a public information piece. I had in my possession a copy of a public document with the opposition member's photograph on it when he was a cabinet minister.

The minister has to understand a little bit about timing. If it is a lead-off question with three parts or an ordinary question with two parts, the zinger has to be used in the last part of the answer so that the questioner has no comeback. Some cabinet ministers are so anxious to get out the information they allow the questioner time to recover and have a response.

In this situation I used the document at the very end. I upset the questioner so much that he left the legislature in a huff. In this game you have to take it as much as give it. Although this episode did not merit a story in the media, it also resulted in no negative story in the media about the government. The tie goes to the home team.

# CHAPTER FIFTEEN

# THE MINISTRY OF BOOZE AND GAMBLING

After the interesting experience of the Ministry of Community and Social Services and when most of the ministries were coming forward with reforms and cost cutting in an effort to balance the budget, Mike Harris made changes in his cabinet. To my relief, I was moved to the Ministry of Consumer and Commercial Relations. To do this, Mike Harris moved Norm Sterling over to the Ministry of the Environment and my parliamentary assistant, Janet Ecker, was elevated to cabinet and assumed my former portfolio.

I had enlisted in the PC team and with that commitment, I had signed on to the reforms that we promised in the Common Sense Revolution. Although I had brought forward the reforms in the welfare system, this was not something that I was comfortable with.

Despite the fact that we had promised to lower the general welfare rates to 10 percent above the national average, it seemed lost in all the fanfare that we had also guaranteed not to reduce the disability allowance. There were many doubts in my mind about the reforms and I was too new to government and my role as a cabinet minister to object. Looking back now, there was absolutely no latitude to alter any of the reforms in welfare because they were the showpieces of the Common Sense Revolution. The only option that I had was not to have accepted the cabinet position in the first place. When I accepted the position, I had no idea what that meant.

The Ministry of Consumer and Commercial Relations is the regulator of government. At the time, the ministry regulated alcohol, gaming, the travel industry, the real estate industry, car dealers, technical and safety standards and the film industry. I was also the Registrar General and in charge of all registrations, from birth, marriages and deaths to corporate and real estate records.

The major reform was the expansion of gaming. Our government had the very difficult task of balancing the budget after years of the tax-and-spend actions of Bob Rae and the NDP. The debt had mushroomed to the extent that Ontario was paying more than $1 million an hour, 24 hours a day, 365 days a year just to pay the interest that was owed on the debt. We had also promised to reduce the personal income tax rate. The additional revenue to balance these commitments was to come from economic recovery. Practically, we needed to generate additional revenue. One of the areas in which we thought could generate more revenue was gaming.

The NDP government under Bob Rae had opened the Windsor Casino and the doors to legal gambling in Ontario. There was relatively little competition from the U.S. side, so it was thought that pulling in American dollars was a good idea. With that in mind, several possibilities were being considered. On the table were options for allowing charity casinos, additional commercial casinos or even video lottery terminals (VLTs) in restaurants and bars.

The Ministry of Consumer and Commercial Relations under Norm Sterling had embarked on consultations on the nature of the expansion of gaming. While on one hand restaurants and bars were lobbying strongly for VLTs, the anti-gambling lobby was characterizing VLTs as the crack cocaine of gambling.

In the middle of this controversial issue, I took over the ministry.

There were a number of other considerations. If the government were to expand gaming into charity casinos, this would have an impact on the revenue that charities and other non-profit organizations made from bingo and other quasi-gaming activities. If we were to increase the gaming activity, we would also need to counterbalance this with additional resources for research, education and the treatment of problem gambling. The municipalities that would host any other gaming venues would need to be compensated for additional infrastructure and policing resources.

Control of gaming activities was important. Commercial casinos and charity casinos would be controlled sites. If VLTs were to be allowed in restaurants and bars, there was a concern about ensuring the integrity of the machines and making sure that no underage gaming took place.

One of the issues that we quickly dealt with was the VLTs, promptly discarding them. Instead we would use slot machines, which for some reason did not have the same negative image as VLTs. Somehow the logic of the difference between the two machines escaped me, but the Opposition was so convinced that we were committed to VLTs they didn't know how to respond to the slight shift in policy. We also decided not to allow the slot machines into restaurants and bars. This was very disappointing to the restaurants and bar businesses.

In order to proceed we needed to deal with the issues we had anticipated could be problematic. The many charities and non-profit organizations that had depended on bingo or break-open tickets would be affected by the expansion of gaming venues. It was imperative to bridge that kind of loss of revenue. The vehicle that we decided to use was the Trillium Foundation. The Trillium Foundation had a budget of $10 million and was supposed to support the charitable sector with programming and special funding. Under the NDP government, some funding started to be approved for political and advocating uses instead of community programs.

To fill the gap we decided to increase the funding for the Trillium Foundation to $100 million annually and to direct it back to its original mandate of supporting community activities like arts, culture and sports. There was to be no political activity allowed.

Major applications would still be processed through the Trillium Foundation main board of directors, who would also be responsible for policy decisions. In order to accommodate more grants and accountability, local Trillium committees would be better able to assess the local community applications. The announcement was received very favourably by the charities and non-profit sector.

We also decided to assist the municipalities that would host the venues with a share of the revenue to help them with their infrastructure and additional operating costs. Most municipalities were smart enough to figure out how large a windfall this would mean to their budgets. We also indicated that no municipality would be forced to host a new gaming venue.

Not surprisingly, there was an uproar created by a small group of people in the City of Toronto, who started a very strong campaign against both charity casinos and casinos in general in their city.

In 1997, as part of the municipal elections, a number of referenda questions were on the ballots. The questions and results were clearly definitive.

The results for a charity casino were:

| | | | |
|---|---|---|---|
| Scarborough: | Yes: | 49, 395 | 35.2% |
| | No | 90,749 | 64.8% |
| Toronto: | Yes | 66,487 | 33.5% |
| | No | 131,786 | 66.5% |
| York: | Yes | 10,201 | 31.4% |
| | No | 22,236 | 68.6% |

The results on the votes on casinos in general were:

| | | | |
|---|---|---|---|
| East York: | Yes | 8,323 | 25.9% |
| | No | 23,757 | 74.1% |
| Etobicoke: | Yes | 25,985 | 27.9% |
| | No | 67,255 | 72.1% |
| Toronto: | Yes | 58,929 | 29.4% |
| | No | 141,353 | 70.6% |

Clearly people had paid attention to the negative campaign. Years later, when the financial benefits are evident, every year there is a lot of talk about a commercial casino for Toronto and how that could aid the city's finances. (In 2012, the McGuinty Liberal government decided to change the policy of slot machines at the race tracks. The impact of that change has yet to be determined.)

The issue of problem gambling was one that the government took very seriously. It was important that the province invest heavily in research, education and the treatment of problem gambling. As gaming was expanded in the province of Ontario, the government simultaneously expanded the investment to deal with problem gambling. The government invested more money than any other jurisdiction in North America and more than all the other provinces and territories combined.

During these discussions, the roles of the various ministries were clearly set out. As the chief regulator of government, I was to combine the Liquor Licence Board of Ontario and the Gaming Control Commission into one board that would be responsible for the regulation and enforcement of alcohol and gaming matters. The result was the creation of the Alcohol and Gaming Commission of Ontario.

Since the government was expanding gaming and was the owner of the casinos, illegal gaming would take revenue from the province, and therefore it was important to clamp down on any illegal gaming.

The Ministry of Industry and Trade was to oversee the operation of casinos and the Ontario Lottery and Gaming Corporation as well as the expansion. The Ministry of Culture would be in charge of the Trillium Foundation and disbursing the expanded budget of $100 million.

As I have discovered, "experts" outside of government who have never worked inside government have interesting theories on how decision-making occurs. Most are wrong and unrelated to reality.

The decision-making for the leadership in the gaming initiative was well thought out. The reality of how I ended up being in charge was completely unplanned.

During Question Period in the legislature, the lead-off question was directed to Bill Saunderson, the Minister of Trade and Industry. The question was about the expansion of gaming. Bill Saunderson had been a very successful businessman and was a chartered accountant and a Ph.D. Unfortunately Bill was not one of our better performers during Question Period. The first part of the three-part lead-off question had not been answered to the satisfaction of Premier Harris, who then said to Bill Saunderson in a stage whisper, "Let Tsubouchi answer the rest of the question."

When the second part of the question was asked of Bill, he then directed the question to me. I responded to the second and third parts of the question to the satisfaction of Premier Harris.

The next lead-off question was directed to my friend Marilyn Mushinski, the Minister of Culture, and it was about some statistical information on the Trillium Foundation. Marilyn is a very smart lady, but for some reason she did not have the statistical information at her fingertips.

I then heard Premier Harris say to Marilyn, "Let Tsubouchi answer the rest of the question." Marilyn referred the rest of the question to me and I answered.

After Question Period, I approached Premier Harris with Troy Ross, my legislative assistant, and said, "Premier, we have a bit of a problem now. I just answered questions on the operational aspect of the gaming initiative and on the Trillium Foundation. Who is going to answer questions in the media scrum?"

Mike Harris turned to me and said, "There's no problem. You can answer all the questions; you are in charge of the gaming file now."

Shortly after we dealt with the charity casinos, I was approached by the horse racing industry about slot machines for the racetracks. The two main people representing the horse racing industry were Jane Holmes and George Kelly of the Ontario Horse Racing Industry Association.

The horse racing industry in Ontario had been in decline for several years. The industry employed around 40,000 people. Public attendance had been declining and as a result the purses were being reduced and much of the breeding was disappearing to the United States. Jane Holmes and George Kelly were very helpful in providing the context and the solution for the industry. OHRIA represented the thoroughbred and the standardbred industries, which generally clashed, but the crisis of the industry made them uneasy and suspicious allies.

I didn't have much knowledge of the horse racing industry. I had only been to the track once years before. I remember the day because all I knew about horse racing was the name Sandy Hawley. So I made minimum bets all day on Sandy Hawley. It happened to be the day he won seven races.

Jane and George arranged for me to tour several tracks and meet the people who worked there. Most people think of horse racing, the sport of kings, as an elitist and privileged sport. The reality is that most of the people who work there are working-class people doing unglamorous jobs. One thing that was evident was their enthusiasm for their jobs.

Eventually we were able to allow the racetracks to have slot machines. The universal view was that this program not only saved the industry but breathed new life into it. Breeding returned to Ontario. Purses were increased and new track improvements were made. A great deal of the credit goes to Jane Holmes and George Kelly.

The Ontario wine industry had some issues as well. The major issue was to create an appellation and standard for wines in Ontario. VQA, or Vintners Quality Alliance, would provide the wine industry with standards and would help market their quality and give that same assurance to the public. The Ontario wine industry had been fighting to get access to markets in other countries. They had been shut out of Europe while European wines had access to Ontario markets.

Ontario wines were very competitive and had been winning awards not only for ice wine but for other wines — both white and red — in Italy, France and England. I was approached by a contingent consisting of Linda Franklin, the executive director of the

Ontario Wine Council, Bruce Walker of Vincor, Paul Speck of Henry of Pelham and Len Pennachetti of Cave Springs.

The year before I became the Minister of Consumer and Commercial Relations, Elaine and I had been out for a drive and ended up in Niagara. As we were driving around I remembered my friend Bob Speck mentioning that some relatives of his owned Henry of Pelham. We had just passed the sign for the winery and decided to drop in and visit. The winery had a little gift shop and we met Paul Speck, who was good enough to give us a tour and explain how wineries operated. This came in handy when I met up with Paul again.

After they explained the issue, it was very evident that this was something that needed to be done. I said it was just a matter of drafting legislation and taking it through the process. This must have been a surprising response to them. Most times government would say we will review the issue and that meant you would probably never hear from them.

On May 4, 1999, an act to provide for the designation of a wine authority to establish an appellation of origin system for Vintners Quality Alliance wine and to administer that system received Royal Assent. I remember signing several copies of the legislation for the people who worked so hard for their industry.

The other issue that Linda Franklin and Bruce Walker approached me about was a puzzling one. They advised me that the Ontario wine industry needed to sell directly to restaurants and bars. This statement alone was curious. I asked, why couldn't the wineries sell to restaurants?

The LCBO, the liquor monopoly of Ontario, allowed the wineries to sell directly to bars, restaurants and hotels, but required the wineries to pay the LCBO retail markup. This did not make sense. It was one thing for the LCBO to charge for services that they provided to the wineries, but it was unfair to charge a fee for no services. This acted as a disincentive. Why would the wineries bother to market their products directly to restaurants and bars if the profits would go to the LCBO?

This had to change, because no government should charge for doing nothing. But our government was still trying to deal with the huge deficit that Bob Rae had left us and this would have an impact on revenue. I explained to Linda Franklin and Bruce Walker that they would need to assist us with finding an offset for the loss of revenue. Logically, if we eliminated the disincentive for wineries, they would ramp up on the marketing and sales. We would be forgoing the retail markup but we would be gaining more income taxes from the people who would be hired for marketing and sales.

When I asked Andy Brandt, the chairman of the LCBO, how much revenue we would be losing, he indicated that it would be just over $1 million. Linda Franklin and Bruce Walker provided me with an estimate of the number of jobs that would be created by the wineries in their marketing and sales departments. The personal taxes and taxes from the additional sales would far exceed the revenue that we would be losing.

On this basis, I moved forward on an issue that would require only a change in regulations. I remember making the announcement at Château des Charmes Winery. We were there for an event that had nothing to do with my announcement. Everyone had assumed that I was just going to give an ordinary speech for the occasion. When I made the announcement there was stunned silence followed by thunderous applause.

In the following years our reasoning proved to be correct. It was fair. Now the harder they worked, the better they could do. Some smaller but excellent wineries like Marynissen Estates hired a whole new sales team.

We received a request for a meeting with Barry Didier of Northern Breweries. Northern Breweries had two major facilities in Sudbury and Sault Ste. Marie. I had some affection for Northern Ontario as well as the far greater task of economic development up north, so we scheduled a meeting with Barry.

When Barry showed up he had a laundry list of changes that he would like to see that would help his business. As we went through the list I sorted the list into three parts. There were things that we couldn't do and I explained why we couldn't do them. There were things that would take a lot of work to do and I gave him some realistic timelines. And there were things that seemed obvious.

One of these issues was Barry's complaint that while his on-site beer store was allowed to be open only from 10 a.m. to 9 p.m., the Brewers Retail beer store in town was allowed to be open from 9 a.m. to 10 p.m. His complaint was that this was not fair competition. I agreed.

The next day I called Andy Brandt and asked him what the authority was that allowed this unfair competition. Andy answered that it was an informal policy of the LCBO.

I said to Andy, "Can I assume that as of this telephone conversation there has been a change in that informal policy?"

Andy agreed.

The next day I called Barry Didier and advised him that as of that day he could open the same hours as the beer store in town.

Barry's comment was, "The government sure works fast."

To which I responded, "Sometimes."

The Ministry of Consumer and Commercial Relations was a very busy ministry. In addition to having responsibility for the Red Tape bills for eliminating unnecessary regulations, I brought in legislation to allow limited liability partnerships, the new Condominium Act and the legwork for the Franchise Act. Several self-managed organizations were created, including the Real Estate Council of Ontario (RECO), the Travel Industry Council of Ontario (TICO), the Ontario Motor Vehicle Industry Council (OMVIC) and the Technical Safety Standards Association (TSSA).

But it will always be remembered as the Ministry of Booze and Gambling.

# CHAPTER SIXTEEN

# ROOTS

It started with a casual conversation in 1996 between Elaine and Consul General of Japan Tsujimoto's wife. As the consul general had just arrived in Canada, Elaine was asking Mrs. Tsujimoto what they would like to see in Canada. Mrs. Tsujimoto then asked Elaine what she would like to see if she went to Japan. On the way home from the consul general's house, Elaine told me about the conversation.

"So what did you tell her that you wanted to see in Japan?" I asked.

"I gave her my wish list for Japan," she said. "I told her I would like to see a Kabuki show and a Sumo tournament. I also said I would like to visit Kyoto and Hiroshima and that you would like to see Fukuoka and Kumamoto, where your family was from. I told her that I would like to see the Tokyo fish market and ride the bullet train. I also mentioned that you liked to golf."

We both had a good laugh. We didn't have any plans to visit Japan. My parents had never been to Japan, but it was nice to dream.

About a year later when I got home, Elaine greeted me at the door and looked very excited about something.

"You'll never believe what came today," she said. She handed me a letter. It was an invitation from the Consulate of Japan to visit Japan. The Japanese government had a program called the Opinion Leaders' Program. Under the program political leaders of Japanese descent around the world were invited to visit Japan. The Japanese government would pay all costs.

I turned to the second page, which had the itinerary, and it looked oddly familiar.

"The itinerary is your wish list!" I exclaimed to Elaine.

"You can thank me now," she said smugly.

When I got to the office the next morning, everyone knew of the letter, as both my staff and the ministry had been advised by the Consulate. This was at a time when the Ontario wineries had been trying to increase their export sales. My deputy minister, Steen Lal, and my staff thought that this might be a good opportunity to promote Ontario wines in Japan. It wasn't long before we had arranged for me to give a speech at the Canadian Embassy in Tokyo to the potential Japanese buyers. I would take several diplomatic cases of ice wine to Tokyo to use for the promotion.

I then realized that I had a problem. I was going to give a speech in Japan to Japanese companies and I didn't speak Japanese. If I was not of Japanese descent it would not have mattered, but since I am it would look very curious.

I decided to take some Japanese lessons from Yukie Nakamura, the reporter from OMNI-TV. When I started the lessons, Barry O'Brien, one of my policy assistants who was going to accompany me to Japan, wanted to sit in.

The only Japanese I learned was when my parents spoke to each other when they didn't think I was around or when they didn't want us to understand what they said. The lessons were progressing well but I felt that Barry was holding me back. When the Japanese do not have a Japanese equivalent of an English word they just use the English word and make it sound like Japanese. Takushi is a Taxi. Supagetti is spaghetti. Kohi is coffee and so it goes. Barry was having problems with these kinds of words. Finally I told Barry that we couldn't spend so much time on these words, otherwise we would never get to real Japanese.

The amazing thing about arriving in Japan was the feeling when I stepped off the plane that I had come home. This must be the feeling that many people have shared when they visit the land of their ancestors, whether they are Greek, Chinese or Scottish. When I arrived at the New Otani Hotel in Tokyo I saw that the hotel was flying the Canadian flag, and the warm feeling that I had when I had arrived was intensified by a huge sense of pride at being a Canadian.

I had been greeted at the airport by Atsuko Kajimura, who was to be our guide during our tour. Atsuko had been educated in Kansas and spoke flawless English. The schedule was to commence the next day with a series of meetings. What amazed me was that unlike in North America, where we make our schedules around each hour or half hour, in Japan the schedule called for me to be picked up at 8:14 a.m. and arrive at 9:07 a.m. In Japan things are run on a precise schedule.

The Japanese government had arranged for me and Barry to play golf at the Summit golf course. The golf course was located just outside of Tokyo, and our driver would pick us up at the hotel at 7:02 a.m. I was told that we just needed to go to the course because the club would provide golf clubs for Barry and me to use.

When we arrived at the Summit golf club we were greeted by our hosts. After we put on our golf shoes, Barry and I were introduced to our caddies. The female caddies in Japan are famous for the first-class service that they supply. After every time I took a stroke, my caddy would clean the club. She would replace any divots. If I hit into a sand trap, my caddy raked the sand. When I got on the green, my caddy would line my ball up with the label pointing to where I was to putt.

It started to rain in sprinkles just before we finished the front nine. When we walked off the ninth green, our hosts told us to follow them for lunch. When we walked into the clubhouse, our hosts told us to follow them into a room where hot air was blowing and we were advised to hang up our hats and coats so that when we finished our lunch, our clothes would be dry.

After a wonderful Japanese lunch we finished the back nine. It was a very unique experience because the four of us were the only golfers on the course. If you have ever been to Japan, you will know that public areas and private property are always perfectly manicured. Multiply that to the nth degree and you can imagine what the golf courses look like.

After golf, we then proceeded to have a Japanese bath. Before entering the bath you scrub and clean yourself and then enter the bath. There is no question that a Japanese bath is extremely relaxing.

Next was a full Japanese dinner and finally, when we finished, Barry and I arrived back at the hotel at 1 a.m. When I walked in the room, Elaine looked at me and reminded me that the schedule called for us to visit the famous Tokyo fish market and that we were to leave at 4:30 a.m. that morning. It was a very short sleep.

I had heard of the bullet trains of Japan, the Shinkansen. Our next leg of the trip was to take the bullet train to Kyoto. Kyoto is a city that was not touched by the Second World War. It is famous for its beautiful temples. Not only were we to visit some temples but, according to Elaine's wish list, we were to attend a Sumo tournament.

It was quite unlike going to a sports event in North America. You don't simply go and buy a ticket for the event. Local restaurants sponsor sections of the arena. You buy your meal from the restaurant for the event and you also receive your admission. When we arrived we received our meal in a large shopping bag. The bag contained several lacquer boxes that held the food. The lacquer boxes also served as souvenirs of the event. We were escorted to a section where Elaine, Barry, Atsuko and I were seated Japanese-style on the covered floor. Shortly after we were seated, a man came around with teacups and green tea, just as in a restaurant.

I am still amazed that Sumo wrestlers, who weighed as much as 520 pounds, could be as fast and agile as they were. In Sumo, the match is ended as soon as one of the wrestlers is forced out of the ring or any part of his body other than his feet touches the ground.

Most matches last just a few minutes. It is intense combat by behemoths. The ceremonial start often takes longer than the match. The experience gave a lasting impression.

In contrast to the violent intensity of Sumo, the temples and gardens of Kyoto bring a sense of serenity and contemplation. We were fortunate that in late March the cherry blossoms, called *sakura,* were blooming early. Many Japanese families wandered through the parks and gardens just to contemplate and admire the blossoms. I was impressed that Japan's complex and busy society took time out just to admire the simple beauty of a cherry blossom.

Our next stop would be Hiroshima.

If every person in the world were to visit the Hiroshima Memorial we would have a better perspective on the impact of nuclear war on human beings. When you see a person's shadow burned into the wall, it gives way to sombre thought. We viewed the memorial without a word and said a silent prayer for peace.

We saw the paper cranes that had been made by schoolchildren in memory of Sadako Sasaki, who suffered from leukemia as a result of radiation poisoning from the nuclear blast. There is a legend in Japan that anyone who folds 1,000 cranes will have her life's wish come true. Sadako folded 644 cranes before she died at the age of 12. Her classmates folded 1,000 cranes in her memory. The tradition continues today of children folding cranes to remember Sadako Sasaki and the horrors of nuclear warfare.

I will never forget this experience. In a way, the memorial is an expectation of hope for the future that we will not forget the consequences of nuclear warfare.

The next day we were to take a ferry ride to Miyajima Island, which is very famous for a torii gate that stands in the water on the way to the island. A torii gate is an entrance to a Shinto temple. Atsuko advised us that on Miyajima Island, the deer are considered messengers of the gods and run around the island wild but are at the same time unafraid of people.

We visited the temple and bought fortunes. I saw a tree with all kinds of paper tied to it and asked Atsuko what that was.

"If you get a bad fortune," she answered, "you tie it to the tree and the wind blows the bad fortune away."

Since we all got good fortunes, we held on to them.

I was looking forward to visiting Fukuoka, the prefecture that had been home to the Tsubouchi clan. Our first piece of business was an official visit to the Governor of Fukuoka prefecture. The meeting was very formal, with our contingent seated on one side of the table and the governor and his staff on the other. I was delighted to see positioned on the desk a miniature Canadian flag. After the formal meeting we took an official photograph and were invited to lunch with the officials of Fukuoka at a local restaurant. The food was delicious and the conversation became much more enjoyable after the formalities were dropped.

I had the chance to meet with some Tsubouchi cousins. The Japanese government had contacted them and arranged for the reunion. We were invited to dine that evening at a French restaurant that I found out later was owned by my second cousin. Apparently that branch of the family had done very well. They owned many business and several apartment buildings.

No matter how much I tried, even my family members could not bring themselves to be less formal. No one would call me by name. They only addressed me as *Daijin*, which means "minister." I did enjoy meeting the family but I wished it was more informal. I wasn't sure if it was because of the culture or the specific people or the title I held. In the end, the evening was amiable and interesting.

We would now travel to Kumamoto, the ancestral home of my grandmother, Ume Hisatsugu. Before meeting this branch of the family we visited the site of the rebellion battleground on which the movie *The Last Samurai* was based, where the Shogun's forces were armed with repeating carbines and cannons and the rebel forces had swords. The curator of the museum gave me a bullet from the battle as a memento.

When we arrived at the house of my great aunt we were greeted with warmth and enthusiasm by her, my great uncle and my second cousins and their children. Despite the warm welcome and although they called Elaine by her name, they insisted on calling me Daijin. We started chatting in a combination of Japanese and English and to each other directly or through Atsuko. Although it must have seemed chaotic, it was a wonderful sharing of family histories and personal information.

Then my great uncle poured a cup of sake for me and explained that this was a Samurai custom. Atsuko advised me to pour a cup of sake for him. Then we lifted our cups to each other, said "Kampai!" and bottoms up.

After that toast, every one of my relatives wanted to exchange sake with me. I felt obligated to do so. As a rule neither Elaine nor I drink alcohol. Elaine took photos as the evening progressed. Two things were evident. As time passed, more food was brought to the table and my face was getting redder and redder. As we drank and ate, we seemed to become closer, but my family never ceased addressing me with formality.

My great aunt showed me a sword and a scroll that had been given to her father by the Emperor for his actions as a naval officer in the Japanese Russian war. It was a source of pride for the family.

When the evening finally came to a close, we all went outside and took a family photograph. My great aunt insisted on standing two steps higher on the stairs so she would be as tall as Elaine. When we left as we looked back, all the members of the family were alternating between raising their arms and shouting, "Banzai!" and bowing. Atsuko said, "That is a tradition. I call it the bowing and waving ceremony. They will continue to do that until we are out of sight." While we watched the bowing and waving I felt sad that the evening had ended.

On the way back to Tokyo we stopped at Kamakura to see the second-largest Buddha statue in Japan. The statue is almost 13.5 meters in height and weighs 125 tons. You can climb inside the statue for 20 yen. Typically in Japan you deposit the money yourself voluntarily, as no one collects it. You are on the honour system.

Back in Tokyo I was scheduled to give a speech at the Canadian Embassy to promote Ontario ice wines. When we arrived the Embassy was filled with potential Japanese buyers of ice wines and many of my friends from the wine industry in Ontario. Giving speeches usually gave me little concern. I seldom referred to written notes, but this was completely different. Half my speech was in Japanese. Japanese at best was my third language and I had no confidence in my vocabulary or pronunciation. There was no question that I was a little nervous. Atsuko had listened to my speech and had given me her nod of approval.

When the time came for the speech, from my end it seemed to go smoothly and the audience was polite, so I accepted that as a success. Of course, Atsuko said it went well but I was happy it was over. More important, the Japanese guests were very appreciative of the ice wine.

The following day was the last day for which I had official duties and a schedule. We were to attend the Tokyo race course to view the races. We were greeted by the officials of the track and taken to the track steward's box. The officials explained that if we wanted to place a bet on the races, the attendants would take our bets and place them for us. The minimum bet was 500 yen, which at the time was five dollars. Since the racing form was in Japanese, the officials described the horses and their record. Elaine made her selection because she liked the name of one of the horses.

The track steward turned to me and said that the horse was a long shot because the horse had never won a race and the jockey had won only twice before in his career.

In Japan, unlike in North America, the horses run clockwise. As we viewed the race Elaine's horse was trailing. Then it started to move up. By the halfway point he was passing most of the field. By the three-quarter point he was neck and neck with the favourite. At the finish Elaine's horse won by a nose. I have the photo of the photo finish.

Elaine had wagered 500 yen and had won 60,000 yen or $600. She had made everyone in the room speechless. Then Atsuko asked Elaine who she should bet on in the next race.

Elaine said, "Your husband works at the University in Yokohama and teaches sciences. This horse, if you translate his name to English, has science in it. Bet on that horse."

Atsuko took the advice to heart and, since Elaine evidently knew what she was talking about, bet 500 yen. It was no surprise to me when the horse won and returned 12,000 yen. Elaine was a superstar.

The next day was our last day in Japan and Atsuko wanted to take us shopping. Elaine wanted to buy an antique kimono, so we went to a specialty shop. Elaine found a beautiful pre-war kimono and was pondering whether or not to buy it. It was priced at $120.

Atsuko walked up to Elaine and said urgently, "If you want to buy that kimono, you should buy it and we should get going."

I thought to myself that it was our day off and wondered what the hurry was but deferred to Atsuko.

After Elaine had made her purchase and we were back in the car, I turned to Atsuko and asked, "What was the hurry?"

Atsuko answered, "That is a very nice kimono and I think they left a zero off."

A few years later I was the honourary chair of the Japanese Antique Show at the Japanese Canadian Cultural Centre, where experts were making evaluations of Japanese antiques. I suggested to Elaine that she take her antique kimono down and see how much it was valued.

The expert on textile took only a few seconds to tell Elaine that she really liked the kimono.

"How much do you think that it's worth?"

The expert said, "I would say around $6,500."

It was amazing how far a five-dollar bet had gone.

The one thing that I wanted to see in Japan was a bookstore. Shoyo Tsubouchi had made the first translation of Shakespeare into Japanese. I wanted to see if I could get a copy of one of the translated plays. Atsuko took us to a bookstore and made the inquiry on my behalf. The clerk reached over to a shelf and brought out three sets of two volumes each in their own case. I looked at the books and they were first editions and had the personal seal of Shoyo Tsubouchi.

I asked the clerk, "Ikura desuka?"

He answered me in English that the price was $90. I thought that the price was fair at about $15 each and agreed to buy the books. At that point he reached back into the shelf and brought out 17 more sets of two. Apparently the price was $90 for 40 books — an astounding bargain at $2.25 each.

The next morning with a little sadness we left Japan. I had done what neither of my parents had: I had visited the ancestral land. I had met our relatives. I left with more understanding of the Japanese people and an appreciation of my heritage and also my country, Canada. It was nice to come home.

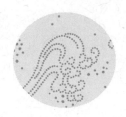

# CHAPTER SEVENTEEN

# OPERATION TRUE BLUE AND DUTY

When we won the election in 1999, I had a discussion with Mike Harris about what cabinet position I would like to have. I advised him that I would love to be the Solicitor General but I didn't really like the Corrections minister part of the job, as they were together as a combined ministry. A few days later I got a call from Mike Harris, who told me that I had gotten both of my wishes. I was being appointed the Solicitor General and he was creating a new Ministry of Corrections that he was giving to Rob Sampson.

Although I had asked for the Ministry of the Solicitor General, I knew that it had been in the past a semi-dangerous place to be politically, as there had been a number of Solicitors General who had to step down for a variety of missteps, including drinking alcohol on a police boat or calling a judge about a current case. I also knew that it was an opportunity to do meaningful things. I was a big supporter of law-and-order issues.

There was also another thing on my mind, and that was the impact of the Japanese Canadian internment and the legal system. I had always felt that it was important to ensure that no group of people, regardless of ethnicity, religion or race, was discriminated against simply because of those differences.

I am told that there are issues that are clearly provincial, federal or municipal ones. I have yet to see these issues. Jurisdiction, either sought or avoided, has been the meat on the bone of contention in Canada as long as there has been split authority and a British North America Act and, more recently, our own constitution. More power and authority had been sought in the past. In today's government, avoidance of jurisdiction meant that there was also no responsibility for the cost of that obligation either fiscally or publicly.

To understand this, one needs only to observe that the federal government has always been careful not to get involved with direct funding to hospitals, as that may lead to more responsibility for a sinkhole of funding.

When the Toronto Police Association embarked on a campaign to get better support from the people of Toronto for the Toronto police, the issue of jurisdiction raised its head.

The gist of the campaign was for people to buy stickers that went on your car windshield to indicate support for the police. The Toronto Police Association's position was that Operation True Blue was a law-and-order telemarketing campaign to raise money to support stronger penalties for young offenders and parole violators. The wailing and the attacks from the left-wing Liberals were caustic. The Police Association was accused of using money to fund spying activities against politicians who disagreed with them. A few politicians indicated that they were concerned they had been spied upon.

Others attacked the Police Association by stating that the association should not be endorsing politicians during an election. I always found this to be hypocritical, as this was the only "union" that the left-wing politicians ever complained about. They never complained about government unions or teachers' unions supporting them with advertising campaigns or straight donations. Somehow police unions everywhere were the exception.

The answer from the left was that they carried guns, therefore they should not be allowed to have an opinion relevant to an election. The sophistry ceased to amaze me years ago.

As I was the Solicitor General, the ministry officials had advised me that this was a local issue and that we should leave it to the Toronto Police Services Board and Toronto Council to resolve it. My own staff had agreed with the assessment of the situation initially. The only problem with this laissez-faire approach was that Queen's Park is located in Toronto. This issue was the lead story in every newspaper and television report. It was the topic of every radio talk show.

The official answer to any media question was that it was a local issue and the local authorities needed to straighten it out. This approach worked for the initial period, but I could gauge by the increase and intensity of the questions after Question Period that it was of greater interest to the media and the public and certainly politically as well.

I had been discussing the issue with my staff and had indicated my concern that there were no negotiations or even civil talk between the Police Association and the Police Services Board. Toronto City Council had waded in publicly. The situation had become negotiation by media press release. The rancour was daily and vicious. I told my staff that I believed that it was just a matter of time before the media started asking us what we were going to do to resolve the situation. My concern went far beyond political. I didn't think that this kind of dysfunctional relationship was good for the health of the City of Toronto.

As we went through the scenarios, my staff who had gathered with me, John Guthrie, Derek O'Toole and Sherri Haigh, agreed that we were going to be drawn into the issue eventually. The party line was that it was a local issue. Both the premier and I had been consistent in answering to the media with that line. The real question was deciding what our level of involvement should be.

I believed that if the parties could get beyond their publicly stated positions and if we could sit them down in isolation somewhere, they would either pound each other out or start to see the other point of view. Then, I hoped, they would begin to become reasonable. I thought that it was important to intervene as an interested third party; however, I did not want to own the issue.

The solution was to hire a mediator. We would pay for the mediator but we would not participate in the mediation. There were two very significant questions. First, who would be a good choice for a mediator? Second, would the parties show up even if we hired a mediator?

John Guthrie suggested that we approach George Adams, a former Superior Court judge. Before his appointment to the bench, George had a respected reputation as a mediator and arbitrator of labour disputes. He was the chair of the Ontario Provincial Police Grievance Board. He had recently been praised for his report on the Special Investigations Unit.

We agreed that George Adams would be an ideal choice if he was available. I asked John to approach George Adams to see if was willing to act as a mediator if we could get the parties to agree to meet. Before we asked the Toronto Police Association and the Toronto Police Services Board to meet with a mediator, however, a bigger decision had to be made. Should I tell the premier what I was intending to do? Normally, it would not only be a good idea to do so, but a very bad idea not to let him know what was going on.

The issue had been raised at Queen's Park by the media. All of us had stuck to the party line when pressed by the media that it was a local issue. This had been the response of the premier and I had answered the same way.

It seemed to me that the issue must eventually land on the doorstep of the province as the media interest rose. I also felt that it would be easier to do something earlier in the process than later. If I got involved and was successful, then it would be no problem, and even if I got involved and it didn't work, at least I would have tried to do something. I decided if the premier did not know and our involvement somehow went south, then at least the premier would have deniability and I could take the blame. But we needed to act.

John Guthrie contacted George Adams and he agreed to act as the mediator. He also understood that neither the ministry nor my staff would be involved in the mediation. This of course would be subject to our being able to get both the Toronto Police Association and the Toronto Police Services Board to agree to be willing and honest participants in the process.

Publicly the temperature had been rising. Mayor Lastman had characterized the situation as hostile — "There is no way this police union executive is going to hold our city hostage" — as he blamed the police association for creating a crisis.

There seemed be no way out of the public showdown. The vitriolic accusations escalated daily in the newspapers, television and radio. Mayor Lastman, who had never been shy about sharing his views, was becoming more and more agitated. If you knew Mel Lastman, you understood that this was not a helpful thing. Out of every situation there is always opportunity. Despite the public posturing, both sides were looking for a solution.

John Guthrie and Derek O'Toole contacted Norm Gardner and Jeff Lyons, the chair and vice chair of the Toronto Police Service, and offered them the opportunity for mediation. They both readily agreed. My communications assistant, Sherri Haigh, had good relations with all the police associations including Craig Bromell and the Toronto Police Association. When she invited them to participate in our process, they also quickly agreed.

The question of where we should hold the mediation session then arose. We decided on the Royal York Hotel. Meetings went on at the Royal York all the time. In addition, it was extremely busy, as the NHL All-Star Game was being hosted in Toronto and many of the players and VIPs stayed at the Royal York. We decided to hide in plain view.

When the day arrived I, along with John Guthrie, Derek O'Toole and Sherri Haigh, greeted the participants in the meeting room that we had reserved. Norm Gardner and Jeff Lyons attended, representing the Toronto Police Services Board, and Craig Bromell and the association's lawyer, Gary Clewley, represented the Toronto

Police Association. After we had made the introductions to George Adams, I told everyone that we would be waiting in the hotel bar until they were finished.

While sitting in the bar, our discussion of the matter was interrupted suddenly when Bobby Hull, NHL legend — I had played golf with him the year before — stuck his head around the corner, waved at me and shouted, "Hey, Dave, Mr. Solicitor General, are you trying to fix the Toronto Police mess?"

Inadvertently, Bobby had revealed our plans. I asked him to join us but he declined as he was heading for an event. The good news was that no one expected that Bobby Hull really had any insight into the situation and no one was really listening.

Six hours later we were told by George Adams that they were concluding upstairs. When we arrived at the meeting room, George Adams advised us that the two sides had come to an agreement. The Toronto Police Association would end Operation True Blue and the Toronto Police Services Board would rescind their bylaw against the association's ability to fund-raise. Both sides would then cool down the litigation and animosity.

This seemed to be reasonable for all parties. Both sides would now need to have the agreement ratified by their boards of directors.

We were advised shortly after that Craig Bromell had convinced the Toronto Police Association to accept the terms. Unfortunately, despite the public pronouncements by the critics who sat on the Toronto Police Services Board, the agreement was voted down by the board.

The matter would rage on for months, creating ill will that would take years to subside between the association and the Toronto Police Services Board. After the expenditure of a lot of the public money in litigation, eventually the matter was settled with essentially what had been the resolution in the meeting room of the Royal York Hotel.

When the mediation efforts became public, when asked to comment, Premier Harris said, "I didn't know he was doing this, by the way, which is fine."

The reason I asked Premier Harris to appoint me as the Solicitor General was that I felt issues of public safety had a direct impact on the lives of the people of Ontario. Every day this responsibility lies on the shoulders of the men and women who serve as police officers and firefighters. I had tremendous respect for people who put their own safety second to that of the public. Unfortunately one of the first things that I had to deal with was the death of Sergeant Rick MacDonald of the Sudbury Police Service. While attempting to deploy a spike belt to stop a fleeing criminal, Rick MacDonald was killed. In a small community like Sudbury, this was a horrific tragedy.

In my entire political career, the most difficult times have been when I lost a police officer in the line of duty. To me, they were very personal losses.

The Ontario Provincial Police had made arrangements for me to join Commissioner Gwen Boniface, Deputy Commissioner Maurice Pilon and Toronto Police Chief David Boothby and be flown to Sudbury in the OPP plane. I was picked up at Buttonville Airport in Markham. The flight was a very sombre one with discussions centring on the best practices and training in the use of spike belts and penalties for criminals who flee from the police.

On the opposite side of the issue, the media discussions centred on police chases and the danger to the public. The consensus on our plane was evident — that the focus should be on the criminal who flees and not on the officers who are trying to stop him.

It was also an opportunity for me to speak to Gwen Boniface, Mo Pilon and Dave Boothby in other than an official capacity. I have great respect for all three of these police leaders. They each had different styles but all possessed great leadership skills and intelligence and carried themselves with dignity and professionalism.

As we neared Sudbury, one of the pilots, whose nickname was Chip, turned back to us and said calmly that it might get a little choppy. No sooner did he say this than the plane hit an air pocket and dropped 100 feet. This was one of those times that I was lucky to be short. Dave Boothby, who is around six-foot-three, hit his head on the ceiling of the plane. At the same time, since it was a police plane, the coffee and doughnuts went flying.

Chip then turned to us again and told us with a snicker to hang on because the rest of the flight was going to be like this. We all sat in silent suffering. For my part, I did not want to throw up in front of the police brass, and for their part, they didn't want to throw up in front of the Solicitor General. When we finally landed I could sense a collective mental sigh of relief. I looked out my window and saw two police vans waiting for us with two smart young OPP officers standing at attention.

Commissioner Boniface exited the plane and told the officers that we all needed a couple of minutes.

When we deplaned I saw my CA, Sherri Haigh, waiting for me. Sherri had been vacationing in the area and was going to drive back to Toronto after the funeral. Sherri proceeded to brief us on the attendees at the funeral and the local issues.

When a police officer is killed in action, the entire brotherhood of policing feels that loss. The officers come from all over Canada and also the United States and other countries to show their support and sympathy for the family of the slain officer and for his colleagues. It is a magnificent display of solidarity. Thousands of officers march in the parade.

What is heartening to see are the crowds of people who line the funeral parade route: mothers and fathers with their children, seniors, and people of all races, religions and ethnic groups. They come to say thank you for protecting all of us; thank you for your sacrifice.

It is sad to see the families of the police officers trying to be brave in a very public forum.

After the funeral, I had the opportunity to speak to Police Chief Alex McCauley and promised him that I would bring in legislation for greater penalties against criminals who flee from the police. I advised Premier Harris, who was there for the funeral as well and he wholeheartedly agreed.

The media of course were looking for their sound bite, but my only comment for them was for my condolences to the family and friends of Rick MacDonald.

After the funeral we were all driven back to the airport, where I saw Chip and asked him if the flying conditions would be the same on the way back as they were on the trip up. He smiled and nodded his head at us. I turned to Sherri and told her that I was driving back with her. I then turned to the rest of passengers and asked them if any of them wanted to come back with us. I realized as soon as I said it that since the commissioner was going back by the OPP plane, so was everyone else. As I got into Sherri's car I could see everybody looking longingly at the car.

Months later at an OPP event, I and the rest of the passengers were presented with a T-shirt that read, "I survived the OPP plane ride from hell."

Tragically, three other OPP officers were killed during my tenure as Solicitor General: Constable Chuck Mercier in September 1999, Constable Jim McFadden in December 1999 and Sergeant Marg Eve in June 2000. All of these officers were killed by bad drivers while on duty. All of their vehicles were parked with lights flashing. Their deaths were senseless.

Chuck Mercier was killed by a truck driver who fell asleep and struck him as he was trying to slow down traffic.

The family of an officer who dies on duty is offered the option of a formal police funeral. In most cases the families opt to do this, both for the detachment and for the community. There are other times that the family wishes to keep the formalities limited and want their privacy respected. In the case of Chuck Mercier, his family wanted his funeral to be private and limited to close family and friends. I felt that it was important to respect their wishes. I also felt that it was important for me to pay my respects. As the Solicitor General I felt that these men and women were a part of my responsibility.

I knew that if I showed up at the funeral, the media would be all over me and somehow I felt that this would not respect the wishes of the family, and that should be the main concern. I spoke to Elaine and we agreed that we would drive ourselves to Welland the night before the funeral and pay our respects as privately as we could.

When we walked into the funeral home, I could tell that our visit was unexpected but greatly appreciated by the family and the officers from the detachment.

It is always shameful when someone tries to make a political point out of a tragic situation. Unexpectedly, at a later event, an opposition MPP decided to criticize me for not attending the funeral. Unfortunately for him, there happened to be a number of OPP officers at the event who straightened him out on the facts.

Jim McFadden was killed while he was sitting in his car at the side of the road and was struck in the rear by a car going 150 kilometres per hour, smashing McFadden's car into another vehicle. I remember the day because it was a very cold day in December. The OPP plane was going to pick up me and my Deputy Minister, Virginia West, at Buttonville Airport at 8:30 a.m. for the funeral in Chatham, Ontario, at 11 a.m.

Virginia and I had both arrived early at Buttonville Airport. At 8:30 a.m. she received a call on her cell phone that because of the conditions at Orillia, the OPP plane could not get off the ground. It was Commissioner Boniface calling from Chatham. She asked to speak to me and she said that she understood why we couldn't make it in time for the funeral and she would advise the family and officers. I thanked the Commissioner and advised her that I was still going to try to get there.

Normally my driver, David Rajpaulsingh, would be with me, but since I had to drive only to Buttonville, I had taken my own car. I told Virginia that I was going to try to get to the funeral. She said that she was coming with me. I told her to hop in and buckle up because I was going to have to hustle to get there. Buttonville to Chatham is just over 300 kilometres. It was 8:45 a.m.

These were the days before GPS and I didn't have a map of Chatham so I was flying by the seat of my pants. As we got on the highway, I had no idea where we were going other than the name of the church in Chatham, but we were committed and off we went.

It would be an understatement to say that I was in a hurry and we were soon at the outskirts of Chatham when I looked at the gas gauge and realized that since I had only intended to drive to the Buttonville Airport, I had not topped up the gas and we were almost on empty. I took the first exit to Chatham, not knowing if I was even heading in the general direction of the church. It was a rural area and there were no gas stations in sight. Luckily, a local man agreed to lead us to a gas station.

As I filled up the tank, Virginia got directions to the church. By chance we were not that far away. As I pulled up, an OPP officer directed me where to park. When Commissioner Boniface saw me she came over and said that she didn't think that we would make it in time and that the family and officers were grateful that we could. She then asked me to drive a little slower on the return trip.

After the service, I remember that it was bitterly cold at the burial. Constable McFadden's wife was so brave.

When I got news that Sergeant Marg Eve and Constables Patti Pask and Brad Sakalo had been struck and injured by a tractor-trailer on the shoulder of Highway 401 near Chatham, my first reaction was anger. I could not understand how a truck driver could not see three OPP cruisers with their lights flashing and still drive into them. They had all been standing outside of their cruisers while questioning possible suspects in a robbery.

Derek O'Toole and Sherri Haigh heard that the officers had been seriously hurt but did not know the extent of their injuries. I felt that I needed to see how they were doing. The ministry staff advised me that this would not be the normal protocol or process, but I didn't care. As far as I was concerned, they were OPP officers and to me that meant they were family. I told David Rajpaulsingh that we were leaving immediately. Derek and Sherri said that they were coming too.

Just as I was leaving we learned that Marg Eve had been taken to the hospital in London, Ontario, with severe head injuries and that she was being operated on. Patti Pask and Brad Sakalo had been taken to the hospital in Chatham. I asked David to go to the Chatham hospital first so I could see Brad and Patti. Both of them had sustained serious but not life-threatening injuries.

When I saw them, I was glad I had been able to check up on them. It was my responsibility to see them, but it also mattered to me and to them that I had been able to. Brad asked me to sign his cast because, he said, otherwise the guys would never believe that I had visited him.

After visiting with them, we went to London to see how Marg Eve was doing. It was going to be difficult because I knew that the prognosis was not optimistic and I also knew that her family were all at the hospital. When we arrived I was met by an OPP officer who introduced me to her family. I asked Derek and Sherri if they wanted to leave, but they were great staff and friends and stayed with me as we sat and waited with the family with as much hope as we could muster.

Hours later, Marg Eve passed away. It was the saddest moment of my political life.

I am not surprised by how much I embraced my relationship with the men and women of the OPP. You can only understand by standing with them in difficult times. They were family.

# CHAPTER EIGHTEEN

# Y2K, Dirty Roots and Muskox

The run-up to Y2K was nothing short of panic. Millions of dollars were being made in the technology field based on "What if." All governments were beyond paranoid that because systems had been built on a two-digit year system, when all four digits changed to 2000, the technology would become non-functional. Fortunately we had a number of steady hands at the wheel. In my case as the Solicitor General, it was Dr. Jim Young. Public order was our responsibility.

The critical date was New Year's Eve, December 31, 1999. Our responsibility was the Provincial Emergency Centre. In the event that there was an emergency of a serious enough nature — either manmade or natural — the Province of Ontario through Emergency Measures Ontario would be the quarterback of the coordinated efforts to respond to these emergencies. This had been the case with the ice storm that had hit northeastern Ontario a few years before.

Within the Centre all relevant ministries and the OPP were represented at their own stations, complete with computers and communications. That evening, the Canadian military and Toronto Police and Fire and all of the other GTA police services would also be present. We had live media feeds from Canada, Europe and Asia. We also had access to all Toronto Police cameras.

Our major concern was the fact that Mayor Mel Lastman had arranged for a big party at Toronto City Hall to ring in the new millennium. On the surface it was a good idea. For Mayor Mel, it was another opportunity to celebrate. To us, it had the potential for disaster. None of us thought that when the clock ticked to midnight the lights would go out. What concerned us was that we were expecting close to 500,000 people for Mel's party and all it took was a handful of idiots who thought it was a good idea to turn over a car and set it on fire and there could be a full-scale riot.

It was the human element — not technology — that scared us.

A few days before the date Dr. Young dropped by my office and delivered a satellite phone in a case. When I looked quizzically at him, he said that if I were going to a party on New Year's Eve, I needed to take the phone with me because if anything happened to the communications systems, they would need to get in touch with me. The case was the size of a suitcase. It was so big it wouldn't have been accepted as carry-on luggage. It also weighed about 40 pounds.

I looked at the phone and case and told Jim that Elaine and I didn't normally go out for New Year's Eve and I asked him where he was going to be. He told me that he would be on duty at the Centre. I told him that I was going to be there too. I wouldn't need the gigantic phone.

On December 31, 1999, I arrived at the Centre around 6 p.m. ready to wait. Nothing happened in Europe. The lights hadn't gone out. Computers hadn't stopped. Then the new millennium reached Newfoundland and again nothing happened. Even though we had believed that nothing would happen, I felt everyone in the room sigh in relief.

Our major concern continued to be the moron factor, especially at Nathan Phillips Square. We continued to observe and wait. All eyes were on the clock as it ticked down to midnight. The last seconds seemed to move in slow motion. Midnight arrived. Nothing happened. We had a brief respite when Mel Lastman's fireworks went off with a dazzling display of colours.

Now our concern was with the aftermath and the dispersal of the crowd. We knew that more than a couple of drops of alcohol had been consumed, but other than minor incidents, the night petered out in a very orderly way. The people of Toronto enjoyed a night of celebration in a civilized manner. I came to appreciate how well the office of Emergency Services Ontario had been running thanks largely to Dr. Young and Neil McKerrell.

Every minister has hundreds of requests for meetings with individuals and organizations. Some issues are related to the ministerial duties, often most are not. I had always felt that it was important to meet with the stakeholders of the ministry. Many times we would have a different perspective from stakeholders on a substantive issue, but I felt that if you didn't meet with them, then you had two problems, one of process and one of substance.

I had received a request for a meeting with the First Nations Chiefs of Police along with a few of the First Nations leaders. The ministry advice was not to meet. They felt that the meeting would be full of demands that we could not fulfill and that there was a greater downside risk with a possibility of worse relations. In addition they said that few, if any, Solicitors General ever met with them.

I said to my staff that not meeting was not an option. How could we resolve any problems if we didn't meet? There would be a far greater probability of worse relations if we didn't meet. I told them to set up a meeting.

The meeting was well attended by both the First Nations Chiefs of Police and First Nations leaders. The meeting started with introductions and with caution on both sides. The two main spokespeople seemed to be Goyce Kakegamic, Deputy Grand Chief of the Nishnawbi Aski Nation (NAN) and Glen Lickers, Chief of Police for the Six Nations in Brantford.

As the meeting progressed, the discussions became more frank. The major issue for the First Nations Police Services in Ontario was the lack of federal funding for the basic infrastructure that supported the policing on the reserves. I was surprised to learn that the entire budget for capital repairs and improvement for all of the First Nations Police Services in Ontario was just over $100,000. This amounted to less than $10,000 a year for each reserve. I had never seen the condition of the police facilities on the reserves, but the issue seemed to be an obvious concern.

If I was to advocate on behalf of the First Nations Chiefs of Police, I needed to see the conditions personally. I advised the chiefs of police and the other leaders that I would like to visit several reserves and observe the conditions for myself. I could see that the delegation was surprised by my offer. The ministry officials were shocked. I could read their thoughts and concerns that I shouldn't commit to anything.

After I made the offer, the meeting instantly became more collegial. I left it then to the chiefs of police, the ministry and my staff to make the arrangements. We decided on a small group. I was to be accompanied by Sherri Haigh, Derek O'Toole and Inspector Hugh Stevenson, who was in charge of the OPP relations with the First Nations Chiefs of Police. Hugh was an unusual policeman in that he also held a Ph.D.

I would visit the Six Nations reserve first at Brantford. It was close and easily accessible. The Six Nations also had a good reputation as a well-run reserve. This reserve was not indicative of the conditions the chiefs of police were concerned about, but it gave me a good idea of what a well-run organization looked like.

We then decided that we would visit the Deer Lake reserve in northwest Ontario. The reserve was accessible only by small plane in the winter and was fairly isolated. Joining us was Goyce Kakegamic.

After we had landed we were met by a reserve police officer by the name of Oscar. He took us for a small tour of the reserve on the way to the meeting with the chief and band council. As we drove past a half-finished foundation, he told us that it was the site of the arena that was likely never to be built.

We then went past an old rundown shack that he explained used to be his house until he finally got a better one.

As we passed the school, Oscar advised us that they had just held a read-with-your-child day at the school. I asked him how many parents had participated. He said that including him and his wife, three parents had participated. When I asked him why, he said that many parents could not read or just didn't care.

He then took us to what passed for a police station. It was just a trailer. The so-called holding cell consisted of plywood nailed to the plaster wall. The door to the cell was also reinforced by plywood. I inspected it with some skepticism. Oscar commented that they had held a prisoner the week before and he just kicked open the door. The rest of the office was barely heated.

Oscar pointed outside to the outhouse that was falling apart with the door hanging half off.

The conditions that they had to work in were unsafe, both security- and health-wise. It was disgraceful.

Our meeting with the band council and elders was very amicable. I agreed to take forward their concerns about the policing conditions to the federal government.

On the plane trip back from the Deer Lake reserve, Goyce turned to me and said that he wanted to thank me. I asked him, for what? He said it was important that I had agreed to meet with them in the first place and that he knew that the advice to me was not to meet. I responded that it was my responsibility to meet.

Goyce then said that they appreciated it when I said that I would visit the reserves and see first-hand the conditions, but they never really believed that the visits would take place. He then looked at me and said they believed me now.

Upon my return, I spoke to John Guthrie, Derek O'Toole and Sherri Haigh about the next steps that we should take. In a few months I would be attending the conference of justice ministers in Iqaluit in Nunavut. I thought that this would be a good opportunity to raise the issue with the federal justice ministers, Attorney General Anne McLellan and Solicitor General Lawrence McCauley. My opportunity would be when new business came up on the agenda.

A surprise attack would bring the greatest advantage. I had already advised Goyce of my intent, but the rest of the strategy I kept close to my vest.

Justice ministers' conferences could either be amicable, parochial or strategic, depending on the representation from the provinces and whether any of the priorities of the provinces meshed. Add into the mix the personalities and level of pragmatism or political fervour of the ministers and you could either have a powder keg or a Trojan horse for the feds.

Representing the Ontario government were Attorney General Jim Flaherty and me. There were a number of issues that we wanted to advance. My priority was to get the federal government to create a national sex offender registry. I had been able to bring in the legislation to create the Ontario Sex Offender Registry, which had been supported by all three parties. There needed to be greater efficiency for the program as people moved around. If a known sex offender moved from Ontario or to Ontario, it was important that the police were aware of this; therefore, a national registry was important.

The other issue that both Jim Flaherty and I were hammering the feds on was for a minimum sentence for any crime involving a firearm, in addition to the sentence for the crime itself. Jim Flaherty was a great partner in the justice portfolio, as we both strongly believed in the merits of law and order, and we were able to work together to press the feds on the issues.

The provincial justice ministers agreed on most of the issues, and among us we were able to work together to press the feds. I credit Jack Anawak, the Justice Minister for Nunavut, for creating a sense of camaraderie among the provincial ministers. Earlier in the week, before the federal ministers had arrived, he had planned a number of events that allowed us to get to know each other on a socially friendly basis. We had all been treated to a walk on the tundra and eating bannock and drinking tea. We found common ground and respect for each other.

As in most of these conferences, it was very difficult to get any commitment from the federal ministers on our issues. In fact, on most of the issues it was difficult to get an acknowledgement that the issue existed. The Liberal federal government was reluctant to move forward on the sex offender registry and had been resisting Ontario's lobbying up until then.

When the issue came up, it was greatly supported by the other provinces, and I remember federal Attorney General Anne McLellan acknowledging and indicating support for the Ontario program and that they would review their position. This was as good as it could get. Any support for the Ontario Sex Offender Registry by the federal government would assist in dispelling doubts about the program.

Now that I had achieved my main goal for my ministry, it was time to see if I could advance the issue for the First Nations Chiefs of Police. When it was time for new business, I raised the disgraceful issue of the funding for capital repairs on reserve for the native policing.

Nobody likes surprises, especially federal cabinet ministers. When I raised the issue, I was supported by my colleagues, and Lawrence McCauley agreed to review the issue and get back to me. In many ways this gave me greater satisfaction than the federal acknowledgement of the sex offender registry because I thought that the federal government agreement was inevitable but the funding for the First Nations Chiefs of Police was not. Since then, funding has been increased for capital and repairs for First Nations policing facilities, including Deer Lake reserve.

When I reflect back on this particular conference, Jim Flaherty and I had certain goals that we wanted to achieve and we were satisfied that we had been largely successful. What set this particular conference above the many others that I had attended was the warmth and welcome of Jack Anawak and the people of Nunavut.

The moment I stepped off the plane at Iqaluit, I was greeted by Jack's beaming face. He took one look at me and said, "Welcome home, Cousin Dave." I didn't know what he meant until I looked around at all the Inuit children at the airport with their parents and I noticed that they looked an awful lot like Japanese children. We shook hands and connected. The great thing about Iqaluit is that the population was around 5,000 people, so that by the evening I was known as Cousin Dave.

I realized after a while that my new friend Jack had a great sense of humour. On our Arctic walk with the rest of the ministers, Jack and I lagged behind as everyone wandered ahead with the guide. Jack turned to me and said, "We can't grow vegetables up here because of the permafrost but we have some berries."

He reached down and grabbed a few berries and handed me half. "Taste these," he said.

The berries were sweet and I said so.

Then he reached down and pulled a root out of the ground, snapped it in two and handed me half.

"Eat this," he said.

I ate the root as instructed, as did Jack.

"What do you think?" he asked me.

I responded, "It tastes like a dirty root."

Jack stared at me for a while and then broke out in a big smile and said, "I think so too. I just wanted to see if you would eat it."

Jack also invited me to join him on a cruise in Frobisher Bay. I wondered what he meant by a cruise. When I showed up I was instructed to put on over my clothes a pair of bright orange coveralls.

I asked Jack why I had to put on the coveralls, which he called a survival suit. Jack laughed and told me that the water in Frobisher Bay was so cold that if I fell off the boat I would be dead in minutes.

When I asked him if I would be dead in minutes why I had to wear the bright orange survival suit, he laughed and said, "This way I can just gaff you and haul your body back into the boat."

Then Jack took me over to his boat. It was just a small boat. After I carefully got in, Jack sped off. The water was relatively choppy and we were bumping over the waves with the cold Arctic water spraying all over. After the warning, I was holding on with a death grip. My gloves were soaked and my hands were freezing but I wasn't going to let go. Every time I looked over at Jack, he smiled and laughed.

Finally he slowed down and steered the boat right up to a huge iceberg so I could reach over and touch it. It was fascinating. Then he drove the boat back to the mainland, where we got off and enjoyed a snack of Arctic tea and bannock made over a fire.

The highlight of the conference was an Arctic feast that was put on for the ministers. It seemed as if the entire population of Iqaluit had been invited. We were entertained by local young people who demonstrated throat singing and various athletic feats. A fashion show of local fur fashions was also featured. In the middle of the fashion show, a political statement was made that for centuries the Inuit people have lived on and with the land. They respect the land. They did not want people from the south — being us — telling them what to do.

In the time I spent wandering around Iqaluit it was evident that when the Inuit hunted, they used the entire animal. They used the meat for food. They used the sinew to sew. They used the antlers and bones. They were true environmentalists. It was difficult to disagree with them.

The dinner showcased the game in the North.

We started with Muktuk, raw whale meat that was cut into small cubes. Surprisingly I discovered that the Inuit were eating the Muktuk by dipping it in soy sauce. Jack wandered over to see how we were doing. He was especially curious of the response to raw whale meat. While he winked at me, knowing that Japanese people were used to eating raw seafood, he could see that the non-Asians were having a range of reactions to the Muktuk.

I asked Jack if he had ever put wasabi into the soy sauce. He asked, "What is wasabi?"

I explained to him what wasabi was. Later when I returned to Toronto, I sent a box of wasabi to Iqaluit. If the Inuit are now eating their Muktuk with wasabi, I can take credit for it.

Platters of heaping food were brought to the table. As it happened, our Ontario delegation was seated together. We were dining on Arctic char, caribou and the most delicious meat I have ever tasted, muskox. The muskox steaks were as marbled as Japanese Kobe beef.

When I asked Jack about this, he said, "The weather is below 40 degrees below zero in the winter, so the animals have a lot of fat."

The consensus at our table was that the muskox was absolutely delicious. I asked Jack if I could let the caterer know how much we enjoyed the meal, especially the muskox steaks. A few minutes later, Jack brought the caterer over to me and I told him that muskox was the best steak that I had ever eaten. The entire delegation added their agreement enthusiastically.

Ten minutes later the caterer brought another platter heaping with muskox steaks to our table. He looked at me and said, "Here are a few more steaks for your group, Cousin Dave."

Our table was the envy of the dinner.

I was amazed at the art and culture of the Inuit people. One day when we were out for a walk, Derek O'Toole, Ian Dovey and I came upon a magnificent display of man-sized soapstone carvings in the middle of town. We also saw a man sitting on the back steps of his house carving. Since there are no real markings of the property, we asked him if we could come up and watch him for a while. He welcomed us to watch.

When we went for dinner on the Saturday night at the Frobisher Hotel, we discovered that the restaurant came with entertainment. All the local artisans and artists brought their carvings, paintings and handiwork from table to table to see if you would buy. The prices were irresistible. The hotel had a shop that sold carvings and art and its prices were less than a third of what you would pay in Toronto. The locals' starting prices were half of the shop prices. All of us bought something and happily supported the local economy.

When it was time to leave, we were all saddened that the time couldn't be longer. Jack, Iqaluit and the people were wonderful.

I found my time as Solicitor General rewarding in the knowledge that I was involved in doing work that would make life safer for people in Ontario. I also made many friends like Eric Joliffe, Chief of Police for York Region, and former chiefs Noel Catney, Ken Robertson and Armand Labarge.

# CHAPTER NINETEEN

# Strike? What Strike?

There are always rumours about cabinet shuffles during the summer break from the legislature. I didn't pay much attention to the chatter because I thought I would be Solicitor General for a while. All of my stakeholders were on side. We had good relations with the chiefs of police, the police associations, the firefighters and emergency services. Our law-and-order agenda had been successfully advanced. I really enjoyed the portfolio.

I had actually talked about the possibility of a change with Elaine.

"There are only three places where I can see being shuffled to," I said to her, "Attorney General, Management Board and Finance. I just don't see that happening and I am not lobbying for any of these positions."

"What exactly does the Chair of Management Board do?" asked Elaine.

"It is largely internal to government. Management Board controls all government spending. It is the equivalent of Treasury Board for the federal government."

"Sounds boring," Elaine commented.

A week later I got a call from Mike Harris. "Congratulations," he began. "I just gave you a promotion. You're now Chair of Management Board."

I was able to mutter a thank you to my boss. To say I was surprised is a great understatement.

I called OPP Commissioner Gwen Boniface to advise her of the change. "We are really going to miss you, sir," she said. "Our people have enjoyed and appreciated having you as the Solicitor General."

Then the penny dropped. "That means you are now in charge of our budget," she added, more to herself than to me. "Congratulations on your promotion."

In fact, this did work out to the benefit of the OPP. Every year each ministry was required to provide a detailed plan of their spending including any new spending and also cost savings. Most ministries file a business plan that is about four inches thick. Education usually had two binders and Health submits three.

Cabinet meetings are run by a process called consensus. Consensus does not mean that everyone votes yea or nay to an issue and the majority wins; it means that the issues are discussed and argued and in the end, the premier makes a decision. Management Board is run in a similar fashion.

When I took over Management Board, I decided to make a few changes. My colleagues had a tendency not to appear at meetings in a timely matter. Everyone was busy, but I always thought that it was discourteous not be on time. If the meeting was scheduled to start at 9 a.m., I started the meeting 9 a.m. sharp. If you weren't there, then tough luck. My colleagues who sat on Management Board with me knew how I ran meetings and showed up on time. Some of my colleagues who were looking for funding learned the hard way. You missed your time and you were bumped to the next meeting. It didn't take long to get the message through.

It was always apparent when the ministers knew the proposal. The good ones — Jim Flaherty, Janet Ecker, Tony Clement, John

Baird, Dan Newman — did the presentation, and accordingly the proposals were approved without a lot of difficulty. It was important that the ministers knew their programs, because after it was passed they would need to communicate it. When the deputy minister did the presentation or if the minister had no clue what was going on, the matter met a lot of resistance and quite often was bumped off the agenda.

When someone is first elected as an MPP, he thinks he is going to change the world. He soon realizes that he needs to be in cabinet to have a greater impact. When someone is elevated to cabinet, he then realizes that decision-making is made at Policy and Priorities Committee or the inner cabinet. When he is appointed to P&P, he then realizes that 90 percent of the decisions are made by three people: the premier, the Minister of Finance and the Chair of Management Board. Simply follow the money.

The major issue that I had to deal with was collective bargaining. The government had almost all of the major unions' contracts expiring at the same time. It was also necessary to hold the unions' feet to the fire in order for us to continue to balance the budget.

The reason why the government was able to sustain the longest civil service strike ever in Canada in 2002 and consequently able to settle the strike on the government's terms was the government's communication strategy, which gave it an advantage.

It's better to be lucky than smart, but it's even better to be lucky *and* smart. I don't remember an occasion when my communications assistant Ian Dovey and I ever disagreed on a communication issue. Ian is smart and has great instincts. As a former member of the press gallery, he had maintained his connections to the gallery and to sources outside as well. Good connections lead to information. Information, in turn, is the currency of communication.

On the day before the scheduled first day of the Ontario Public Service Employees Union (OPSEU) strike, someone leaked to Ian a copy of an OPSEU internal memo. The memo was addressed to the radio dispatchers who answered 911 calls. The memo advised the radio dispatchers, all of whom belonged to OPSEU, not to answer the 911 calls. Aside from their intent to use this as a communication tool, it was disgraceful, in my opinion, as it endangered public safety.

The union leadership had scheduled a press conference for 4 p.m. the following day. We decided to hold a press conference at 3 p.m. for the same day.

I had anticipated that the union was going to have a communication plan for the strike attacking the government on the issue of public safety. This was not rocket science, as the union had already been running radio ads for the previous two weeks in anticipation of the strike doing exactly that. They were planning to use the tragedy of Walkerton as an example of the government endangering public safety.

At our press conference I attacked the union leadership for endangering the safety of the citizens of Ontario. Ian distributed copies of the memo to the press gallery.

Because we called our press conference for an hour before the union's press conference, by the time the press gallery had their questions answered, there were only a few minutes until the union's turn. This accomplished several things. First, the media went to the union press conference with our message and our agenda on their minds. If the union had to talk about our message, they had lost before they started. Second, even though the union had monitored our press conference, they had forgotten that a lack of communication always has the potential to create bad situations. Instead of immediately advising the union leadership of the crisis they now had on their hands, the union's communications staff continued to monitor the entire press conference. I'm sure that they had an in-depth and full record of the conference, but they left very little time for the union leadership to prepare a response.

The union leadership may have also forgotten that the media are not their friends when there is the potential for a juicy story. The unions had been used to having their way with the media over the years. They had never been on the hot seat. The media had sought them out for their views on government cuts or outsourcing, and the union probably didn't anticipate that the media might turn on them.

It was hugely predictable. The union was not able to convey its message during what they thought was going to be a successful launch of their strike; they were too busy putting out fires and defending themselves about the issue of endangering the public. Their explanations were feeble and included outright denial of the memo, which the media had in their hot little hands. All the television, radio and newspaper coverage severely criticized the union. Fortunately for us, the union was not smart enough to take their lumps and go on to other strategies.

Despite being forced by the public outcry and the media outrage to back off on their direction to radio dispatchers to refuse to answer 911 calls, that night they stupidly sent out another memo to the radio dispatchers. The memo instructed the radio dispatchers to answer 911 calls but not to hang up after the calls were made. This would effectively tie up the phones and once again endanger public safety.

Once again, Ian was leaked a copy of this subsequent memo. We held another press conference the next day and provided the particulars to the media. The union lost the communications battle on the first two days of the strike and was never able to recover. These two bad days of media coverage also destroyed their credibility as defenders of the public's safety, and they were forced to pull their radio ads.

Whenever I spoke during press conferences, I had two audiences: the general public and the rank-and-file government workers, most of whom I suspected did not want to be on strike. To both groups I had to sound reasonable. Whenever I was critical of the union, I was critical of the union leaders, not the union members.

There are two basic and distinctly different approaches to negotiating union contracts. The first approach is the more traditional one. The employer lowballs the offer and the union increases its demands. As negotiations proceed, the two sides make concessions to each other and eventually meet somewhere in the middle, where they both thought they would land in the first place. This approach can be painstakingly long. It also allows each side to accuse the other of pushing forward unreasonable positions because of their respective starting points. Each side understands that the other has to start with an extreme position but each will take every opportunity to criticize the other to get public support.

I discussed the strategy with Ian and Derek O'Toole, my senior policy adviser, and we thought it was important to show that the government was being reasonable from the start, not only to the public but also to the rank and file. We felt that if we were to provide a reasonable first offer, it would send the right message to employees who might consider crossing the picket lines or who might eventually put pressure on the union leadership to settle. This conclusion was endorsed by the excellent negotiating team of the government headed by Kevin Wilson, the assistant deputy minister in charge of HR for Management Board Secretariat.

As we had already settled two other labour contracts earlier in the year with PEGO (the professional engineers) and AMAPCEO (the middle managers of government), we had a general sense of what a reasonable settlement would be.

Bearing in mind that you always have to hold back some negotiating items to get to a final position, we felt we should start with an offer that almost mirrored the other two contracts that we had settled without strikes. We could then communicate to the employees that there was no need to strike, as all that would then be needed was some minor tinkering.

As expected, the union made outrageous demands equivalent to a 26.25 percent raise. When I remarked on this to Kevin Wilson, he said quite seriously that I must have scared them because in previous negotiations, the union had started their demands at 40 percent.

Part of our deliberations concerned our areas of vulnerability and the approach we would take with those weak spots. As it turned out, we had identified many of these areas as job classifications for which we needed to offer an immediate top-up to remain competitive. There was concern that we might lose some of these employees to the private sector or to other levels of government. These included radio dispatchers, government nurses, water technicians, scientists and jail guards.

Generally, these classifications that might require an immediate increase would be addressed at the tail end of negotiations and used to get the various bargaining units on side after the major items were negotiated by the central bargaining unit. I felt that if we made the top-up offer at the beginning of negotiations, it would accomplish two things. First, the public would see that we were addressing the areas that they considered essential to public safety. Second, the employees in these bargaining units would immediately receive bump-up increases for nurses, radio dispatchers, water technicians and scientists and jail guards. This would be in addition to the general increase that would be offered over three years to all employees. I thought that most people would put their own interests before the political interests of the union. Divide and conquer.

The strategy seemed sound, but now the task was to communicate our message. As there had not been any communication blackout agreed to at this point, we had free rein to take whatever steps we wanted. Our initial offer had to be conveyed immediately. We did this by press release and over the government website. It was also necessary to hold a press conference.

Ian suggested that instead of reserving the media studios he would alert the gallery and we would do an informal media scrum. The advantage to this would be that the union would not be notified if I did an informal scrum and would not have anyone present to either interfere with my message or have anyone present to monitor the scrum and spin the story their way. They would learn at the same time as the general public on the six o'clock news and in the newspapers the next day. If we reserved the media studios, it would be announced to one and all that we were having a press conference. There's a lot to be said for the element of surprise.

At the time of the previous OPSEU strike, Dave Johnson had been the Chair of Management Board. He decided that he personally would make daily reports to the media for the duration of the strike.

Unfortunately, not every day do you have new information for the media, or at least new and interesting information. My view has always been if you have a press conference and do not have news for the media, they will feel that you have wasted their time and will either challenge your information or start to ask questions in unintended and strange areas.

Remembering the lessons of the past, we decided to take a different approach from what was done in 1996. The media would be expecting daily reports, but having me delivering statistics about the number of employees crossing the picket lines or the number of cases before the Ontario Labour Relations Board didn't make any sense. It would just give the media a chance to create political stories, which we might not want to arise. It would be better to have some degree of control over the message being delivered.

It was decided to have a ministry spokesperson — a Management Board employee — provide the day-to-day technical briefings. As expected, initially there was good attendance by the media, but as the strike wore on, their interest started to wane.

My role would be different. If there was a particular piece of information that we wanted to convey to the media, or if we wanted to deliver a new message or simply to provide the government perspective on a union spin, I would meet with the media, generally by prearranging a time for a media scrum.

One of the advantages that we had during the OPSEU strike was that the strike had relatively little impact on the public. Unlike in a municipal employees, strike, there were no mounds of uncollected garbage or idle public transit buses.

The government had an essential services contract with the union, under which the union was obligated to provide the employees we had mutually identified as being essential. We also took out newspaper ads to inform the public of how we were dealing with the services they were looking for. For example, we were extending the date for renewing drivers' licences until the end of the strike.

The essential services agreement, although it was intended to safeguard essential government services such as 911 dispatchers and jail guards, did not ensure that OPSEU members would comply with the agreement. During the previous strike, some of the essential employees did not show up for work or, if they did show up, would not do their job. We anticipated wildcat strikes, noncompliance and highly insubordinate behaviour.

On a lighter note, one employee actually showed up for work as a jail guard wearing a Superman outfit, including a cape. He argued that it was acceptable attire. My thought after the strike was not to have him disciplined other than make him wear the Superman outfit to work for as many days post-strike as he had worn it during the strike. It would be a kind of rough justice. I eventually conceded, grudgingly, that it would be neither possible nor desirable.

As expected, the union decided to ignore the essential services agreement. As a lawyer, I felt that the only response to this was either through the courts or the labour relations board. I instructed our lawyers that we would have zero tolerance for any noncompliance. This resulted in more than 130 court or labour relations board actions.

These events created some interesting facts and figures, which we thought would be strategically good to share with the public and the government employees.

During the first week of the strike, the union approached the government to see if we would continue the benefits of the union members if the union paid for the cost. This seemed reasonable, so we agreed. This would cost the union $1 million a week.

We also estimated that it was costing the union $5 million a week for strike pay. In addition to all of the foregoing, and because I had instituted a zero-tolerance policy for breaches of the essential services agreement, the legal proceedings that we were instituting were costing the union about $2 million per week for their legal fees. This led to a cost to the union of about $8 million a week.

On our side of the ledger, because we didn't have to pay the employees, I was given estimates of savings of about $6 million a day, or between $30 and $40 million a week. From a purely financial perspective, the strike was very sustainable.

This was a message we wanted to get out, but it was important that we didn't gloat about it. Ian Dovey performed his magic once again and planted a question with the media to which I could then respond. Once delivered, it was the story of the day and of the strike.

While the communication battle with the union was going well, the negotiations had bogged down. Both the government and the union negotiators had taken up entrenched positions. Each side accused the other of lying and bad faith bargaining.

Despite its poor bargaining position, however, the union demands were starting to become greater instead of coming closer to the government position. This was curious, because we had estimated OPSEU's war chest at about $25 million. This would have meant that after about three weeks they were effectively broke.

The only danger I could see was if the union put itself in such an untenable situation, it felt that it could not win and therefore had nothing to lose. This could lead to a situation like in the movie *War Games*, where the conclusion was that in a thermo-nuclear war there would be no winners because everybody would lose.

There is also a point in a public service strike when the public, and therefore the media, expect the government, as good managers to end the strike. I could feel that we were nearing that point. We were at a stalemate.

There is a wonderful book written by Roger Fisher and William Ury of the Harvard Negotiation Project called *Getting to Yes*. In the third chapter, entitled "Focus on Interests, Not Position," there is an example of how to deal with an impasse situation. Two men are arguing about a window — one wants it open for the fresh air; the other wants it closed to avoid the draft. A librarian walks in, hears their arguments, and opens a window in the adjoining room. Problem solved. The authors go on to say, "For a wise solution reconcile interests, not positions . . . Since the parties' problem appears to be a conflict of positions, and since their goal is to agree on a position, they naturally tend to think and talk about positions —

and in the process often reach an impasse." They conclude, "Behind opposed positions lie shared and compatible interests as well as conflicting ones."

This was a classic example of how we would need to get both sides to see the areas of commonality of their interests rather than their entrenched positions. Unfortunately the battle lines had been drawn by our negotiating teams and neither side could unlock their horns without being gored.

In order to break the deadlock, I believed that we needed to think outside the box. I instructed my chief of staff, John Guthrie, to set up a face-to-face meeting, completely off the record and sub rosa, with Leah Casselman, the president of OPSEU and her executive assistant, Mike Grimaldi.

I believed that Casselman truly did understand the difficult position that she was in, but because of the public posturing would have difficulty accepting the government's offer without at least some fiction of a win for the union.

There were a number of concessions that I believed I could give to Casselman that would allow her to save face and to say that she forced them out of the government. Even if we were to reach a consensus, Casselman had a more difficult row to hoe. The union negotiating team negotiated only by committee, and the committee was composed of all the various bargaining units, including the jail guards, who we believed were the most militant.

On the other hand, all I needed to pull the trigger was to get the blessing of the premier, who had given me carte blanche to negotiate.

We wanted the meeting to be confidential and away from the prying eyes of the media. If we met at a downtown Toronto location it would be very obvious that something was going on. My intention was to try to find a solution in good faith. We suggested meeting at the Hilton Suites Hotel in Markham.

To her credit, Casselman accepted the offer to meet without hesitation. It was to be a meeting just among the four of us, totally without prejudice, unless we could find consensus.

The meeting was slated for the next day, Sunday. I immediately contacted Kevin Wilson, my point man on the negotiations, to get his opinion on the areas that I might have some leeway and the priorities that I needed to obtain. The key issues, of course, were wages and benefits.

Regarding wages, I wanted to contain the base rate of increase. It was important to do this, not only for the further contract negotiations I would have with other unions later that year but also for the impact it would have on broader public service negotiations, for cities, colleges and so on. I needed to keep the rate of increase under two percent per year on average. I had some leeway in that I could front-end load the increases in the first year and still stay within my overall mandate.

I also had some flexibility to increase wages in areas where the government was not competitive with the private sector or other levels of government. This could cover jail guards. If we could move the very militant jail guards to accept the offer, that it could be very significant. It was worth noting that before Leah Casselman became the president of the union she was a jail guard. In the benefits areas, I could concede many items if I could get containment on others. The benefits containment could cover the cost of much of the wage increase.

I give full credit to Casselman for putting her union's interest ahead of her ego. She had agreed to drive from Hamilton to Markham in an attempt to settle the strike. This told me that she understood the difficulty of her position. I also understood that in order for any agreement to be reached, I was going to have to compromise as well. She had to save face with her members.

The meeting was long but went the way I had anticipated it would. We conceded what I thought we might have to. They agreed to our requests with respect to benefits. As an afterthought, I asked for containment on another category not strictly related to benefits. They agreed because it seemed innocuous. The small point that they had agreed to saved the government significant money. I don't believe, to this day, they understood what they had given away.

The meeting lasted for about four hours. At the end, we all shook hands with the understanding that an agreement was at hand and with the commitment that we would advise our negotiators of the outcome and instruct them to iron out the details.

I've always said that the devil is in the details. Monday the talks bogged down as the lawyers and negotiators on both sides started to argue about interpreting what I had thought was straightforward and simply stated. This is the nature of negotiations. The lawyers interpret and make complex what is simple and straightforward.

Tuesday was even worse. The previous attitudes that were created during the entrenchment part of the negotiations were starting to raise their ugly heads again.

I finally decided that things needed a push. I told John to indicate to the other side that unless the matter was settled by midnight Tuesday night, the deal was off. I believed that both Casselman and I thought that the strike would be settled by Monday. No one thought that it could be dragged into Wednesday.

Wednesday was significant for a good reason. Wednesday was the day of the by-election in Orangeville for Ernie Eves. The Progressive Conservative Party of Ontario had newly elected Premier Eves as its leader. It would be helpful to have the matter settled. We also had a by-election in North Bay to replace Mike Harris with Al McDonald, the former deputy mayor of North Bay.

On Tuesday night, the minutes were slowly ticking off. This is the problem when you are playing a game of chicken. Casselman and I were seeing who was going to be the first to blink. At around 11:30 p.m., I received a phone call at home asking me if Casselman could talk to me.

From about 11:45 p.m. to 3 a.m., Casselman and I went back and forth with intervening calls to our negotiators. Finally we agreed on all the details. My end of the negotiations was simple. I would instruct our negotiators on the settlement details and tell them to close the deal. Casselman's end was a lot more difficult. She had to convince all the various bargaining units to consent to the terms of the agreement. This was not a certainty by any means.

At about 3:15 a.m, I decided to get a little sleep but I advised my negotiators to call me, regardless of the time, when the deal was completed. At about 6:30 a.m., I received confirmation that the union had signed the deal. I advised Ian Dovey and Derek O'Toole of the successful completion of the deal and instructed them to set up a press conference for that morning.

It was necessary to be a little cautious at the press conference, as the union membership still had to ratify the agreement. The chances were pretty good that the agreement would be ratified by a large majority, but it would not have been smart to gloat at the press conference.

The facts were fairly straightforward. The union settled for a contract that was not much different from the original offer I had made at the outset. By going on strike for such a long time, the union members actually lost money. The money that we saved by not paying the employees paid for a great deal of the contract. The union was also in great debt. These were the facts.

I decided that it would be better for me to say that the agreement that was reached was fair to both the union and the taxpayers. I knew that the union would say we capitulated, but unfortunately for the union, I had kept the media up to date with any changes in the offer during the strike. The media also knew what my starting offer was. This would eventually come out. The fact of the matter was that despite the difficult negotiations, the government still had to maintain somewhat of a relationship with the union.

Things turned out as we had anticipated. The union claimed victory over the government. I congratulated the union and their leadership on coming to terms. The government saved millions of dollars and had set the stage for other negotiations in the broader public sector. Because of the length of negotiations, the union was in great debt and had borrowed money from other unions. As a result of a lack of resources, the union had a shortened negotiation with the colleges and universities later that year. The contract was a fair one that, if accepted weeks before, would have benefitted the union members, but politics — even union politics — do not always result in logical actions.

While the union negotiations were happening, I was dealing with an issue that had begun earlier in the year. There is a process in government called a cabinet walkaround. This is process that is exercised when a matter needs to be dealt with and there are no cabinet meetings scheduled for a period of time. It occurs during the summer break. The regulation will need four cabinet ministers to sign it, one of whom must be either the Minister of Finance or the Chair of Management Board.

Just as the government was transitioning from Premier Mike Harris to Premier Ernie Eves, a cabinet walkaround was brought to my attention. The regulation called for a health tax credit to be given to professional sports teams. The reasoning was that most of the professional athletes were seasonal and most did not spend the off season in Ontario. The regulation didn't seem to be a big deal, but because we were in a period of transition of power, out of caution I wanted to confirm our direction with both the outgoing and the incoming premiers.

I contacted Premier Mike Harris, who supported the regulation. I advised him that I would be confirming Ernie Eves's assent before I signed it. Mike Harris had no problem with that. My office got the head of Ernie's transition team on the phone for me and he confirmed that Ernie had no problem with the regulation. I had checked with both the outgoing and incoming leader. Based on my conversations, I signed the cabinet walkaround.

The matter was forgotten for months until one day in Question Period, NDP Leader Howard Hampton brought up the regulation, since it had appeared in the *Ontario Gazette*. Premier Eves's response was unexpected. He went on at length that he didn't know about the regulation and that it shouldn't have gone through the process.

Houston, we had a problem! Either the head of Ernie's transition team had been misinformed about the issue, or Ernie had forgotten the matter. Issues management in politics is simple. The higher the issue goes up the food chain, the bigger the problem.

Now that Question Period was over, we had to go out into the scrum. The way Premier Eves had framed his answer made it a problem. I needed to answer the question and I couldn't say what had actually happened, because then it would land in the premier's lap, but I also didn't want to sound silly.

The media were gathered around, ready for a feeding frenzy. The question was, who had signed a regulation behind the premier's back.

I walked out first. The first question was: Did you sign the regulation? My answer was simple. I said that I had done my due diligence (I didn't say what that was) and I signed the regulation and I took full responsibility for signing it. After my answer, there wasn't a lot more to ask me. No probing was necessary. I had not used an evasive answer. Also in my favour, the media knew that I never avoided tough issues and I never lied to them.

The real problem lay with my colleagues. The ones who signed were not sure that they had signed it, and the ones who hadn't, thought that they might have signed it. This led to some very awkward answers including, "It wasn't us. It was the previous administration." Other than the change in premier, it was still us.

The media had a field day over a non-issue. It was the lead story on the television coverage that night. It was the headline in all the major newspapers and the topic of all the radio shows.

The next morning we had a cabinet meeting. After seeing the media attention, I was fully prepared to run the gauntlet. As usual I was the first person to show up for cabinet. The media — print, television and radio — were all camped out in force. As I approached the cabinet meeting room, I expected a flurry of activity to set up the scrum. I reached the door and no one had even stood up.

I walked into the room without incident and put my briefcase down. My curiosity got the better of me. I walked back up to Richard Brennan of the *Toronto Star*, who was the president of the press gallery.

"Richard," I said. "It's not that I want to be in the stories again, but why didn't anyone get up when I walked through?" He looked at me and told me that I had taken full responsibility yesterday for signing the regulation, so what was he going to write today?

Unfortunately for the rest of my colleagues, it was a zoo. Many of them arrived completely frazzled from the grilling.

I thought that that was going to be the end of the story until the following week, when one of my colleagues who had been away and had been one of the signatories to the regulation answered that she knew that Dave Tsubouchi had done his due diligence and checked with both premiers, so she had signed it. The cat was out of the bag.

When I passed through the media that day, one of them said to me, "I thought there was more to what you were saying, because you are too careful to just sign something without checking."

That was a lesson that I learned well years before, from the regulatory error made by legislative counsel during my Community and Social Services days. Other things had changed since those days as well. I didn't really care whether I remained in cabinet and so I did things the way I thought they should be done. If I got resistance from the premier's staff, I simply went over and spoke directly to the premier. I had been given the benefit of the doubt by the press gallery because they knew I never lied to them or ran away from a bad story and, moreover, because I was still around and had not only survived but had been promoted.

Since my early, inexperienced days the media had acknowledged that my approach to media scrums was polished and rock solid.

# CHAPTER TWENTY

# CULTURE: ALL'S WELL THAT ENDS WELL

After I supported Ernie Eves in the leadership campaign to replace Mike Harris and settled the OPSEU strike on the day before Ernie's by-election for a seat in the legislature in Orangeville, Ernie Eves decided to "reward" me. I was still the Chair of Management Board and controlling expenses for the province. Ernie Eves felt that this did not give me enough profile and appointed me to be Minister of Culture in addition to my duties as Chair of Management Board.

Although I appreciated the gesture, Management Board was one of the busiest ministries. Four ministries were allocated the maximum number of staff: Finance, Health, Education and Management Board. I had never taken the maximum number of staff, as the staffers that I had were extremely efficient, motivated and loyal. Now that I was assuming the Ministry of Culture as well, I had to take on new staffers and I had to learn the issues of a new ministry as well.

Fortunately, as the Chair of Management Board, I was familiar with the programming of the Ministry of Culture from a fiscal perspective, as I had reviewed and approved its spending for the previous year. I was not, however, familiar with the policies and implementation status of the ministry. Staffing was not a problem. We were able to take on new eager staffers mostly from other members or other ministries. Training these new staffers was simple. John Guthrie, my chief of staff, took on a dual role. We maintained one office at the Management Board offices and my experienced staffers took on the responsibility of showing our new people how we did things.

Our new staffers included Jennifer Blitz, a lawyer who took on policy; Marc Boudreau, stakeholder relations; and Barb Burrowes, communication. My new deputy minister was Don Obonsawan, an experienced deputy and someone whom I knew and respected. There was only one problem with Don — he was just about to retire. Fortunately for me, when Don did retire, my new deputy minister was Terry Smith. Terry, to my great fortune, was very smart and creative. These talents would become very important in our issues in Culture.

My most immediate problem in Culture was resolving the impasse about the cultural infrastructure negotiations with the federal government. The infrastructure grants were to provide the stimulation to revitalize arts and culture, mainly in Toronto, and provide a much-needed boost to the economy based on cultural tourism. Ontario and the federal government would provide matching dollars. For the past year after the initiative had been announced, the cultural institutions had been lobbying to be on the priority list.

Since the Province of Ontario backstopped the Art Gallery of Ontario (AGO) and the Royal Ontario Museum (ROM), it was important to us that these two institutions were at the top of the priority list. Every other museum, gallery, cultural centre and arts and cultural organization lobbied diligently. Even before I became the Minister of Culture, I had been the object of a lot of the lobbying because I was the Chair of Management Board and because I sat on the board of the Superbuild Corporation — the agency in charge of all infrastructure financing in Ontario, through which the decision-making for the infrastructure grants were being made.

There had been two major stumbling blocks to getting a consensus on the main grantees. Since no agreement had been made on the biggest parts of the deal, all the other smaller grants had not been dealt with as well. Also, the negotiations had eroded into near brinkmanship between Premier Mike Harris and Prime Minister Jean Chrétien. Discussions were markedly cool at best.

The two major subjects of disagreement were the Canadian Opera Company's application for a new opera hall and the application of the National Ballet School for an expansion and upgrade to its facilities.

The Canadian Opera Company's application was being supported by the Province of Ontario through the land upon which the facility would be located and by a grant of $25 million by the federal government. The obstacle was the fact that the land was appraised for $36 million. The whole principle of the Canada Ontario Infrastructure Program was that the funds had to be matching amounts. This was the only instance that was not based on cash. The province had dug in its heels and was insisting that the feds match the $36 million, but that was not about to occur. In order to provide an alternative, the province suggested that the difference of $11 million become a vendor take-back mortgage. This solution did not appeal to the COC and the feds, and hence there was a deadlock.

The National Ballet School could not even get through the front door. The rationale for the culture grants for the Province of Ontario was that the grants would support cultural tourism and therefore the jobs creation agenda of the government. The province did not stumble upon this theory, as almost every application for a grant espoused with authority the principles of cultural tourism that had been set out by the province. The National Ballet School, although a cultural institution in Canada, had zero aspects of cultural tourism. The National Ballet School had been turned down flat.

There were a few smaller issues. There was a limited amount of money, so not everyone was going to get in on the good news. The

Superbuild board had to prioritize the applications. If you were too far down the line, you were out of luck. The federal list and the provincial list were different. The majority of the money was going to be taken up by the big three — the Royal Ontario Museum, the Art Gallery of Ontario and the Canadian Opera Company. That meant most applicants were likely not to get all the money that they applied for, and some wouldn't get any at all. The Gardiner Museum of Ceramics, for example, a very popular tourist attraction in Toronto, was not even on the A-list.

Even without this impasse, there was a lot of animosity between the Harris provincial government and the Chrétien federal government. Many of the MPs and MPPs did not like the policies of their counterparts and continually blamed all their woes on the other government. Relations had deteriorated so much between many of the members that they amounted to personal dislike. One-upmanship seemed a normal part of the process.

These two issues polarized the caucuses and set the parties on a head-on collision course. This was the reward I got for supporting Ernie Eves in the leadership race. The good news was that other than asking that I "fix" the situation, there was no interference by the premier's office.

As I had sat on the Superbuild board, I had some familiarity with the applications and had met with most of the major institutions lobbying the government, but I had not made a site visit to all of the locations.

Most of the delegations put together by the applicants were large. They included the executive and influential board members along with the architect and other friends who might have some degree of acquaintance with the person being lobbied.

The delegation that made the greatest impression on me was from the Gardiner Museum of Ceramics. It was a delegation of two — Helen Gardiner, who had founded the museum along with her husband, George, and the executive director, Alexandra Montgomery. There were no bells and whistles but only a healthy dose of sincerity and commitment. I came out of the meeting with a great deal of respect for both Helen Gardiner and Alexandra Montgomery. I agreed to visit the museum.

I had already met with the groups from the ROM, the AGO and COC but I had not met with the National Ballet School, as they were not even considered a legitimate application. Out of fairness I felt that I needed to meet with them and at the very least do a site visit, so I could show them that there was some fairness in the process.

We arranged to meet at the National Ballet School with Executive Director Robert Sirman, Chair of the Board Marie Rounding and Karen Kain. The National Ballet School had a strong advocate in my house. Elaine was a great ballet lover. She insisted on accompanying me on my site visit.

When we arrived at the school we first had a discussion of the issues. The school pleaded its case to be recognized on the basis of the impact that the school has on the culture of dance and not to be excluded because of a lack of tourism. Most people assume that ballet is a performing art for the elite and rich. They also make the incorrect assumption that the young people who attend the National Ballet School are all from families of privilege. This is not true. I was able to learn that fees for most of the young people who attend the school were subsidized. Entrance to the school was based on merit and talent, not on ability to pay.

We saw students and staff enthusiastically engaged in school-work and practice. They were all doing what they loved to do. As we toured the facilities, we couldn't help but note the rundown condition of the school, and yet that did not deter anybody's spirit. The justification for cultural tourism made sense in that it fit within our economic growth and jobs philosophy. The logical extension was that if the government supported infrastructure projects like the Canadian Opera Company's new performing centre, we needed world-class organizations to provide the performers. The National Ballet of Canada had been a partner of sorts with the COC, and the National Ballet School was the leading producer of ballet per-formances in Canada. If we didn't have a steady stream of new and talented young dancers, what would become of the National Ballet?

In addition to these considerations, I knew that the federal government was pushing the Royal Conservatory of Music because Mrs. Chrétien was on their board of directors. Like the National Ballet School, the Royal Conservatory would not fit the criteria of cultural tourism. Therein lay the kernel of an idea.

We met and were impressed by a number of the students, who had a maturity beyond their years. Robert Sirman, Marie Rounding and Karen Kain all made impassioned pleas for assistance.

When we left, Elaine continued the arguments on behalf of the school. After seeing the National Ballet School for myself, I was sold. I just had to figure out how it could be done.

I have always been fortunate in the quality and intelligence of the deputy ministers with whom I have had the pleasure of working — people like Steen Lal, Sandy Lang and Virginia West. At the time I was working with Deputy Minister of Management Board Kathy Bouey and Deputy Minister of Culture Terry Smith. Both deputies had been supporting me on the Superbuild projects, and I consulted with them on how we could resolve the impasse. We concluded that the problem was a political one, externally with the federal government and internally with my colleagues.

The animosity between our government and the federal government seemed to be the greatest stumbling block. The good news was that both Premier Eves and I did not have bad relations with our counterparts. There was also the intervention of fate when we were trying to resolve the political problems. I had been invited to the Stratford Festival for a special event and performance, as had David Collenette, the federal transportation minister who had responsibility for the Greater Toronto Area and the Toronto infrastructure issue.

My previous interactions with David Collenette had been very congenial. He had never been my counterpart federally for any of my ministries, but I liked him on a personal level. I thought that there might be an opportunity to chat about the infrastructure issue at some point in time.

As we were the only ministers present from both the federal and provincial governments, we were seated together at the dinner. We had a chance to chat casually, but the dinner had a lot of formalities and speeches so we didn't have much of an opportunity at dinner. The Stratford Festival seated us next to each other for the performance. It was at this time that we started chatting about the issues, the obstacles and the priorities for both of our governments. The conversation continued throughout the intermission.

Together we decided that we could work together to resolve the issues. We both had respect for each other and for our abilities to problem solve. In short, we liked and trusted each other. We committed to continue the dialogue. We also knew that neither of us was a pushover and that some serious horse-trading would ensue.

Appropriately the Shakespearian performance that we attended was *All's Well That Ends Well.*

Now that I had cleared a path for building a better relationship with the federal government, I needed to turn my attention to the two major stumbling blocks: the Canadian Opera Company and the National Ballet School. Throughout this process, Premier Eves had been supportive and had basically given me carte blanche to deal with the negotiations. The two paths that I took to resolve the issue would not have been possible without his support and consent. I needed to find reasons to justify what would be changes in the process for both of these issues. The COC application was one of the highlighted projects of the Superbuild, and the National Ballet Schools was an important institution in Toronto and in Canada.

In trying to resolve these issues I had brainstorming sessions involving both my staff and the ministry staffs of both Management Board and Culture. Both of my deputy ministers were essential. I had an idea what I wanted to do, and they needed to let me know if I was on the right track, if I could do what I wanted and how we could justify it.

The COC issue involved a lot of money on paper. We were $11 million apart. One of the principles that we had followed in our relationship with the feds was matching dollars. It didn't make any sense, however, for a major fundraising campaign for the COC if $11 million of the funds raised were going to be spent to pay back the mortgage to the province. In my view, we would be taking a good story — supporting the arts and culture in Toronto — and creating a bad story and making our government look mean spirited.

Our contribution, although important, was on paper. It did not affect our cash flow. The value of the land was based on an appraisal of the property. The value of land could change depending on the economy and when the appraisal was made. I hoped that I could convince my colleagues that if we were to forego the difference in the contributions, we would be perceived as doing the right thing and being more generous than the feds. It was not a strong argument, but it was one in which the premier would support me.

The National Ballet School seemed to be a tougher nut to crack. We had been messaging that our rationale for the arts and cultural infrastructure was cultural tourism. Our government had a priority of job creation. My predecessor, Tim Hudak, had been very clear on the message and in conveying to the National Ballet School this reason for not even processing the application.

I asked my staff who had created this rationale for the grants. They responded that we did as a government and a ministry. I suggested that we could change the rationale. We then worked with the ministry to amend the process so that we could accommodate both the National Ballet School and the Royal Conservatory of Music. Premier Eves went along with the change and so did my colleagues at Management Board, Superbuild and cabinet.

Knowing that I could proceed with the COC, the National Ballet School and the Royal Conservatory of Music, my staff contacted David Collenette's staff. David was going to have to meet us partway on some of our priorities as well. The province wanted the Royal Botanical Gardens to participate in the infrastructure grants, even though the Gardens were located just outside of

Toronto. As with the ROM and AGO, the finances of the Royal Botanical Gardens were backstopped by the province and we were anxious to have matching federal dollars.

Most of the projects appeared on the priority lists of both the province and the federal government. Each side also had different favourites that were not shared, and therein began the horse-trading. All the projects had been ranked by their relative importance. Both offices mutually agreed that a few like the Gardiner Museum of Ceramics should be moved up in the pecking order. When the consideration went to some of the smaller projects, David Collenette and I both liked the cultural centres.

Once the major projects and obstacles had been cleared out of the way, the rest of the approvals fell into place. On both federal and provincial levels, we needed to get stamps of approval from Prime Minister Chrétien and Premier Eves and then we needed to get support from our respective caucuses. None of these negotiations could have been possible without the full support of Premier Ernie Eves.

It is unfortunate that Mike Harris has been vilified by so many critics as someone who did not support the arts. The actual criticisms of him were much worse. This is patently unfair. Mike Harris actually started the ball rolling on the cultural renaissance of Toronto. It was his initiative. What Mike Harris expected was value for his money. In all my discussions with Mike Harris on the issue of the infrastructure grants for the cultural community, he was consistently positive. He was looking for accountability, but he was positive.

As you gain experience and perspective in government, you gain more of an ability to find solutions. Early in my mandate as the Minister of Culture I was advised of a problem that would impact the Ontario publishing industry. Major publishing company Stoddart Publishing and its book distribution arm, General Distribution Services, was in financial trouble. Stoddart going down had a ripple effect on all the smaller publishers in Ontario, who relied on GDS for distribution, and it would affect the authors too. The big issue was that our government did not believe in corporate welfare and bailouts.

The ministry had been inundated with communications of concern for the publishing industry. My deputy minister, Terry Smith, and I met with our staffers. My perception of the Ministry of Culture civil servants was that they had been underused and had not been given anything challenging to work on.

I told Terry the challenge was that we needed to fix the situation but that it could not be construed as corporate welfare. When we came up with a program, it was important that the premier's office did not think it was a bailout. In effect, we needed a bailout but it couldn't walk or talk like a bailout. Terry is a smart woman and I knew that she had some very smart people working at the ministry.

Months later we announced the Ontario Book Initiative, which would be administered through the Ontario Media Development Corporation. It was described in the OMDC annual report as a "dramatic new program" that was launched,

> . . . providing much needed support for Ontario's book publishing industry in the wake of distribution and retail challenges through $1.5 million of working capital to Ontario's book publishers. The OBI provided an immediate investment of up to $100,000 per eligible publisher, with the goal of enhancing the book publishing sector's ability to attract investment, generate employment and be competitive. Forty-six Ontario book publishers received support from the OBI in 2002/2003.

We were able to make the announcement with great fanfare and nobody knew that we had bailed out the industry.

In many ways, my short stint as the Minister of Culture was very rewarding. I believe that my love of reading has given me a thirst for learning and knowledge. As a young boy, I never had money to buy books and so I knew how important libraries were and are today. Libraries are safe places to meet and read and discuss. They are viewed that way by new Canadians and people who are like me when I was young. A library is one of the greatest institutions of democracy. Everyone has access and equal rights to be there. It doesn't matter how much money you have or how important you are or what colour your skin is or your religion or beliefs.

It is unfortunate that all levels of government minimize the value of libraries. Libraries seem to be at the bottom of the food chain when municipal budgets are discussed. People will complain if their streets are unplowed or garbage is not picked up. No one complains when their libraries are not current or have their hours pared down. They are easy targets for cuts. Many Canadians assume that because most families have computers or books, that it is the norm. Libraries fill that gap.

The problem for funding becomes greater in smaller and northern and First Nations communities. The logical place to look for funding was the Trillium Foundation, which had an annual granting budget of $100 million. The problem was that municipalities were not eligible for any grants from the Trillium Foundation.

After much negotiation with the premier's office, I was given the leeway to make a one-time exception to the rule if I could convince my colleagues to support the initiative in Management Board and cabinet. Contrary to the popular view, my colleagues did support libraries and I was able to obtain the support for the program.

We called it the Strategic Granting Initiative for Library Boards. The program gave one-time grants of up to $15,000 to libraries serving municipalities of 20,000 or less and to First Nations libraries. In the first year of the grants, 214 libraries received in total $2 million for collections, community programming, training, technology and equipment. The program was welcomed by libraries.

My hope was to gradually expand the program to all libraries, but the 2003 election intervened and that is when the library grant expansion initiative ended.

The other small adjustment I was able to make was to the Trillium Book Awards, which is a competition and recognition of the best authors in prose and poetry in Ontario. It was one of the events I was looking forward to attending with great anticipation.

I was given copies of all of the finalists in the competition and I was going to give a speech and present the awards. I would also be meeting all the authors at a reception preceding the event. I thought that it would be appropriate to read the books of the finalists before to the event. The only problem was time. The schedule of a minister runs from about 6 a.m. to 10 p.m. every day and I had two portfolios. I read every night in bed, but even with that time I would be hard-pressed to read all the books.

As the Minister of Culture and the Chair of Management Board, I rarely got questions during Question Period, so I decided to read the novels during QP. This idea seemed to be a good one until one day during QP, Helen Johns elbowed me and said, "The question is to you!"

I said to Helen, "What was the question?"

She said, "I don't know. It was your question so I didn't pay attention."

I looked up and saw that Jim Bradley, the member from St. Catharines, was taking his seat. Jim was my critic for Management Board and he usually asked me about government advertising. I made the assumption that he had asked about government advertising and apparently I was right. After that, I kept one ear on the question until I knew that it wasn't to me.

At the reception, to the surprise of many of the authors, I was able to discuss their respective books and my view. John Ota, one of the Ministry of Culture officials, commented to me that I was the first culture minister to read any of the books before the Trillium Awards, but to me it was a pleasure.

The one thing that became apparent to me when I was reading the finalists' books was that it was very difficult for a book of poetry to compete with a novel. As a result, I created the Trillium Book Award for Poetry.

One of the perks of being the Minister of Culture is that when you go to see a performance you are introduced to the performers.

I've met some very interesting people during my brief acting career and many after.

In October 2002 I received an invitation to attend at the home of the British Consul General, Geoffrey Berg, to meet the Rolling Stones. I was thrilled at the opportunity to meet these rock icons. I was a little disappointed to find out that there were to be no photographs allowed. Elaine is no fan of rock and was not keen to go. I thought it would be a waste not to use the extra invitation. One of our OPP security officers, Beth Hollihan, who used to accompany Elaine, was a smart young officer, and I knew that she would be delighted to go. Elaine thought that it was a good idea and also solved the question of security for the evening.

Although the invitation made it clear that no photos were allowed, it was not stated that no autographs were allowed, so I brought with me an old album that I bought when I was a teen in the '60s. As the evening progressed, Keith Richards wandered over to chat with me. I thought to myself that here was a rock icon and world-famous person who seemed so down to earth. I took the opportunity and asked Keith if he would sign my album and he said yes.

When I handed him the album, he looked at it and said, "This is a really old record."

I replied, "Keith, you know we are both getting old."

Keith then signed "B4 my time, Keith Richards."

As we continued to chat, Ron Wood walked over and joined in.

I asked Ron, "What would you do if you had a night off?"

Ron Wood replied, "I am an artist, so I would love to visit the Art Gallery of Ontario, but we would just get mobbed."

It was about 9:30 p.m. at the time.

I said to Ron Wood, "Ron, I'm the Minister of Culture. Let me call the AGO."

I called the AGO and asked if they would mind giving a private tour to the Rolling Stones, to which their answer was an enthusiastic yes.

I turned back to Ron and said, "The tour is on." They asked me if I was coming but I had early meetings and couldn't. It was a small gesture to thank them for all that they had done over the years for Toronto.

Earlier in the year, Elaine and I had been invited to Stratford to see a performance of My Fair Lady featuring two very well known actors, Cynthia Dale and Colm Feore. Anthony Cimolino, the general director of the Stratford Festival, had indicated that there was a possibility that Julie Andrews would be attending as well.

When we arrived, we were a little disappointed to find that Julie Andrews had not been able to attend but we were very excited to see both Cynthia Dale and Colm Feore. During the intermission Elaine and I were discussing how talented Cynthia Dale was and, although she was best known as an actress, how wonderful a singer she was. I realized that we were seated just behind Peter Mansbridge, the well-respected newscaster and husband of Cynthia Dale, so we chatted briefly with Peter.

We were seated next to two girls who looked like they were around 16 years old. They were very happy about being there and the young lady next to me started talking to me. I noted that she seemed very excited to be there. She told me that it was her birthday and all she wanted from her father were tickets to the performance because Cynthia Dale was her idol and she loved everything that she did, especially her TV show, Street Legal. She then told us that after the performance she was going to wait with her friend at the stage door and try to get an autograph and, she hoped, a photograph with Cynthia Dale. I turned to Elaine and said to her that it was closing night and that there would probably be a cast party after, and that she was going to be out of luck.

When the performance finished, I turned to the girls and told them to come with us. After the theatre emptied, a member of the Stratford Festival staff came over to escort us backstage. I told them that the girls were with us. Both Colm Feore and Cynthia Dale were very gracious, and when I explained to Cynthia why the girls were there, she kindly agreed to pose with the girls. Elaine took the shots.

As we were leaving through the stage door, the birthday girl stopped suddenly and said that she forgot to get Cynthia Dale's autograph. Elaine handed her a program that she had gotten Cynthia to sign.

During the Toronto International Film Festival, I was invited to all the openings and the best parties. I was at the party for *Between Strangers* starring Sophia Loren and directed by her son Edoardo Ponti.

I was chatting with Edoardo and said to him, "Will you do me a favour and when your mother arrives, would you introduce me to her?" He agreed to make the introduction. A little while later Sophia Loren walked into the room. At the time she was 68, but I have yet to see a more elegant woman. She was still stunningly beautiful. I have no idea what I said. All I can say is that when she walked into the room all eyes were on her. My friend asked me if I saw Mira Sorvino, but I had no idea that she was even in the room.

I also had the opportunity to introduce David Cronenberg's movie *Spider* at TIFF. David had given me my first speaking part as an actor years before, and I was able to tell the story during my introduction.

Elaine and I also had the good fortune to see and meet Tony Bennett when he performed at Roy Thompson Hall. At one point during his performance he said that he wanted to show how good the acoustics were and asked the crew to turn off the microphone. That man can sing.

When we met him in the green room, I asked if he could sign my CD. He said sure, and then I added, "Could you sign it the way I want?"

He said, "Sure, how do you want me to sign?"

I said, "Could you sign it 'To my friend Dave's father, Tom. Happy Birthday.'"

When I gave it to my dad he turned to me and asked, "You know Tony Bennett?"

The Ministry of Culture had challenges, but I was lucky in that the people who worked for the ministry were good and smart people. By and large, *All's Well That Ends Well.*

# CHAPTER TWENTY-ONE

# Saving Parliament

An invaluable skill in government is the ability to sniff out sensitive areas that could flare up badly and to pay attention to your instincts. The difficulty many ministers have is that even though they may figure out that a local or ministerial issue may be the harbinger of critical problems, their colleagues and the premier's office could have a very different view. It may be that others either don't care or don't think it's a priority. Or they may feel that even if it does flare up, it is not their responsibility. Most don't think corporately. They have blinders on unless it has a direct impact on them.

An issue that was bubbling under the surface when I was appointed as Minister of Culture was the site of the first parliament building of Ontario. The site had been discovered under a car dealership when the dealership was excavating to expand. The matter was before the Ontario Municipal Board to decide whether or not the car dealership could proceed with its construction, which would mean not preserving the site for the public.

The Ministry of Culture was advising me to continue with the position that it was a local issue and that the City of Toronto had taken the leadership in their attendance at the OMB. Although this was technically true, the argument was very weak.

The municipalities are responsible for local historic sites and I had no power as the Minister of Culture to designate a site as provincially significant. The province could expropriate the site, but I couldn't do that without the approval for the money or consent from the premier's office. We were in a very tight budgetary time and I anticipated huge opposition.

There were a lot of reasons why we shouldn't get involved. There were even more arguments why it couldn't be done for financial reasons. I would be in competition for funds with all kinds of other priority areas for government — health care, education, agriculture. Most people relegate heritage issues to the bottom of the priority heap.

Despite all the logical reasons why we shouldn't get involved, the issue was gnawing at my gut. It seemed to me nonsensical to have to stand up and say that the first parliament building site was a local issue and of no interest to the province. This was the site of the first Ontario Parliament! How could I say that I had no interest in our first site?

To add to the complexities, a seemingly unrelated issue did not appear unrelated to me. The government had just been soundly criticized by everyone — the media, the opposition and stakeholders — for holding the budget announcement outside the legislature at Magna's corporate head office. There had been ample precedent for doing so. The criticism had been that it was undemocratic to do so because the budget had been traditionally announced at Queen's Park. The government would be disrupting the normal process that the media was familiar and comfortable with. The opposition parties were also extremely upset because their access to the media would be more challenging. The moaning of the Opposition reverberated through the rafters of the legislature. The media stories were relentless.

Public opinion was abetted by the media stories. In reality there was nothing undemocratic about the process. With the budget, the government had found itself in a box. On one hand, the premier had promised to have a budget before the end of March. On the other, the government was not ready to commence sitting in the legislature until after the end of March. The premier's staff had come up with the idea. I remember hearing assurances that there had been precedents for holding the budget outside the legislature; one example was Robert Nixon under the former Liberal David Peterson government and another was Floyd Laughren under the former NDP Bob Rae government. I also remember the assurances that there would not be a problem.

The key perception in this issue was that it was undemocratic.

So if you juxtapose the issue that almost everyone considered undemocratic with a failure to protect the original seat of democracy in the province, I believed that this would soon become a hugely difficult problem. I also believed that it was just a matter of time before the heritage stakeholders began to ask why the province was not stepping forward. The City of Toronto, which did not want the issue to begin with, would soon be pointing fingers at the province. This all meant that the media would soon be aiming at us as well.

But above all that, I thought that protecting the site of the first Ontario Parliament was the right thing to do.

At a recent lunch with a friend of mine, Larry Keating of Keating Technologies, we were discussing the changing framework in the world of high tech. I said to Larry that it was like shooting sporting clays. If you aim at the target, you will always miss it because it's constantly moving, but if you aim where the target's going to be, you'll hit it.

Larry agreed, adding that Wayne Gretzky always said that he goes where the puck is going to be, which is how he became so successful despite being smaller in stature. Larry is one of those self-made men who went from delivering dry cleaning as a teenager to being one of the most successful entrepreneurs in the high tech industry because he too learned to go where the puck was going.

Even if we were a moving target, I expected us to be targeted soon.

The City of Toronto had been pressuring the province to attend the OMB hearings as an interested party. That would imply to the OMB that the province had an interest. It may not technically have obligated us to participate but it gave the perception of the province coming to the table. It would, however, give us some time to try to find a solution and, secondarily, give the impression that we were trying to find a solution.

Our participation would also allow me to change the message track from it's not the province's problem and it's a local issue to we are actively trying to find a solution. It moved us from inaction to pro-action.

If things worked out and a solution were to be found, we had set the scene to get credit for moving the situation from a stalemate to an everybody-wins scenario. By going down this path, however, I was obliged to come up with a solution.

As a result of the matter being before the OMB, the relationship between the city and the car dealership was not good. The city had been painting a picture of the dealership as a less-than-good corporate citizen. Some city councillors were specifically pointing their fingers at the dealership.

My strategy was quite different from the city's. I didn't believe we could get a consensual agreement by finger pointing. I tried not to criticize either the city or the car dealership. Someone had to act as mediator and solution finder.

Not surprisingly, there was almost no communication between the city and the dealership that didn't have an element of animosity and advocacy. Lines were being drawn in the sand.

As I got deeper and deeper into the details of the situation, it became very apparent that the dealership was willing to be as cooperative as possible. Several deferrals of time were granted by the dealership. They were looking for a solution that would allow them to cooperate without losing their investment. It was up to us to find it.

The first thing that we did was open up the communication channel with the dealership. In the meantime we needed to find out what the city was willing to do to cooperate.

Some context is necessary. The City of Toronto was asking the province to assist the city with their deficit. They estimated that they were going to be around $80 million short. They had already started with their usual wailing at the province. They claimed, as they did every year, that their deficit was the result of provincial downloading. The amalgamation of Toronto was several years in the past, and the city politicians — with some exceptions like Rob Ford or Doug Halliday — were not that interested in fiscal responsibility. In fact, they still had not sold one of the six former city halls and Metro Hall. To make matters worse, they had not repaid any of the outstanding $120 million that they had borrowed from the province that was due and owing.

I thought that there might be some good opportunities here to get the city to give to the province as part of the debt they owed us some of their excess real estate holdings, including a piece of property that might help us with the first parliament situation.

An alternative solution lay in the fact that the first parliament lands were located in an area called the West Don. The province held substantial lands in the area, which were extremely marketable but were currently under a "hold" designation by the city, which meant that no development could occur. If we could get our lands released, it would allow us economically to give up a piece of our land for the deal because we would have enhanced the value of the remaining lands. This would cost the city nothing.

As straightforward as the solution seemed, the roadblocks started to appear. I approached the premier's office with my suggestion to get back some of our debt by taking real estate in return. Everyone thought that it was a good idea. I even suggested that I participate on the bargaining team with the city. I had just concluded the OPSEU strike at no cost to the government and had a reputation of being difficult to push around. If anything, I thought that this might enhance our position. The city was begging for millions more dollars and they owed us another huge debt. This was the time to strike for a good deal for the province.

Time went on with no word. Eventually, unexpected news broke that my good friend and colleague, Chris Hodgson, the Minister of Municipal Affairs and Housing, was not going to run for re-election and was stepping down from cabinet. This was a fairly significant happening. Chris Hodgson was widely respected as being quietly competent. As a former municipal politician, he was held in high esteem by the Association of Municipalities of Ontario and the mayors and municipal politicians around the province. Chris had left big shoes for someone to fill.

It was decided at the time to temporarily appoint Minister of Agriculture Helen Johns to the post until a more permanent minister could be appointed. This meant basically that Helen was simply caretaking the ministry until her replacement was named. This also meant that there was likely to be no action on the City of Toronto negotiations. In the meantime, my staff had been in very close contact with the premier's office because I felt this would be my path to a settlement of the first parliament situation.

More time passed and then David Young, a very competent minister, was moved from being Attorney General to the Municipal Affairs portfolio. David is a highly intelligent person but had obviously not been in the loop with my concerns with the City of Toronto debt. Very soon after David's appointment, the City of Toronto was given relief of its debt and was given a grant for the money that they were asking for. I understood at the time why this had occurred. It demonstrated that David Young could come in and settle a situation quickly.

No consideration had been given to accepting assets from the City of Toronto. In fact, what the city had given the province was absolutely nothing. When I asked the premier's office what had happened, it was indicated to me that the province could still negotiate after the grant for the transfer of assets. I don't know what school of negotiation that came from, but it's hard to negotiate when you have no bargaining power. This was a huge loss of opportunity. Not unexpectedly, whatever the province had requested from the city as a repayment of their debt was refused. As the negotiations ended with a whimper not a bang, the province ended up with, you guessed it . . . nothing!

This effectively closed the most effective possibility for an alternative site for the dealership to locate to so that the first parliament site could be saved and not paved over.

The second possibility was more dependent on goodwill and, I hoped, logical thinking by the city officials. We had had ongoing conversations with the president of the car dealership that clearly indicated that he still had an intention to cooperate and find a solution.

The city had so far stonewalled us. We were receiving no feedback on the matter of releasing the "hold" on the West Don lands. Every suggestion that the car dealership made with respect to alternate properties was turned down flat by the city. It was clear that they thought we had no bargaining power and that the problem was now the province's.

What angered me was that despite the non-cooperation and stonewalling by the city, City Councillor Pam McConnell and local Liberal MPP George Smitherman held a rally on the site to get people to pressure the province into taking action. What hypocrisy!

As angry as I was and even though some of my staff wanted me to correct the record and reveal that the problem was that the city was blockading all solutions, I felt that we would still need to bring all the parties together to get a consensus.

At this point I decided that if the city and some of the councillors were going to play games while feigning seeking a solution, I would see if we could go it alone. Time was passing, and as it did there was a danger that the car dealership would decide that the city and the province were not dealing in good faith and start excavation. There would be two costs if we decided to go this route: first, there was the cost of the land for the exchange and the question of whether an appropriate piece of land was available; second, there would be the cost of retrofitting the current building as a temporary measure until new accommodations could be built.

The cost of land could be straightforward. As long as the value of the land we would be giving up equaled the value of the first parliament lands, it would be equal value for equal value and therefore would have no impact on the fiscal plan of the government. Unfortunately, the dealership was looking for a piece of property in the same general vicinity as the current dealership. This meant that the city would eventually have to cooperate in order to release the lands from both the "hold" designation and also the waterfront plan.

The second cost, the retrofitting, would have to be approved as a new expenditure. That meant it had to be approved by Management Board and then by cabinet. I was confident that I could push through the cost at Management Board, but in order to move forward through cabinet I would have to deal with the premier's office. I believed the cost of the retrofitting would not be inexpensive. I considered the amount of flack we would receive for not saving the first parliament site. I also believed that it was a now or never situation. I knew that I was not going to be the culture minister at the helm if this site was lost. This is the stuff that appears in history books. Politicians never get credit for doing the right thing, but they are lambasted for making the wrong decisions.

The premier's office was briefed on our intentions. Meanwhile, stories were starting to appear in the media indicating concern that the site may be lost. I was continually haranguing John Guthrie to follow up with the premier's office. When no feedback was forthcoming for a month, I knew that we had a problem. I knew that the staff member who was in charge of briefing the premier was not particularly kindly disposed to the issue. I also knew that the way in which the premier was briefed could sometimes affect the outcome.

If I were to say to the premier that this matter was not a particular priority and that it was not on the media's radar screen, and that the people who were lobbying for the first parliament site were all wealthy, elitist people, I can imagine the response. Of course, none of that was true. On the other hand, if I were to say that this could be highly problematic tacked on to the claims of an undemocratic budget process, and that the media were generating stories and that the people who were clamouring for a solution were all ordinary citizens, it would be a very different result.

The direct feedback that we finally got was that the staff person in the premier's office did not like the idea. I decided that I needed to speak directly to the premier. I called Sandra Comisarow, the premier's long-time and very loyal assistant who without hesitation slotted me in to see him just before cabinet. The downside of this was that I knew that he was going to be briefed on the matter again just before I had my meeting.

When I got to see Premier Eves, I discovered that he had been told quite a different set of facts than the ones I was presenting. By the end of our conversation, he had agreed to go along with an allocation of $5 million to assist me in my negotiations. Thus armed, and with the support of many of the members of cabinet, I was able to get approval for something I still believe was a no-brainer.

In the meantime, despite having no assurance that a solution could be approved, the car dealership had been extremely cooperative in deferring time after time the start date of excavation. Once we had the approval to negotiate, we were able to move towards a resolution. The next step was getting a piece of property that could work in a land swap. We were still at a roadblock because the only properties that were in the general area and suitable were owned by the city.

Eventually, the city cooperated and a land swap was worked out that required the province to provide a piece of property in exchange. There should have been absolutely no problem at this point, as the land to be given up had the same value as the first parliament land. Unfortunately, I couldn't get by the attitude in the premier's office that they had already given us $5 million so nothing more was forthcoming. The deal was in danger of being unravelled because of stupidity.

An additional factor was that the province was just about to have a general election and our candidate, John Adams, a former Toronto councillor, believed that this was a critical issue in the riding. Once the election was pending, the premier's office was otherwise occupied. Despite my warnings, no action was taken.

The premier's office decided that no announcements could be made during elections. This meant that I could not officially announce a new MRI for my hospital or additional lands given to the Rouge Park, even though the approvals had all been completed. This especially applied to the first parliament lands, as the approval for the land swap had not been given.

Somewhere during the election, someone must have finally awakened. I was asked to sign a cabinet walkaround to approve the land swap. My CA, Carolyn Knight, informed me that even though we had approval of the swap and therefore the deal, we could not make an official announcement. What this meant was that the city, even though it had caused most of the delay and animosity, was going be able to make the announcement and steal the credit for a solution it had very little to do with.

I told Carolyn to advise John Adams of the details of the deal and to let him know that although I could not make the announcement, I would not hold him to the same restriction. The result was not the best from a communication standard, but it was better than nothing. A year and a half was spent crafting a solution, but because of the continual inability by people not under my control to recognize a problem, everyone else got the lion's share of credit.

The end result was that the site of the first parliament of Ontario was spared from becoming a car dealership. At the farewell party the Ministry of Culture gave for me and my staff, my deputy minister, Terry Smith, presented me with a mock newspaper. The headline read "Tsubouchi Saves First Parliament." We all knew what we had done behind the curtain.

# CHAPTER TWENTY-TWO

# FRIENDSHIPS, POLITICS AND FUNNY STUFF

Politics was never my life's ambition. My real friends were never from that world. The people I would spend my spare time with came from different walks of life. High school friends, neighbours, golfing buddies — our house was always full of friendship and laughter.

When there was a break in the political calendar, I spent time with Elaine. Very few politicians had ever been to my house. There are two politicians that Elaine really liked as people: Al Palladini and John Snobelen. They were always welcome at our house.

Al Palladini was my closest friend in the legislature until his untimely death. At least he died doing what he liked — golfing in Mexico. I could never say no to Al. As a result, I participated in some very wonderfully strange adventures with him.

One day after Question Period we were sitting in the East Lobby. We both had evening House duty.

"What are you doing for the next couple of hours?" he asked.

"As it turns out I am actually free," I answered. "I had a couple of appointments but they were cancelled. I thought we might grab some dinner."

"I have a better idea," Al said with his usual mischievous smile. "Let's go down to the Food and Wine Show at the Convention Centre."

I didn't really feel like going down to the Toronto Convention Centre and walking through a big crowd, but it was Al and I couldn't say no.

So off we went to the Food and Wine Show, without any staff. When we arrived, Al walked purposely towards something. We soon arrived at an area that was set up for a demonstration with TV cameras. Al walked behind the cooking counter and grabbed an apron and chef's hat.

"Put this on," he said as he donned his own apron and hat. Then James Barber, the Urban Peasant, showed up. Al had just put us in a cooking demonstration.

Al had a good heart and I believe he would inadvertently get me involved in these sitcom situations. He called me one day to invite to go golfing.

"Meet me at Lionhead," he said as he named the date. When I showed up I realized that Al had invited me to the Michael Jordan Celebrity Invitational golf tournament. Almost every major sports personality was appearing in aid of Michael Jordan's charity. I caught up to Al and he advised me that we were golfing with the irrepressible owner of Lionhead, Iggy Kaneff, and Dave Johnson, our cabinet colleague. We were waiting for Dave Johnson to arrive, which he did, just before the golf carts were supposed to leave to take us to our tee off.

Dave Johnson was a very cerebral man, a mathematician by trade and very low-key and fiscally conservative. He hopped on the cart next to me holding on to his golf clubs. They looked like a range set from the 1960s. He was wearing some grey dress pants, a short-sleeved white work shirt and running shoes. Dave looked a little uncomfortable.

"Al never told me that this was a tournament," he muttered. He had pulled the same trick on both of us.

In a normal tournament, at the first tee, you will have a few people watching you golf. Michael Jordan had a gallery of thousands. We were nobodies, but even we had a gallery of about 500 people.

The first person to tee up was Iggy Kaneff.

Iggy turned to the crowd and said, "I'm Iggy Kaneff. I'm 70 years old. Watch me hit the ball."

Iggy then hit a nice drive up the middle of the fairway.

Al Palladini went next. Al hit a beautiful drive and chuckled as he turned back to me.

I managed to hit a nice drive.

Dave Johnson was to go next.

"Dave," I asked. "When was the last time you went golfing?"

"Two years ago," Dave said softly.

Dave Johnson teed up the ball, took a mighty swing and hit the ball five yards to the right.

"Take a mulligan!" yelled Al Palladini.

Dave retrieved the ball and hit it five yards to the left.

"Take another mulligan!" yelled Al Palladini.

The next ball Dave hit went about 100 yards down the fairway. If I were Dave Johnson, I would have probably been saying a lot of uncensored things to Al. But Dave Johnson was a very understated person and the worst expletive he could manage as he got into the golf cart was, "Darn that Al Palladini."

John Snobelen was the master of droll. He has a wonderful sense of humour and irony. Elaine always liked John and would trust him with anything. With John Snobelen, what you see is what you get. He is another self-made man and a real cowboy.

I was on a radio call-in show in Thunder Bay the morning after the black bear spring hunt had been cancelled by Natural Resources when John Snobelen was the Minister of Natural Resources. I was there to talk about the new programs that we had instituted to make obtaining birth certificates and records easier and faster. Every call to the radio station was on the black bear hunt cancellation.

One caller started his question by, "Mr. Tsubouchi, I wish that you were John Snobelen . . ."

To which I responded, "I don't."

The caller laughed and hung up.

I liked John because of his honesty, the same quality that held him up to scorn from the media. He also became a convenient whipping boy for the teachers. John is quick and has a lot of common sense. Or, as he might call it, horse sense.

One day in the legislature during the debates I could hear Al Palladini screaming at Bud Wildman of the NDP. It took a lot to get Al's goat, but I think Bud Wildman owned the milking rights. He just seemed to know how to push all of Al's buttons. Normally I didn't pay too much attention to this, but then I saw John Snobelen, who was sitting next to Al, with both of his hands restraining him. Al was getting so angry that his face was turning red. John was no weakling but I could see Al straining to get away. It would not be a good thing if Al crossed the floor and punched Bud Wildman in the nose.

I stood up and walked over to Al and stood in front of him, blocking out the TV cameras.

"Al, sit down!" I said firmly.

Al continued to strain and yell.

I raised my voice. "AL, SIT DOWN!"

Al glanced at me with a very aggressive look and then he really looked at me. I could see the anger leave his face and he grinned sheepishly and sat down. After a few minutes, John let go of his arm.

"I really was going to punch him in the nose," he admitted.

I was forced into a peacemaker role another time. Doug Ford Sr., the father of Toronto Mayor Rob Ford and Toronto Councillor Doug Ford, was, like his sons, a big man. He used to sit next to another friend of mine, Doug Rollins from Belleville. Doug Ford and Doug Rollins looked like half of the Toronto Argos offensive line. Both Dougs were gentle giants and nice guys.

Again I could hear someone from the NDP caucus yelling some insulting comments and directing them at Doug Ford. I saw Doug Ford stand up, straighten his jacket and start to march purposefully towards the NDP caucus. I got up from my seat and walked over and blocked the aisle.

"Doug, go back to your seat!" I said to him.

Doug looked down at me and, only because he liked me, turned around and sat down. It's a good thing he liked me because he outweighed me by about 100 pounds.

Whenever I was on tour and had an official function, I made sure that the local MPP was a part of the formalities. When I was in Sudbury for an opening for Science North, I noticed that the program did not include the local MPP, Rick Bartolucci. I made sure that Rick was a part of the official party, helped cut the ribbon and gave a speech. Rick appreciated the gesture. When I was asked why I made sure that an opposition MPP was recognized in such a way, I answered, "Manners and courtesy."

I always remembered Tony Roman's words to me to share the credit. It does not feel good when you are the one excluded. One of my cabinet colleagues once showed up in Markham to make an announcement. Not only was I not part of the formalities but I had not even been notified of the event. I was very unhappy.

Rick Bartolucci is a good guy. Every year he had a little party in his Queen's Park office just before Christmas. The only Tories who were invited were Al Palladini and me. Once when asked by one of his Liberal colleagues why I had been invited, Rick simply said, "He's a friend."

Jim Bradley is a charming rascal who is quick to utter a very amusing heckle in the House. Jim has elevated his little asides to an art form. He is not mean with his quips and is very witty. He is also a well-respected representative for St. Catharines and another nice guy. When Prince Charles was visiting Niagara College, Jim was escorting him along with Dan Paterson, the president of Niagara College. Since everyone was pushing to meet the prince, I thought I would stand in the back and observe. I had dined before with Prince Andrew and Prince Michael of Kent and Prince and Princess Takamado of Japan, and I thought it would be nice for others to have the opportunity.

I was standing near the wall with renowned chef Anna Olson when I could see Jim Bradley and Dan Paterson making a beeline towards me with Prince Charles. Jim introduced me as a former colleague and cabinet minister. It was a classy gesture.

I was fortunate to have friends on both sides of the House.

I used to watch my cabinet colleague Chris Hodgson's son Cody play bantam hockey with Chris. You could see that he had talent. The Markham Waxers bantam team had one of the best coaches, Paul Titanic. On his team he had some pretty good hockey players along with Cody, Steve Stamkos and Michael DelZotto. I still have a game of golf with Chris every year.

My big golf buddy is another cabinet colleague, Dan Newman. Dan is a scratch golfer and a great addition to a scramble team. I enjoy golf but Dan loves golf. Dan and I play on a fairly regular basis. We became friends at candidate school in 1994 and car-pooled together. I never missed any of Dan's fundraisers and he returned the favour.

In the old days of the legislature, before the televising of the proceedings, there was a lot more camaraderie between members and parties. When it became showtime it became a lot more personal. I have always stuck to the issues and never personally attacked any politician, even when it was justified. It's not that I have a Pollyanna view of the world, but when you make it personal it costs you more than it costs them.

# CHAPTER TWENTY-THREE

# BEGINNING OF THE END

When Ernie Eves won the leadership race, he was riding a brief wave of popularity. However, after settling into his office, he suddenly seemed like Joe Btfsplk from the *Li'l Abner* cartoon, who walked around with a black rain cloud over his head and brought bad luck to everyone around him. It seemed like the government was rocked by disaster after disaster.

First Ontario was beset by SARS (Severe Acute Respiratory Syndrome). The outbreak that affected many areas in the world had a particularly big impact on the Greater Toronto Area. Premier Eves did all the right things. He was on the job. He was visible to the public. He was everywhere. There was no precedent for the outbreak. When the World Health Organization issued a travel advisory for Toronto, it affected the economy of the city in a disastrous way.

All the resources of the province were directed at dealing with the outbreak. From my perspective, Premier Eves did everything that was possible to do. The other person who did heroic service was Dr. Colin D'Cunha, the Ontario Medical Officer of Health.

Unfortunately there were a number of deaths that were a result of SARS. Ultimately blame had to be assigned by both the media and the opposition parties and it was unfairly directed at Ernie Eves, who had lived every minute of every day during the crisis trying to fight SARS.

On August 14, 2003, the lights went out in Ontario and most of the northeastern United States. I was on my way to a meeting. I was driving on the 407 when I heard the news. As I drove by some of the intersections with the highway I could see that there was a huge disruption. I turned around immediately and headed home so I could find out what was going on.

As I got off the highway, I could see that all the traffic lights were out. All the store and business signs were out and people were just standing around outside on the sidewalks. Ordinary people were directing traffic. As soon as I arrived home I called Elaine, who had been staying for a few days with Jacquie in Virgil to look after our grandson Ethan. I asked her how she was coping with the blackout. Elaine was genuinely surprised. The Niagara area had been untouched.

I then contacted Derek O'Toole. As Chair of Management Board, I was in charge of all government buildings. I was assured by both Derek and Kathy Bouey, my deputy minister, that we had everything in hand. There was no point in coming downtown as I could deal with decision-making from home on my phone. There was a lot of finger pointing by officials on both sides of the border and by political opponents who took the opportunity to blame the government of Ernie Eves. As it turned out, the problem had originated in the United States.

Ernie Eves never really had a chance. When he won the leadership race he was riding high in the polls. There was much discussion among his advisers about when to call an election. Legally we had five years from the 1999 election to call a new one. I believe there would have a very different result if there had been an earlier election. Ernie would not been blamed for SARS or the blackout. It's all about timing.

These events caused a lot of difficulty. Generally, a new party is not voted in but rather a government is voted out. Voters usually get tired of a political party after two terms. When a party gets voted out, it is either for incompetence or scandal.

A series of Freedom of Information (FOI) requests by the Liberals gave cause for concern to the government. The Liberals were looking for information on the expenses that had been claimed by all cabinet ministers and their staff since 1995. The party had already started attacking Cam Jackson publicly about his expenses as a minister. Cam was under fire daily in Question Period and in the news. As long as the media would cover the story, the opposition parties would keep up the attack.

Discussions began about how this could be defended in light of the FOI request for everyone's expenses. I suggested that since the opposition leaders' expenses have never been subject to FOI, there were sure to be some abuses and misuse of public money. If we were to bring in legislation making these expenses subject to FOI, they might start to back off. The other option that was favoured by the premier's staff was that since everyone's expenses had been FOI'd then we should just give them all the information and overwhelm them rather than die the death of a thousand cuts.

This option made no sense to me. Why make it easy for them? We should make them go through the process. By making all records available to everyone, even legitimate expenses would be subject to attack. The media had not requested this information and simply giving it would provide fodder for weeks.

As the argument raged back and forth, Cam Jackson continued to be under attack. The idea that Cam should be removed from cabinet began to be discussed. I gave my unsolicited opinion that nothing had surfaced to show that Cam had broken any rules. It didn't look good, but he hadn't broken any rules. My pragmatic view was that if Cam were to be forced to resign, the opposition parties would be encouraged by their success and would immediately look for the next victim.

Eventually the anti–Cam Jackson voices succeeded and Cam resigned. Immediately the opposition parties started attacking Chris Stockwell for his travelling expenses. The intensity and volume of attacks started to escalate to an alarming rate. Finally the word came down from Premier Eves's staff that the legislation for expenses would make all expenses public for all cabinet ministers and their staff and also for the opposition leaders. The expenses would be made public going retroactively back to June 1995.

Now that the decision was made, the logistics would have to be determined. It was decided that the Integrity Commissioner of Ontario would be responsible for reviewing the expenses and that I would be the government liaison. This additional work would increase the responsibilities and work of the Integrity Commissioner exponentially, meaning we would have to allocate more staff and office space to the Office of the Integrity Commissioner.

Politically it would be smart to examine all expenses and make sure any questionable expenses were repaid before the legislation was passed. This meant reviewing almost nine years of paperwork and tracking staff, some of whom no longer worked for the government.

Then the other shoe dropped.

I was going to make an announcement to increase the prize amount for the Trillium Book Awards and to add brand-new awards for poetry in both French and English. This should have been, on the face of it, a straightforward, good news announcement attracting nothing but good press.

The ministry staff, my staff and the staff of the Ontario Media Development Corporation chose the library at Hart House on the University of Toronto campus as the site of the announcement. They liked the location because it was close to Queen's Park and the media. They also liked the backdrop of a university versus a commercial bookstore or a publishing house. It would be difficult to choose one commercial outlet over another.

I didn't like the venue because it had the potential for trouble unrelated to the announcement. University campuses have had security breaches in the past for some of my cabinet colleagues.

I relented, against my gut instinct, as I didn't have any controversial issues with university students. I had no difficult issues in my cultural portfolio. I did, however, have a fairly high-interest issue that I was managing under my Management Board portfolio dealing with expense accounts of the premier and some of the cabinet ministers. The media reporters who covered the culture beat were not the same ones who covered Queen's Park and the day-to-day events of the legislature. Hart House, however, is only a five-minute walk from Queen's Park.

The first sign that something was up was when the CBC television crew asked if they could interview me before the announcement. They then proceeded to ask me about details of Premier Eves's expenses. I managed to answer the question on a high level, indicating that I was bringing in rules to bring in transparency and accountability. The rules would apply not only to the premier and cabinet ministers but also to the leaders of the opposition. The object was to have the toughest rules in the country.

As I was wrapping up with the CBC, they were followed in short order by CTV, Global and CITY. The print media — the *Toronto Sun*, the *Star*, the *National Post* and the *Globe and Mail* — were hot on their heels. I just kept repeating myself.

What had gone wrong?

Earlier that morning, one of the opposition MPPs had held a press conference to criticize the premier's expenses, which they had obtained through a Freedom of Information application. The whole tone of the Liberals' conference was holier than thou. Both my legislative assistant and my CA had been notified of the press conference. They had decided to check out the references to the premier's expenses for accuracy with the premier's staff before they notified me because they wanted the information to be accurate. Mistake number one: My staff members didn't think there was any urgency to notify me because my press conference was off-site. They should have taken into consideration that I was just a stone's throw from Queen's Park.

They finally decided to call me just as one of the two staff members I had with me at the press conference was informing me that CBC wanted to talk to me. Mistake number two: My accompanying staff member who took the phone call did not realize that there was a problem as soon as she started talking to the other two back at the office. She did not realize what the issue was, and then she did not make the connection that the CBC interview was regarding this problem and not the cultural announcement.

Mistake number three: When she finally connected the dots and realized that we had a problem, she should have immediately pulled me from the interview so that the two staff members back at the office could brief me before I went on camera.

The difficulty this placed me in was that if the media started stating as fact some of the allegations against the premier, I wouldn't know if they were true or not. If I had known that the facts were wrong, I could have summarily dismissed them as being factually incorrect. If they were true, I'd have to phrase my words very carefully. It is a sickening feeling when you don't have the facts and you are on the spot and must respond to the media. Looking at the interviews retrospectively, I would have answered the questions exactly the same, but with a lot more confidence.

The only staff member who didn't screw up was the brand-new employee who was dutifully holding my tape recorder, blissfully unaware of the chaos surrounding her.

Once Premier Eves was under fire, we were forced to accelerate the timetable to table the legislation. When the expenses for the opposition leaders surfaced, there were many examples of inappropriate spending. Taxpayers' money was spent on high-priced political advisers from the United States, luxury food items and, curiously in the case of Dalton McGuinty's staffers, an unusual amount of orange juice. When asked about the orange juice, he responded, "It's good for you."

Just as I had anticipated, even small expenses were mocked in the newspapers. One of my colleagues had been on business in Windsor and instead of having a decent lunch bought a Big Mac, thinking that he would save money for the taxpayers. Instead he was criticized for not paying for the hamburger out of his own pocket.

By bringing in this legislation, we had given the media and opposition parties fodder for weeks leading into the election. This was a really bad decision.

We had handed the opposition parties the other reason a government is voted out: scandal.

The writing was on the wall for the election. Given the circumstances, it was not surprising that the government fell.

A small footnote was that Cam Jackson was eventually exonerated of all claims of illegal expenses. In the slaughter of the PC Party in the 2003 election, Cam Jackson was re-elected.

The Common Sense Revolution was over — not with a bang, but a whimper.

# CHAPTER TWENTY-FOUR

# AFTERMATH

I had never planned to be a career politician. I got involved in politics for a reason. Before the 2003 election, I had actually decided to retire from politics the year before, much like my friend Chris Hodgson did. This would have allowed me to get a leg back into the private sector while our party was still in power and would have made me in demand.

Privately, I was worn down from the continual and unceasing demands of politics. I give a lot of credit to anyone who serves at any level of government. You are on call 24 hours a day, 365 days a year. It is even more demanding today than it was when I served. The internet has increased the pressures exponentially. As much as I thought there could have been better ethics in the media, at least there was some accountability for what was written or stated. Now any anonymous blog can unleash relentless libelous statements without any accountability. A thick skin is a prerequisite for standing for office.

I once said to someone that if you want to find out about your family tree for free, run for political office.

I was getting tired from the increasing demands on my time, both in government and in politics. As one of the better-known members, I toured a lot and gave speeches and raised money. I was home maybe five nights a month.

I no longer had the burning desire to do the job. If you don't have that fire in the belly, you shouldn't be there. I shared my feeling with a few people and was pressured to run again. I was running for all the wrong reasons — for my colleagues and my party; not for myself or my constituents.

When we lost the government, it was a relief in many ways.

When you retire on your own terms, you can control the circumstances better. There is also a grace period during which the community or the many organizations and people that you have aided over the years have a chance to say thank you. When you lose an election, you need to be careful that the door does not hit your behind too hard.

One of the things that I was grateful for was that both of my ministries — Culture and Management Board — held appreciation parties for both me and my staff. At the Management Board party, my deputy minister, Kathy Bouey, presented me with a miniature chair from the ministerial staff to the Chair of Management Board. Terry Smith, Deputy Minister of Culture, gave me a mock-up newspaper with the headline, "Tsubouchi Saves First Parliament." I always appreciated the high calibre of the people who work for the civil service of Ontario. They are hard-working people who never get the respect or appreciation that they deserve.

When you leave government because the people have spoken, you quickly learn who your friends are. I am fortunate in that a number of people have given me an opportunity with no other motive than being a good person.

You also find out that there are many people and organizations that want to exploit your network for their own means, with only a small benefit to you. About a month into my new stage in life, I was approached by a medium-sized law firm. After meeting with them, I didn't think that there was much in their offer that would be to my advantage. By chance I happened to chat with a friend, Peter Van Loan, who had been the president of the PC Party of Ontario for most of my time in government. Peter had been the best party president that I have known. He supported the MPPs across the province. I can't recall many events where he was not present.

Peter is one of the two most ardent participants and students of politics that I know (the other being Tony Clement). Peter eats, sleeps and exists for politics. He is also one of the most intelligent people that I know. He is also one of best municipal lawyers in the country.

Peter suggested that I come in and talk to the folks at his law firm, Fraser, Milner, Casgrain. I came down and was soon working at FMC as part of the real estate development department, and as I became involved in investment banking, gaming regulation and nuclear energy, my practice evolved into a range of quite different specialties. FMC had a great working atmosphere and culture. FMC also had its share of political people. On the Conservative side there were a lot of good people — Blair McCreadie, who at the time was the president of the PC Party of Ontario; Aron Halpern; and Andrew Jeanrie. The corner office belonged to Senator David Smith, who is a key Liberal strategist and a classy man. We had many a healthy discussion on politics; insiders might have been shocked at how frankly we discussed issues. I came to know and work with Andrew Jeanrie, and we made a pretty good team. After a while, Peter began his run for MP and was successful. To the delight of all of his friends, he was appointed to cabinet in the Harper government.

Another friend, Aris Kaplanis, was the CEO of Teranet, the company that converted the records of the Land Registry Offices in Ontario to electronic records. Aris is a great philanthropist and has raised millions of dollars over the years. Aris is a very modest man. I was at a fundraising dinner with Aris for an organization called "Operation Springboard" that helps at risk youth and adults. The lady sitting next to me asked me if I was going to an event that weekend at the Aris Kaplanis Centre. I didn't know that Aris had a community centre named after him.

Aris asked me if I was interested in sitting on his board of directors. Teranet was an income trust and was listed on the TSE. Since the provincial government had an interest in Teranet, I would have to be approved by the new Liberal government. Aris told me not to worry because they all liked me. Sure enough, I was approved.

Indirectly through Aris I came to know a real lovable character, Ted Manziaris, one of the most upbeat people I know. I was waiting for my appointment to show up for lunch in an Il Fornello restaurant in Etobicoke when a young fellow walked up to my table, handed his cell phone to me and said, "I have someone on my phone who wants to talk to you."

I said, "Hello?"

"Dave, it's Aris," said Aris Kaplanis. "This phone belongs to Ted Manziaris. He saw you come in and wanted to meet you."

That is how I met Ted. Ted is one of the most generous people I know. It was no surprise that I met him through Aris. If Ted walked into any room, he would light up the room. Ted owned a company, Turtle Island Recycling, that he had started after he graduated from university. When he began his entire resources consisted of Ted and his mother's K-car.

Ted is a great marketer and handed his card to everyone. He received a call one day from Maple Leaf Gardens. The Gardens was holding a concert on the weekend and their regular waste company could not do the job and so they asked Ted if he could do it, not realizing of course that it was just Ted and his mother's car.

Ted worked all night and day and made more than 300 trips to the dump and got the job done. Maple Leaf Gardens was so pleased that they offered Ted the work after their contract with the other company expired. From that willingness to work, Ted parlayed Turtle Island into a multi-million dollar business.

It was through Ted and Aris that I met Dr. Paul Casano, Father Rennick and Father D'Souza of Assumption University. The Basilian Fathers, who run many learning institutions, are terrific people who dedicate their lives to education. Aris was the Honourary Chancellor for Assumption University. It was a pleasant surprise to learn that they had put my name forward for an honourary doctor of laws for my contributions as a politician and a fundraiser. It was also an acknowledgement that I was both the first Japanese Canadian to be elected as a municipal politician, an MPP and cabinet minister. I received the honour in 2006.

Ted has his zany side. We were golfing one day at my club with a couple of friends. When we got to the first par three hole Ted went to his golf bag and pulled out a Toronto Maple Leaf banner that was signed by Mats Sundin.

"The closest to the pin wins the prize," he announced. "But you have to be on the green."

Unfortunately no one was on the green.

When the next par three came around, Ted pulled out the banner and a bottle of wine.

"Winner takes all," he announced. "But you have to be on the green."

Again, no one drove the ball on the green.

The third par three brought another announcement, "The winner gets the banner, the bottle of wine and this great prize." Ted then pulled out an ordinary T-shirt. Finally someone got the ball on the green.

Ted is full of surprises and never refuses to support any good cause.

The scariest thing about restarting your career after being voted out of politics is that it is unplanned and unstructured. It takes you back to the challenging time when you were looking for employment after school. After being on top, it is difficult to imagine starting from the bottom. There have been some very tragic stories about ex-politicians not being able to cope. Just after we were elected in 1995, one of the reforms we passed was doing away with the gold-plated member's pension. The end result of this reform was that we never got credit for doing this and the public still believes that Ontario MPPs have a pension. I can tell you definitively that we do not.

Some of the older politicians got paid out for their years of service and got a big payday. MPPs like Bob Rae benefitted, but MPPs newly elected in 1995 were left holding an empty bag.

Within my own community of Markham, my years of service and lobbying for infrastructure projects and funding for the people of Markham went largely unacknowledged. You don't take on the responsibility and commitment of public service for the accolades. but it would have been nice to hear a simple thank you.

There were a number of organizations who did thank me for what I had done. My alma mater, York University, presented me with the Bruce Bryden Award for leadership. The Japanese Canadian Cultural Centre gave me the Award of Merit for Outstanding Leadership and Service to the Nikkei Community and Canadian Society. My friends at the Governor General's Horse Guard made me an honourary member of the GGHG Officers Mess.

When you are in politics and you are approached by organizations for your help, you basically say yes to everyone. Now that I was out of politics I could decide who to help. While I was building my career again I decided to do what I had always done — raise money for non-profit organizations as a volunteer. I was partial to education, as that is what gave me my chance in life.

As I was contemplating this, I was approached by Maureen Loweth, the Dean of Fine Arts and Business for George Brown College. I was familiar with many of the people at George Brown College because they had been part of a contingent, along with Albert Schultz of the Soulpepper Theatre group, who had lobbied me for a grant for a new theatre that both organizations would share in the new arts and cultural area in Toronto called the Distillery District. Their request had been successful. Maureen asked me if they could invite me to lunch.

At lunch, I was asked to chair a campaign to raise money for the new theatre. I had raised money before, but not with numbers that were defined by "millions." I knew it would be challenging but I believe strongly in the importance of arts and culture, so I agreed.

The first point of order was to recruit a fundraising cabinet. The best thing to do is ask your friends. I started with Ted Manziaris and my friend Baron Manett, who has an absolutely brilliant creative mind and is an ad and marketing genius. Baron has created major buzzes with some of his marketing for clients such as Virgin Mobile, Facebook and Unilever. Baron had never failed to volunteer whenever I need a fundraising cabinet.

The campaign was challenging but it was interesting and because of the people both on the cabinet and at George Brown, it was a lot of fun. We raised a lot of money for the theatre and we also enjoyed the journey.

Shortly after we had completed the campaign for George Brown College, my friend Larry Keating asked me to go to lunch. Larry and I became friends when I asked him to chair the Minister's Technology Advisory Committee when I was the chair of Management Board and in charge of technology for the government. We met for lunch from time to time, but Larry was acting mysteriously.

At lunch he asked me if I would consider becoming the honourary chair of Seneca College's $10 million campaign for the Markham campus. Now I knew how much work it was and I said, "Larry, I don't have a lot of spare time. I'm not so sure that I can do it."

Larry apparently was prepared for this and responded, "You would be the honourary chair and would just have to help us with introductions and wouldn't have to go to all the meetings."

I felt an obligation to help Seneca College since it was the only post-secondary institute in York Region — and specifically Markham — so I agreed. As things turned out, the chair of the campaign stepped down before the completion of the campaign and of course I was asked to step in. I learned a lot about the largest college in North America. It had great people and the students were very representative of the ethnic mix of York Region.

After the campaign was completed, there had been a change at Seneca and an old friend, David Agnew, who had been in charge of the civil service under the Bob Rae provincial government, took over as president. David asked me to join the Board of Governors.

At the time I was sitting on the Board of Governors of York University and that time commitment by itself was a lot. I had been recruited to sit on the York University board by the then-president Lorna Marsden, a former Liberal senator who also became a good friend. Lorna had since left and was succeeded by Mamdouh Shoukri, whom we had recruited from McMaster University. I didn't think that I could handle both. York had a who's who of Canada on the Board of Governors, people like former Chief Justice Patrick LeSage, publisher Anna Porter and business leaders like Guy Burry and Mark Lievonen of Sanofi Pasteur. So I knew that they could easily get along without me.

I decided to meet with Mamdouh and explain that I was going to leave the York University board and go on the Seneca board. When I made the suggestion to Mamdouh, he peppered me with a million reasons why I should not leave his board and finished by stating that he was sure that I could handle both. When I left his office somehow I had agreed to continue on for another two years. It helped that I had a lot of respect for Mamdouh and liked him.

The other offer that boosted my post-government life came through another connection with the Japanese community. I had known Howard Shearer and Rose Chojnacki through my connection with the Japanese Canadian Cultural Centre in Toronto. Howard is the president of Hitachi Canada and Rose is the CFO. Howard is also the son of the former prime minister of Jamaica, Hugh Shearer. One day Howard and Rose approached me and offered me a seat on the board of directors of Hitachi Canada.

It's a little like trying to get a loan from the bank. When you need it, you can't get it. When you don't, you can get one. Once I had board positions on Teranet and Hitachi, other offers soon followed. After chairing two major fundraising campaigns, I was continually being asked to do more. The fundraising efforts brought much personal satisfaction.

When I consider that in my early life we had to struggle and fight to move ourselves forward by inches and we had no role models or connections or easy ways, it was rewarding to get involved to give others the opportunities I never had.

My greatest piece of fortune in my post-political life was becoming friends with Danny Leung. Danny is my closest friend and business partner. He is typical of my friends. He came from Hong Kong as a young man years ago. He got a job as a door-to-door salesman of vacuum cleaners. There were two problems — he did not speak English, and in Hong Kong, where he was brought up, no one had a vacuum cleaner. He was dropped off in a middle-class white neighbourhood.

At the first house where the people let him in, he tried to demonstrate the vacuum but was hopelessly unable to do so. He had attached the hose to the wrong hole and blew the dirt around the house. The lady then showed him how to operate the machine and then felt so sorry for Danny she made him lunch. Danny started to pack up his vacuum after lunch. When the lady showed interest in buying the vacuum and asked the price. Danny gave her the price of the vacuum less any commission he would have earned. It was the only sale he had that day.

The next day at the sales meeting, the sales manager congratulated Danny on selling a vacuum on his first day.

A few years later Danny applied for a job for seasonal help at Simpson's for the Christmas season. His job would be to stock the shelves. Being the conscientious young man that he was, Danny showed up early every day for work. He then noticed that the deliveries of new stock usually sat until people showed up when their workday began. He started taking the initiative and putting away the new stock before everyone arrived. This came to the notice of the manager, who offered Danny a job on a permanent basis as his assistant.

While he had been working Danny had noticed that the salesmen in the men's clothing department worked on commission and he thought that he could do the job. Danny then asked if he could have a job as a commissioned salesman instead of the job as the manager's assistant, because he thought he could make more money on commission. The manager liked Danny but was concerned. He told Danny that he could give him the job as a commissioned salesman, but if he didn't succeed the manager would have to let him go. He tried to convince Danny to take the safer job as his assistant. He then told Danny that being a commissioned salesman was not easy and a very cutthroat job.

Danny asked for the job as a salesman. During the monthly sales meeting, the manager of the department would announce the sales for the month in descending order. The top salesman was acknowledged first.

After a month, Danny was attending his first sales meeting. As they announced the sales results he waited anxiously for his name to be called. The sales staff had all been announced except for Danny. At the end of the meeting the sales manager asked Danny to stay. As they filed out a few of the salesmen teased Danny about not being called and it was nice knowing him.

After they left, the sales manager looked at Danny and told him the reason that he did not call his name was that Danny had the most sales for the month and was the top salesman. He didn't want to announce it, because then all the other salesmen would be gunning for Danny. The manager wanted to give Danny a few months' grace before he let it out of the bag.

I once asked Danny what was the greatest number of suits that he sold in one day. The answer? Two hundred.

Danny continued to look for opportunities. When the first wave of wealthy Chinese came to Canada from Hong Kong, he got into the gambling junket business. He became so successful that he was pursued by and went to work for Donald Trump as a VP of marketing. Danny was never fired by Trump.

When I was the Minister of Consumer and Commercial Relations and was heading the effort to expand gaming, Danny sat on my advisory committee. Later, when I left politics, Danny and I got together and started developing an international resource and infrastructure business. Our adventures have taken us to many strange and exotic places. We have traipsed through a jungle in Cambodia with armed soldiers and wandered through sandstorms in the Gobi Desert. We have been appointed to be the co-chairs of the Canada Vietnam Business Council by the Vietnamese government to create opportunities for both countries for economic development. Through our relationship with the Republic of Mongolia, I was appointed to be the Honorary Consul General for Mongolia in Toronto.

Danny is my trusted friend. There are very few people that you meet during your life that you trust 100 percent.

In 2009, I got my shot for the H1N1 flu. A couple of days later I passed out at my house seven times. I only remember passing out twice.

Jacquie had been visiting with us and said, "Dad, you did pass out again. Mom and I had to lift you up."

As I lay in bed I couldn't breathe, so Jacquie called 911. When the paramedics arrived I was feeling a little better and convinced them against the better judgment of everyone else to let me stay home.

I didn't have any context for the situation. I had never been seriously ill before and had never been admitted to a hospital. The next day I knew that I wasn't right and asked Elaine to take me to the Markham-Stouffville Hospital.

When I got to the emergency department, the doctor took my blood pressure and ordered a number of tests. I was put on an intravenous drip almost immediately. I was thoroughly convinced that after a little while I would be sent home to sleep it off. I was puzzled when I started getting transfusions. I was told I was going to be there for a while.

After a night in ER I was lucky to get a bed. I then was scheduled for an ultrasound test and when that didn't reveal anything, I underwent a gastroscopy exam, where a thin telescope is passed through the mouth down into the stomach. The test revealed a pinpoint ulcer that I had been bleeding out through. Later I found that I had bled out almost half the blood in my body and my blood pressure had been falling to dangerous levels.

Finally after days in the hospital I was told I could be released. When I was talking to my doctor, amateur gastroenterologist Elaine, wanting to make a point, asked him, "He wanted to sleep it off at home. What would have happened if he did?"

The doctor answered, "He would have been dead three days ago."

I got the point.

A month later when I had a follow-up appointment I asked him, "How did I get an ulcer?"

He answered, "About 50 percent of the people your age have a kind of bacteria in their stomach that gives them a disposition for ulcers or acid reflux."

I said, "Dr. Selucky, I have a cast-iron stomach. I can eat chili just before bed and not have acid reflux."

He said, "The good news is that you don't have the bacteria. Another cause could be if you were taking an anti-inflammatory, but you weren't doing that either. The last thing was that it was an old ulcer from stress but this was very new."

"So what was it?" I asked.

"I can't say," he said.

"The only new event that happened was my H1N1 shot," I said.

"I can't say that that was the cause," he answered.

"But you can say that it wasn't," I concluded.

The bad thing when you are lying on your back in the hospital with tubes stuck in you is that there is nothing to do but think. That is also a good thing as well. It allowed me to think about what I was doing with my life and if I was truly enjoying it. I also decided that I was not enjoying life at the law firm where I had been working at the time. There had been a change in management and the place felt very different. I decided that I would concentrate on other businesses and that the practice of law had lost its shine. Elaine agreed with the decision.

A few months later my friend Adam Szweras had heard that I was no longer with my former firm and asked me if I might be interested in joining Fogler Rubinoff. I wasn't really looking. After a few meetings with the firm, I decided that I liked the upbeat, progressive and entrepreneurial nature of the firm. It had a decidedly positive culture. That positive attitude led to great people and new friends like Howard Rubinoff, Lou Natale and Scott Venton.

Business makes for strange bedfellows. When I was down at Queen's Park for a visit, I was approached by Marc Kealey, who took the time to reintroduce himself to me. We had met before on a number of occasions when I was in government, and we agreed to get together and chat. Marc is a former staffer for John Turner when he was Prime Minister and a big "L" liberal.

When we met we realized that we had a lot in common and we could help each other out. Marc has since joined Danny and me in our international infrastructure projects. He has travelled with us and has become a close friend and business partner.

Marc still does a lot for former Prime Minister Turner and has always supported all the community and charitable work that Danny and I do. When Marc was in charge of John Turner's book launch at the Economic Club in Toronto, he asked us to buy a table.

We couldn't say no but I did say to Marc, "I bet I'll be the only Conservative there."

Marc just smiled and said, "Don't worry about it."

What he meant was that he had placed me at the head table with John Turner, me and every Liberal cabinet minister.

Steve Paikin of TVO approached me with a puzzled look on his face. I knew what he was thinking. "Why are you sitting there?"

I said jokingly to Steve, "I have pull." Then I pointed to Marc.

I have a special place in my heart for the Japanese Canadian Cultural Centre and the Japanese Canadian community. The Japanese Canadian community has always supported me, no matter what kind of political crisis I had on my hands. It was as if I had hundreds of uncles and aunts and cousins. When I hear of some accomplishment by a member of our community, I feel in a way as if I am sharing in that accomplishment. I feel proud of her or him. For a small community in Canada, we have had many very successful and prominent people — Raymond Moriyama, Vicky Sunahara and Bruce Kuwabara, just to name a few.

I also have great respect for the leaders in our community, who have carried on the daunting task of promoting Japanese culture to a dwindling group. I am proud to call them my friends and wish that I had not lived my life in isolation from other Japanese Canadians, as did many of them. I wish that I had been able to connect with other Japanese Canadians when I was growing up. I have come to realize, when I talk to my friends Ron Yamanaka, Marty Kobayashi, Connie Sugiyama, Gary Kawaguchi and Bill Hatanaka, that they all have had similar experiences. They too felt as if they had grown up alone and different.

When I was approached by a contingent from the Japanese Canadian Cultural Centre that included Sid Ikeda, our ambassador at large for our community, and was advised that I was to be honoured by the Japanese Canadian community, it was the greatest honour that I could ever receive.

At the event, I felt like I was giving a speech to my family. All of the family was there. My father was seated next to Elaine. My speech was all about how my father and my mother gave us the opportunity to do something with our lives. My speech was all about thanking them. As I spoke I watched my father. He was glowing. He was surrounded by his friends and family. I had a chance to express to him what I had not had a chance to say to my mother before she died. I could see that he was happy.

I never thought that this was going to be the last time I spoke to my father. The very next day, while he was out for a walk in the morning, he was tragically struck and killed in a hit-and-run incident. The criminal was never caught.

The small blessing is that I had a chance to say to my father that it was his perseverance that taught us how to live our lives.

Every morning I remember my father's advice to himself, to try to make life a little better each day for him and his family. My father began each day with purpose. "Gambatte!" he would say. I truly hope I've done my best.

ACKNOWLEDGEMENTS

It is impossible for us to live our lives in isolation. It is only with the help and support of family and friends that we somehow manage to muddle through and hopefully find some small piece of happiness. My wife, Elaine, treasures her privacy and I have tried to minimize her appearance in this book on her instructions, but without her support and strength I doubt that I could have been able to accomplish and experience the life I have had. My great fortune in falling in love with an intelligent and strong woman can never be overstated. Somehow she has managed to tolerate my eccentricities for most of our lives together. I don't think I have ever heard her take credit for her many sacrifices and accomplishments. That speaks volumes.

My hopes for the future lie in my grandson, Ethan Seaver. He has learned values that I treasure through my daughter Jacquie — loyalty, generosity and kindness. When he was six, he asked, "Grampy, if I ran for Prime Minister, would you vote for me?" I told him that I would run his campaign.

My last chapter would have been a lot longer if my editors didn't nudge me a lot as there are so many people that I need to acknowledge and so little space, like with an Oscars speech with only a brief allowance of time before the music starts to play.

I would not have survived without my family. My brother, Dan, and sister, Lynne, have been important to me as have my second set of "parents," my Aunt Haruko and Uncle Tosh Bando, two of the kindest people in existence.

I had many friends in politics. With great admiration and respect, I call former Premier Mike Harris my friend. The entire PC caucus that was elected in 1995 shared a truly unique experience that joined us together as comrades in arms. There were a few who became close friends, the ones I used to hang around with or sit with in caucus or consult with: John Baird, Tony Clement, Dianne Cunningham, Garfield Dunlop, Janet Ecker, Barb Fisher, Jim Flaherty, Doug Galt, Chris Hodgson, Julia Munro, Marilyn Mushinski, John O'Toole, Al Palladini, Lillian Ross, John Snobelen, Norm Sterling, Wayne Wettlaufer and my golf buddy Dan Newman.

Much of what I learned in politics was from the late mayor of Markham Tony Roman who taught me how to share the glory and shoulder the responsibility. My colleagues on Markham Council knew how to argue on the issues and after a debate amiably have a game of euchre and a cup of coffee.

I mentioned the teachers who had a great impact on my life, Margaret Britain and Ed Vine, but there were others who were wonderful role models and educators. John Rutherford was my music teacher and showed me how to play and appreciate all kinds of music. Ken Smith taught me history, and I enjoyed the debates and discussions that we had. I just really liked Bill Fry, my mathematics teacher, who showed a lot of patience especially when I cut his class. Ed Collins was my English teacher and my football coach. He was a big, intelligent man who showed by example that it was cool to like Shakespeare. Teachers do have an enormous impact on students. Politics, on both sides, gets in the way of what teachers really want to do — open the doors to opportunity for young people.

My eternal gratitude to York University; without the education I received there, there is so much I would not have been able to do. I strongly believe that education is the greatest equalizer in life. I continue to work with my friends Mamdouh Shoukri and Harriet Lewis at York University. I also work with my friends at another great institution, Seneca College, to improve opportunities for students. I am still continually learning and am fortunate to be associated with such wonderful people like David Agnew, Bill Hogarth, Daniel Atlin and Krishan Mehta.

My friends have always told me their unvarnished points of view. Some of us have been friends since high school — Dave and Anne Forfar, Bob Speck, Bud and Myra Chepack, Bob McTaggart, Craig McOuat, Dave Subotic, Ron Yamanaka, Nancy and Victor Toran, Marc Kealey and my closest friends, Danny Leung and Angela Chiu.

I have been fortunate to have friends who have also been friends in business. Luck and karma are always welcome friends as are Aris Kaplanis, Ted Manziaris, Frank Bellotti, Wally Hunter, Bill Petruck, Shawn Saulnier, Avinash Bal, Howard Shearer, Rose Chojnacki, Viraf Kapadia, Mike Aymong, Andy Chan, Steve Michalopoulos, Jay Safer, John and Diane Gibson, Scott Gibson, Ted Langdon, Adam Szweras, Jeremy Goldman, Yannis Banks, Baron Manett, Jim Kabrajee, Larry Keating, Stephen Chait and Waqaas Siddiqui.

There are a few friends who don't really fit into any particular box but are there when you need them — Catherine Mitchell for her insights on my fiction writing, Floyd Jack, Chris Stewardson, Gus Riddell, Mario Belvedere, my former Deputy Minister of Culture Terry Smith, MP Paul Calandra, Bill Fatsis, Ragui Ghali, Neil Fernandez, Merle Jacobs, Susanna Kelly, Jeff Lau and Stephen Brickell.

I have been blessed by smart and dedicated political staff over the years who understood that giving me the best advice and not what they thought I wanted to hear was the priority. It started with my Chief of Staff for most of my provincial career, John Guthrie, whose calm, clear thinking set the tone for all of our people. My thanks for their loyalty go to Derek O'Toole, Troy Ross, Sherri

Haigh, Ian Dovey, Barry O'Brien, Paul Burns, Bill Campbell, Deb McCain, Barb Burrowes, Sam Eldiriny, Jennifer Blitz, Bernie Yeung, Alex Kyriakos, Brett Bell, Caroline Knight, Mark Borer, Bill Moore, Andrew Ens, Jason Okamura, Mark Boudreau, Al Sakach and especially David Rajpaulsingh who spent so many early mornings and late nights driving me around.

My friends in the Japanese Canadian community have supported me throughout my life. It is comforting to know that you have hundreds of "aunts," "uncles" and "cousins" who are in your corner. I appreciate my heritage more and more the older I get. Most of my Japanese Canadian friends I have made later in life, but we share so much in the way we grew up that it seems like we have been friends since childhood. I have mentioned them in the body of my book, but we all work continuously together for our community — Sid Ikeda, Ron Yamanaka, Gary Kawaguchi, Art Ito, Bill Hatanaka, Connie Sugiyama, Marty Kobayashi, Ann Ashley and our honourary Japanese Canadians, Bill Petruck and James Heron.

I want to thank my publisher, Jack David, for putting the idea of writing this book in my head and then working with me. Working with editors was a new experience for me and I have much respect and appreciation for Jen Hale, Kathy Fraser and Crissy Boylan for their gentle art of persuasion.

Lastly I wish that my mother and father were alive to read their story. I miss them deeply. Their guidance and lessons live on in my heart and in the pages of this book. Gambatte!